CAMBRIDGE IBERIAN AND LATIN AMERICAN STUDIES

GENERAL EDITOR

P. E. RUSSELL, F.B.A.

EMERITUS PROFESSOR OF SPANISH STUDIES,
UNIVERSITY OF OXFORD

Christian Córdoba

Christian Córdoba

The city and its region in the late Middle Ages

JOHN EDWARDS

LECTURER IN MEDIEVAL HISTORY,
UNIVERSITY OF BIRMINGHAM

CAMBRIDGE UNIVERSITY PRESS

CAMBRIDGE
LONDON   NEW YORK   NEW ROCHELLE
MELBOURNE   SYDNEY

Published by the Press Syndicate of the University of Cambridge
The Pitt Building, Trumpington Street, Cambridge CB2 1RP
32 East 57th Street, New York, NY 10022, USA
296 Beaconsfield Parade, Middle Park, Melbourne 3206, Australia

© Cambridge University Press 1982

First published 1982

Printed in Great Britain by
Western Printing Services Ltd, Bristol

Library of Congress catalogue card number: 81–24213

British Library Cataloguing in Publication Data
Edwards, John
Christian Córdoba: the city and its region in the
late Middle Ages. – (Cambridge Iberian and Latin
American studies) Includes bibliography + index
1. Córdoba region (Spain) – History –
Ferdinand and Isabella, 1479–1516
I. Title. II. Series
946'.8403   DP402.C7 E35 1982

ISBN 0 521 24320 3

1. Cordoba (Spain)--
History

WP

In loving memory of L. N. E.

Contents

Maps

Tables

Preface

To use a religious category to define the limits of a study of a city and its region is, perhaps, to widen the scope of enquiry beyond the conventional. The notion of undertaking the detailed investigation of a small geographical area as a way of approaching the problems of a whole society is well enough established. The technique has the attractions of an easily understood theme and, generally, a manageable amount of source material. These advantages may be counteracted by the danger that the region in question will have too many peculiar characteristics to be of general interest. It might appear that in the case of Spain this danger is especially acute, indeed that it applies to the whole country. Responsibility for the fact that the Iberian Peninsula is still largely excluded from the normal scope of European historical studies must be shared by the Spaniards themselves. Since the Muslim invasion in 711, which turned the country into an Islamic colony, Spain has been uncertain of the relationship between its role in European Christendom and its place, over so many centuries, in the Muslim world. While it might be possible to conclude that such problems of identity make Spanish history unique and hence of limited general interest, the intention here is to adopt a more positive approach, and the society of late medieval Córdoba provides an excellent opportunity to do so.

The period of the city's history which will be studied is that which saw Spain's sudden rise to prominence as first a European and then a world power. When Isabella came to the throne of Castile in 1474, Córdoba had been in Christian hands for over two hundred years. It contained small Muslim and Jewish communities, but it was primarily a Christian city, of the second rank in contemporary Iberian terms, dominated by a military aristocracy and living mainly from the disposal of surplus agricultural production. Other cities, notably Seville, were more dynamic in the late fifteenth century, but Córdoba is probably representative of the inland towns of the Peninsula. The city's government was in the hands of a council consisting of nobles. Córdoba was represented in the Cortes, the Castilian parliament, as the capital of the kingdom (*reino*) of Córdoba, which was, after the thirteenth-century Reconquest, a purely notional territorial unit, but still survived in one of the titles of the rulers of Castile.

It has not proved possible to give a full account of the life of Córdoba's citizens in the period around 1500. Most of the sources are either administrative or legal in character. A great deal is known about the day-to-day operations of the city council and its official relations with the royal government, but much interesting detail may have been excluded from the town clerk's minutes, and legislation and administrative regulations, two types of document which are not clearly differentiated, indicate more of what was intended to happen than what actually did. At the local level, there are notable gaps in the evidence. No records survive of the court cases heard by the city's magistrates. The only municipal accounts extant are those of 1452–3 (see Table 2) and there are no tax-lists. Guild records do not survive, so that trade, industry and lay religious activity can only be studied from external and bureaucratic sources. The notarial archive, on the other hand, contains great riches in the spheres of individual property, family history and citizens' obligations, both fiscal and military. Although the records of only one office out of about thirty are complete for the period, the notarial registers have still not been fully exploited as a source for the economic activity of the city and the same applies in the case of the records of the Cathedral, which was one of the most important landlords in Córdoba itself and in the surrounding countryside.

Another problem is the shortage of information about the region outside the city. There are no notarial registers for these areas and the available sources in the municipal and Cathedral archives are all written from the urban and institutional point of view, although it is argued here that this state of affairs very probably reflects the reality on the ground. A similarly external view is all that is generally available of the activities of the secular nobility and in particular the lords. Only two noble families, the house of Belalcázar and the house of Aguilar, have been systematically studied, by Emilio Cabrera and Concepción Quintanilla, respectively. It is clear, though, that much more still needs to be done in the seignorial sector, which was so important in late medieval Castile in political, economic and social terms. The account which results from the nature of the available sources is thus urban and authoritarian in bias and it is only in the sphere of religious affairs that an attempt can be made to delve more deeply into individual beliefs and attitudes.

There is obviously matter of considerable interest to be found in the study of a large town with a comparatively sophisticated economy and an important regional political role. Much may be learnt about the distribution of power and wealth. However, it must be clear that there was far more to the life of Córdoba's citizens, at whatever social level, than political or economic activity. The use of the word 'Christian' in the title of this book is not merely decorative. The identity of individual Cordobans was shaped to a considerable extent by religious, as well as political or economic, affiliations. The life of the city in the late Middle Ages was enriched by the coexistence of adherents of Christianity, Islam and Judaism, and although in this area it is inevitable that the evidence must be external to the question, it nonetheless appears that belief in each of these religions was largely defined by the fact of the existence of the other two. External observance, in other words, may have been a true expression of the religious feelings of the people of Córdoba, so that the impossibility of entering into the private religious experience of individuals appears less of a handicap.

In the late fifteenth century, Córdoba was the scene of important episodes in the breakdown of coexistence between the three religions. It was the second Castilian city to receive an Inquisition and its Muslims and Jews were generally among the first to feel the effects of increasing royal hostility. Thus it may be argued, paradoxically, that it is the very particularity of Córdoba's social problems, rather than the obvious parallels between its political and economic structures and those of other areas of late medieval Europe, which provides the main justification for looking at the city's history. Nowhere can a better example of the joys and pains, the successes and failures, of relations between different religious groups be found than in the city of the caliphs.

Many people have assisted the progress of this work. Particular help and support was received from Don José de la Torre and his staff at the municipal archive in Córdoba, from Don Salvador Jiménez, the custodian of the notarial archive, and from the Cathedral archivist, Don Manuel Nieto, who kindly offered the use of his card-index to Córdoba sources, the *Corpus mediaevale cordubense*. The facilities of the Casa de Velázquez in Madrid, which were generously offered by the then director, M. François Chevalier, and secretary-general, M. Jean-Paul le Flem, were of great value in the completion of bibliographical work. Later stages of research, in Madrid and Córdoba, were effectively supported by the Small Grants Fund of the British Academy. The original concept of a political and administrative study of late medieval Córdoba was initiated and guided to fruition by Dr Roger Highfield, while invaluable advice and encouragement have since been received from Prof. Miguel Angel Ladero, Dr Emilio Cabrera and other historians of Andalusia, too numerous to name individually. Many members of staff and students of the University of Birmingham have provided inspiration, advice and criticism, in particular, Dr Christopher Wickham, who has kindly read the manuscript and succeeded in obtaining some alterations and improvements. The maps were drawn by Mrs Jean Dowling.

Moseley, Birmingham, on the Feast of St James the Great,
Patron of Spain, 25 July 1981

Abbreviations

ACC	Archivo Catedralicio de Córdoba
Actas	*Actas capitulares*
AGS	Archivo General de Simancas
AMC	Archivo Municipal de Córdoba
APC	Archivo de Protocolos de Córdoba
BL	British Library
BN	Biblioteca Nacional, Madrid
HID	*Historia, Instituciones, Documentos*
MCV	*Mélanges de la Casa de Velázquez*
Montalvo	A. Díaz de Montalvo, *Leyes de España*
Morales	Morales collection in RAH
RAH	Real Academia de Historia, Madrid
RGS	Registro General del Sello
Salazar	Salazar y Castro collection in RAH

Citation of references

The minutes (*actas capitulares*) of the town council and the Cathedral chapter are normally referred to by date and folio number, respectively. Documents in the municipal archive are cited by section, series and individual document numbers, in accordance with the archive's manuscript catalogue. Notarial documents in the Archivo de Protocolos are referred to by office number, volume number, section (*cuaderno*) and individual folio. Documents in the Cathedral archive, other than the chapter minutes, are referred to by bundle (*cajón*) and individual document number. Entries in the published calendar of the Registro General del Sello are referred to by date. Direct references to folios from this source are taken from the *Corpus mediaevale cordubense* (see Bibliography).

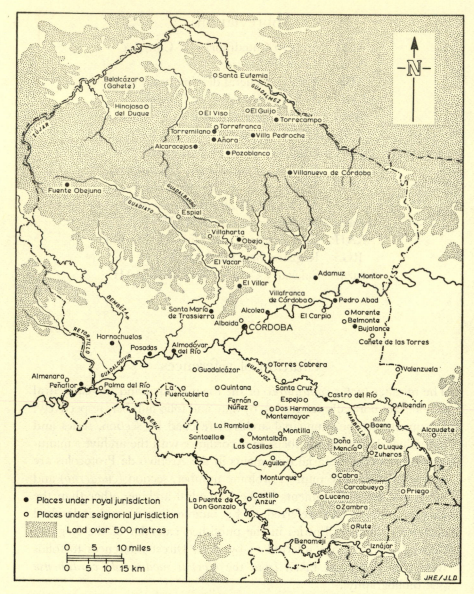

Map 1 Córdoba and its region

Places under royal jurisdiction
Places under seignorial jurisdiction
Land over 500 metres

| 0 | 5 | 10 miles |
| 0 | 5 | 10 | 15 km |

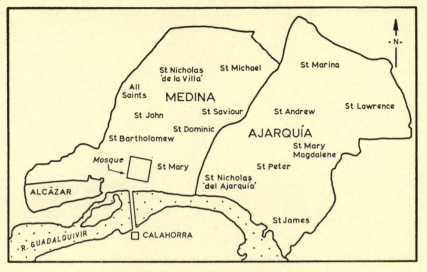

Map 2 The parishes of Córdoba

The kingdom of Córdoba after the Reconquest

GEOGRAPHY AND SETTLEMENT

When Córdoba was reconquered by the Christians in 1236, the chroniclers viewed Ferdinand III's achievement as primarily a religious and military victory. Not much attention was paid to the natural assets which had been taken over. However, the *First General Chronicle* records that, on his death bed, the monarch himself adopted a more practical attitude towards his conquests. He is said to have told his son, the future Alfonso X, 'Son, you are rich in lands and in many good vassals – more so than any other king in Christendom.'[1] Before looking at the political entities which the Christians established in the kingdom of Córdoba, it is best to examine the geographical conditions which did so much to determine the options which were open to late medieval Cordobans and their rulers.

The city of Córdoba lies on the right bank of the 'Great River', the Guadalquivir, which is the axis of the natural region of western Andalusia. This region conforms to the triangular shape of the Guadalquivir delta, with mountain ranges to the north and to the south. The former kingdom, and the modern province, of Córdoba lie across the middle of the Guadalquivir's course. Emilio Cabrera has calculated the area of the former as 14 100 km², compared with the latter's 13 718 km². The difference is explained by the transference of Chillón to the province of Ciudad Real and Peñaflor to the province of Seville, while the lands beyond the Zújar, in the north-west, are now in the province of Badajoz.[2] The climate of the whole western Andalusian region is influenced by the Atlantic, but the inland areas, including the kingdom of Córdoba, receive a much lower rainfall than the parts nearer the coast. Also, summer and winter temperatures inland are more extreme than those on the coast and the spring is generally the most temperate season of the year. On average, rain falls in the Córdoba area on between sixty and seventy days in the year, and, as a general rule, there is not enough rainfall in the region to counteract the high summer temperatures. This fact has clearly influenced the agriculture of western Andalusia, particularly as, in the medieval period, irrigation seems not to have been developed to the same extent as in, for example, the kingdom of Valencia, on Spain's east coast. The Córdoba region is not, however, a geographical unity. It may be divided into three areas, each of which assumed distinct economic, and even political, characteristics, in the late Middle Ages.

The Sierra

The mountain system which forms the natural boundary of Andalusia, to the north of the Guadalquivir, comes close to Córdoba in the shape of one of its lesser chains, the Sierra de Córdoba. The Cathedral is, at 107 metres, over 400 metres below the hill known as the Cerro de las Ermitas, five kilometres away. To the north of the Sierra de Córdoba lies the region known as the Pedroches.

The geographical characteristics of the Pedroches are more akin to those of La Mancha, to the north, than to those of the rest of Andalusia. The climate is dry, especially in the summer, and the prevailing winds come from the north and north-east. The entire plateau is at a height of about 600 metres, with peaks rising to nearly 1000 metres. The natural vegetation varies according to the height of the land. On the highest ground, known as *monte alto*, the main plant is the holm-oak, or ilex (*encina*), producing acorns in profusion. After this, the most common is the *coscoja*, which was used as a dye-stuff by the Romans and Arabs, and there are also some cork-oaks. The vegetation of the lower ground, the *monte bajo*, consists of strawberry-trees (*madroño*), rosemary, white heather and other mountain plants. Oleanders are to be found beside the streams. Thickets are scattered over the area and consist mainly of cistus (*jara*), surrounded by gorse, broom and lavender. There are also meadows, in which wild oats, white clover and lucern grow. The Arab name for the Pedroches was *Fahs al-Bollut*, or the plain of acorns (in Castilian, *bellotas*). The twelfth-century Arab writer Edrisi refers to holm-oaks as the main vegetation in the area and states that the inhabitants found the acorns particularly useful in years of scarcity.[3]

Agriculture seems to have made little impression on the natural state of the Pedroches, either in the Middle Ages or in more recent times. Most of the area remains forested, in the form of *monte alto* or thickets (*chaparrales*). Until the nineteenth century, the seven towns of the Pedroches, Villa Pedroche, Alcaracejos, Añora, Torremilano, Pozoblanco, Torrecampo and Villanueva de Córdoba, which were all subject to the jurisdiction of Córdoba, held their municipal lands in common. These consisted of *dehesas*, which in this area were generally fenced-in parts of the *monte*. Further to the north and west, in the region of Gahete and Hinojosa, Guijo, El Viso, Santa Eufemia and Chillón, the use of land was similar. The soil is generally sandy and does not encourage cultivation, which means that although subsistence crops of wheat, barley, beans and vines were grown, the predominant activity in the Pedroches was the rearing of livestock on the *montes* and in the *dehesas*. The most intensively cultivated lands were the *ruedos*, which immediately surrounded the centres of population. The best land might be cultivated every other year (*año y vez*), but most would only support crops every third or fourth year. Cultivation was generally by the method known as *rozas*, which involved broadcasting seed over a wide area and covering it by means of a ploughshare. The land was burnt in August, after harvesting, and left for the next sowing. The technique had a disastrous effect on the *chaparrales* which found themselves in the path of the flames, but the crops produced were apparently adequate.

However, the greatest scourge of crops in the Pedroches was not the *rozas*, although the damage they caused to the wood and fruit of the natural vegetation was unfortunate, but rather the depredations of livestock. All towns found it necessary to protect their cultivators with ordinances, forbidding flocks to enter vineyards, olive-groves, gardens and orchards (*huertas*) and other cultivated ground, but the extent of stock-breeding activity to the north of Córdoba made it particularly difficult to satisfy the conflicting interests of graziers and agriculturalists. The 1435 ordinances of Córdoba contain a long section, entitled *La corta e quema* (cutting and burning), which referred to the town council's duty to protect both the *montes* and the cultivated areas in the Sierra de Córdoba. The 1500 ordinances of Torremilano refer specifically to vines, which were apparently suffering from the incursion of all kinds of livestock. Owners were fond of bringing their flocks to the vineyards when the grapes were on the vines and feeding them to their dogs. All ordinances on this subject were phrased in a similar way, allowing cultivators to exact fines on the spot from offenders, according to a set scale of charges. In Torremilano, money fines were laid down, but Córdoba revised its own ordinances in 1478, specifying as a penalty the confiscation of one-fifth of the flock concerned, the *quinta de los ganados*. In each case, magistrates and council officials were ordered to support cultivators in applying the law.[4]

Further to the south, the valley of the Guadiato is more fertile, providing Belmez and Fuente Obejuna with pasture, vineyards and arable land. To the south-east, towards Espiel, the valley becomes narrower and more rocky, as it begins to cut through the Sierra. The extensive modern municipal territory of Espiel contained some olives and fruit-trees, but consisted largely of *monte bajo*, on rough, stony soil. This is even more true of Obejo, which is 700 metres up in the mountains, between the Cuzna and Guadalquivir valleys. In this area, cultivation has always been a problem because of the large area of barren rock, but there is some evidence of pasture, probably consisting of *monte bajo*.

The river valley

The asperity of the Sierra Morena gave the region to the north of Córdoba a very different character from the valley of the Guadalquivir. Towns to the north of this mountain wall have in the past had a tendency to look as much to the Campo de Calatrava and the north as to Córdoba, the mother town of the Pedroches. However, some of the valley towns have far more land in the mountains than in the plain, because of the Sierra's proximity to the river. Hornachuelos, for example, still has a vast territory, which consists, apart from some fertile land on the Bembézar and Guadalquivir, of a large area of holm-oaks, *dehesas* and *monte bajo*, as found further north. The same may be said of the neighbouring lands of Posadas and Almodóvar del Río, which consisted largely of *monte alto* and *monte bajo*. There was also arable cultivation, with some *dehesas*, and some vines, olive-groves, fruit-trees and gardens in the river valley. To the east of Córdoba, the picture in Adamuz, Villafranca and Montoro is similar. Although Montoro is on the left bank of the Guadalquivir, most of its land lies to the north and in the nineteenth century three-quarters of this was still *monte bajo*, including holm-oaks and pines.[5]

As might be expected, the area immediately surrounding Córdoba is better documented in local archives than many of the more distant parts. Columbus's son, Hernando Colón, in his 'Itinerary' (*Itinerario*), states that he saw *huertas* around the city, in which oranges, lemons and other fruit were grown, and vineyards to the west and north.[6] It appears from contemporary documents that a great many vines were grown on the south-facing slopes of the mountains to the north of Córdoba, particularly around Santa María de Trassierra. Vineyard properties generally also contained olive-groves and often a *huerta*. There would be presses for the olives and grapes and *bodegas* for storage. The intense cultivation of fruit and vegetables in the immediate vicinity of Córdoba was a survival of the rich agriculture which had supported the city in Muslim times. There were *huertas* on both banks of the river and also in the city itself, where they were frequently sold with houses. Just outside the walls were market-gardens, which supplied the population with a wide range of fruit and vegetables.[7]

The Campiña

The Campiña, to the south of Córdoba, stretches as far as the Sierras of Lucena, Cabra, Rute and Priego. The countryside here is undulating and has a very different character from the Sierra and the north. As in the Pedroches, arable and pastoral use of most land alternated. Generally, grain was grown every third year, the land then remaining fallow for a year as *barbechos*, with a year of use as pasture to follow. According to Colón, the Campiña was primarily a grain-producing area by the early sixteenth century, though there were also important concentrations of vines and olives, especially around La Rambla and Santaella. There were *huertas* in the valley of the Guadajoz, near Castro del Río. *Dehesas* were not mentioned by Colón, but they clearly existed, both to provide grazing for plough-animals and for stock-raising, in the territories of Guadalcázar, Santaella, Fernán Núñez, Montemayor, Castro and Monturque. The uniform character of agriculture in the Campiña was somewhat altered at its southern extreme, where the mountains begin to rise. As in the towns on the Guadalquivir, the type of cultivation varied from valley to mountain slope. On the flatter lands, for example in the valleys of the Guadajoz and Río de Cabra, vines and olive-trees could be grown, while the hills around Aguilar, Alcaudete, Baena and Cabra were partly barren and partly made up of *dehesas*. The southernmost extreme of Córdoba's influence, the area around Luque, Zuheros, Priego and Iznájar, is quite distinct from the Campiña. Some land in this area was cultivated with grain, olives or vines, but much of it is too rocky. Each town was provided with *dehesas* on the mountain slopes. The one fertile part of this southern fringe is the territory of Lucena, which includes some of the Campiña and the valley of the Genil, with its orchards, arable land, olives and vines.

RECONQUEST AND RESETTLEMENT

As Angus MacKay has recently suggested, there are two themes which help to explain much of the history of the medieval Iberian kingdoms. One of these is the Reconquest, which provided a unique spur to action and factor in social development from the moment of the Muslim invasion in 711 until the surrender of Granada in 1492. The other is the more subtle process whereby, during the superficially chaotic and meaningless fourteenth and fifteenth centuries, the Spanish kingdoms, and particularly the Crown of Castile, developed the institutions and the political and religious uniformity which were to provide the basis for Spanish imperial expansion in the sixteenth century.[8]

The cataclysmic event which determined the future development of the whole structure of western Andalusian settlement, cultivation and social relations was the thirteenth-century Reconquest. In the case of Córdoba, this mighty happening took place more or less by accident. It seems that in 1236 some non-Muslim bandits, or *almogávares*, who lived in the Sierra to the north, made contact, as was often their practice, with the highly mixed population of the Ajarquía, the eastern walled division of the Muslim city of Córdoba, this time securing control of it. The religious and administrative quarter, the Medina, held out for some time, but the 'official' armies of Ferdinand III of Castile and León were called in almost as an afterthought. One consequence of the haphazard way in which the city fell was that many areas to the north, in fact the home of the *almogávares*, took a number of years longer to conquer.[9]

The course of the conquest of the city of Córdoba and the process whereby it and its kingdom were first settled have been established satisfactorily by Julio González.[10] In the initial stages, the city was vacated by its existing population, but the surrounding countryside, particularly the Campiña, remained in Muslim hands. The actual *conquistadores* were on the whole more interested in going home to the north than in settling in Andalusia. Nonetheless, the word soon spread and Córdoba rapidly filled to overflowing, with the result that problems of housing and nourishment quickly arose. The need to expand into the countryside became imperative, but it took four years for the Christians to gain control over the Campiña. This was done largely by means of pacts, which allowed all Muslims who wished to stay to retain their own law-officers, mosques and property, while the Christian settlers took over all fortifications and shared out the rents and lands of the fugitives. Very little Christian settlement in fact took place in the Campiña until the Muslim revolts of 1264 put an end to the pacts and the area to the south of Córdoba became the defensive frontier of Christendom against the Moors, known as the *banda fronteriza* or *banda morisca*.[11]

Study of the thirteenth-century settlement of the kingdom of Córdoba is hampered by the lack of the original document of *repartimiento*, whereby the Castilian Crown allocated the conquered lands to their new inhabitants. Nonetheless, an ecclesiastical tithe-book of 1364, the *Libro de las Tablas*, gives a fairly clear idea of what happened in the Campiña, though not in Córdoba itself, and the procedure of *repartimiento* can be described by analogy with that of Seville, which was conquered in 1248 and where full documentation survives. As in the earlier stages of the Reconquest, there was no doubt in contemporaries' minds that the absolute priority was colonisation. Land should not go to waste and the vanished or evicted Muslims should have no chance to return to it. In Córdoba, Ferdinand III set up a commission of *partidores* immediately, in 1236. Donations of lands and urban properties to individuals, such as members of the Court and royal family, began in 1237 and continued up to 1244. The Church was set up at the same time, with grants of newly conquered lands. Some people probably occupied the largely urban property which they had seized when the city was first captured in 1236, but most waited for the grants made by the royal *partidores* before moving in.[12]

Clearly fundamental to any consideration of Cordoban society after the Reconquest is the size and nature of the area's population. The first problem is to discover what happened to its Muslim inhabitants. It is very difficult to say more than has already been stated, that the existing rural population largely remained until the failure of the revolt of 1264 and then emigrated, either to the kingdom of Granada or to North Africa. In the city itself, there is evidence that, after an initial expulsion, certain specialised artisans, particularly building-workers, were reimported to continue plying their trade. Nonetheless, it is clear that Christian settlement took place between 1236 and 1264 in an entirely, or almost entirely, vacant city and a largely vacant countryside, though the latter took until after 1264 to clear, if it ever was completely cleared, of Muslims. The cautionary phrase is needed because this question is still an open one. Clearly the fate of the rural population of the Muslim kingdom of Córdoba is a matter of some importance, yet extraordinarily little is known about those who worked this land, as opposed to those who held it, in the late Middle Ages. Had there been a massive emigration, it would obviously have been to Granada and North Africa, but there is little or no information available at present about the arrival of exiles in these two areas. In the case of Granada, there is little hope of more coming to light on the spot, but private libraries in North Africa may eventually provide a solution to the problem. There is evidence that even in the nineteenth century some lands in the Campiña had still not been cultivated since the thirteenth-century Reconquest, though they had been before. It is possible that at least some of the rural population, which was in any case a mixture of Celtic, Gothic, Berber and several other strains and had changed its religion more than once before to suit new conquerors, did in fact remain in the countryside. The absence of documentation makes it impossible to establish to what extent the rural population changed in composition and to what extent it declined as a result of the Christian conquest of Córdoba, though it is undeniable that both phenomena occurred.

How successful was the resettlement? In recent years, Andalusian historians have begun to question Vicens Vives' judgement on the attractiveness of the region to settlers in the thirteenth century, pointing to a crisis in the resettlement which began almost immediately. In fact, Ramón Carande long ago noticed that royal documents of Alfonso X begin as early as 1255 to refer to the departure, and hence the shortage, of settlers, in the case of Seville.[13] However, the main advocates of the view that the settlement of Andalusia was in large part a failure, at least in the initial stages, are Manuel González Jiménez and Antonio Collantes de Terán. It now appears that it was never very easy to attract settlers to Andalusia and that the efforts which were made received a severe setback in the Muslim uprisings of 1261–6. Grave economic difficulties were a feature of the whole of Castile from the middle to the end of the thirteenth century and were reflected in the unsuccessful price-control measures of the Cortes of Valladolid in 1258 and Jerez in 1268. A demographic decline in Castile at this time cannot be proved but is in any case not necessary to explain the unwillingness of settlers to move to Andalusia. The danger of Muslim attack and the difficulty of occupying assets which had only recently been vacated by an enemy population were no doubt powerful deterrents.[14]

Population

The pattern of late medieval demographic trends in Andalusia is gradually emerging. Thanks to the difficulties of settlement in the mid- and late thirteenth century, the Andalusian population was in a weak position to face the general European demographic crisis in the first half of the fourteenth century. While not particularly affected by the famine of 1315–17, Castile, including Andalusia, suffered major famines and shortages in 1310, 1335 and particularly between 1343 and 1346.[15] No sound figures are available for the effect of the Black Death on Castile, though it was clearly great in many areas. However, Andalusian patterns of population change, as reflected in deserted villages, have many interesting features. According to Manuel González's figures, which amplify those published by Cabrillana in 1965, the number of villages abandoned in the kingdom of Seville was thirty-eight in the thirteenth century, only eleven in the fourteenth, and thirty-three in the fifteenth and sixteenth. Unfortunately, Cabrillana's figures for the kingdom of Córdoba were compiled from eighteenth-century documents and cannot be dated to any particular century, though the total mentioned, for what it is worth, is thirty-two. If documentary evidence for deserted villages is poor, archaeological evidence is virtually unexplored.[16]

It appears, however, that in Andalusia only limited settlement, with setbacks, took place in the thirteenth century, while losses in the fourteenth century were counteracted by a fairly sizable effort at resettlement. The evidence available so far is for the kingdom of Seville. Manuel González has discovered about twenty-five new settlements, mostly to the west of Seville, in the rich, olive-growing area known as the Aljarafe. However, it seems unlikely that this movement was caused by an increase in the overall population of the kingdom of Seville. It was probably the result of pressures on land-use and on the economic situation of landlords. Similar new settlements in the kingdom of Seville in the late fifteenth and early sixteenth centuries, a total of twenty-two cases, have been described by Antonio Collantes.[17] These later settlements, however, while also apparently taking their population from among the existing inhabitants of the region, do seem to have happened during a period of demographic advance in Andalusia, which began in the early fifteenth century and probably involved considerable immigration from the rest of the Peninsula, at least to the developing port of Seville. As far as the distribution of population is concerned, the figures of Vicens Vives and his disciple, Sobrequés, have been reduced by recent research on the basis of *padrones*, or lists of urban tax-payers, in the case of Seville, where Collantes has found 2613 *vecinos*, or citizen heads of household, in 1384, 4893 in 1426–51, 6896 in 1483–9 and 9161 in 1533, totals which cannot approach Sobrequés' estimate of 75 000 inhabitants in the late fifteenth century.[18]

The *padrones* for Córdoba do not survive, so that the only source for the population figures of the kingdom of Córdoba is the later fiscal census of 1530, which has been studied by Emilio Cabrera.[19] Using Cabrera's coefficient of 4.5 for the number in each household, although as he rightly points out the figure was probably higher, for example 5.0 or 5.5, in rural areas, the total of 33 417 *vecinos* recorded in the 1530 census would amount to approximately 150 000 people. The Córdoba evidence, although from a slightly later period, does confirm Ladero's suggestion that Sobrequés and others have tended to underestimate the importance of middle-sized and smaller centres of population.[20] The city of Córdoba itself had 5845 *vecinos* in 1530. The next largest town, Baena, had 1467 and the other larger centres of population – Bujalance, La Rambla, Fuente Obejuna, Pedroche, Priego, Montilla, Aguilar, Cabra and Lucena – had between 1100 and 1500 *vecinos*, apart from the estimated figure of 2000 for Lucena, where no *padrón* was provided.[21] Whatever the inadequacies of the evidence, this Andalusian demographic pattern – a resettlement crisis in the late thirteenth century, a small advance with setbacks in the fourteenth, and a fairly steady surge in the fifteenth and early sixteenth centuries – makes an interesting comparison with the better-known trends in the rest of Europe, where the demographic crisis is generally placed in the fourteenth century and where the recovery is on the whole later than in this region.

Land-holding

The question of land-holding in Andalusia after the Reconquest inevitably involves a discussion of *latifundia*, which are often supposed to be a Roman feature which survived both the Muslim and the Christian conquests. If, however, the break-up of social structures at the Reconquest in the thirteenth century was in fact as complete as has been suggested up to now, it may be presumed that the development of *latifundia* was a consequence of the *repartimiento* of that period. For the structure of land-tenure as the *partidores* left it in the mid-thirteenth century, the González model, based mainly on Seville and to a lesser extent on Jerez, Ecija, Carmona and Córdoba, is the only satisfactory one. As a general rule, all lands were in the hands of the king. When he disposed of them, not all *conquistadores* received grants and not all recipients of grants were *conquistadores*. González divides the grants of rural property into two main categories. The first, the *donadíos*, were grants made to those who were obliged, as king's vassals (*vasallos del Rey*) to aid him in the Reconquest. A *donadío* was effectively a special jurisdiction, whose possessor had complete freedom of disposal, though the larger grants carried the requirement that the holder should not absent himself without leaving a military substitute. The recipient was normally a nobleman. The second category, the *heredamientos*, were redistributed portions of *donadíos*, normally granted to settlers who were not the king's personal vassals, in return for certain obligations and services. The size of these two kinds of property varied, but the *donadío* was very much the larger and could consist of more than one *alquería* or farmstead. Thus González sees it as the precursor of the *latifundium*. Valuable property such as vineyards or fruit-orchards, which was available in smaller quantities, was normally only included in *donadíos*.[22]

Nonetheless, Julio González's work on Seville and later research on Seville, Carmona and Córdoba has shown that, despite the size and significance of *donadíos* in the Reconquest settlement, there was always considerable room for small and medium-sized holdings. Indeed, the fourteenth-century resettlement in the kingdom of Seville seems to have helped to create a new group of small peasant cultivators, juridically free and with the usufruct (*derecho útil*) of the land concerned, without being subject to any form of contract involving short-term, or ground-rent.[23] Much of this settlement took place in the heavily commercialised olive- and vine-growing region of the Aljarafe. Developments here may not have been typical of the region as a whole, as the more general trend in the kingdom of Seville in the late Middle Ages, described by Collantes, is a gradual and fairly continuous concentration of land in the hands of a small number of great landowners. In other words, the *latifundium* was there from the start, in the form of the *donadío*, but it only gradually became the normal form of land-holding in western Andalusia in the period up to and beyond 1500.[24] Thus while *latifundia* increasingly dominated the scene in the fourteenth and fifteenth centuries, especially with the development of the *mayorazgo*, or entail, as a means of keeping together the lands of noble families, smaller estates also flourished, though they were less frequent near the larger centres of population. Nonetheless, in the early sixteenth century, forty-one per cent of the *vecinos* of Carmona still owned some land, and small properties were particularly common in recently settled areas. The letting of land by major landowners, ecclesiastical or secular, for ground-rent (*censos*) was common, providing an opportunity for the small cultivator to retain considerable control over his land, including the right to dispose of it to designated heirs. Share-cropping (*medianería* or *aparcería*) and *complantación*, in which a peasant agreed to cultivate a lord's land within a certain period and thereafter shared the plot equally with the lord, were methods whereby landless peasants could become cultivators.[25]

These generalisations need to be tested in specific cases. Various examples from the region of Andalusia will be considered here, while the Córdoba evidence will be studied in greater detail in later chapters. Collantes describes the typical *latifundium* in the kingdom of Seville in the fifteenth century as a large property exploited as a unity – a *hacienda* if used for olives and vines and a *cortijo* if used for cereals. The commercialised olive-growing *haciendas* tended to have more buildings and to remain under the lord's direct exploitation. Vines were normally cultivated on the same estates as olives and facilities for the pressing and storage of wine and oil were included in each property. Typical *latifundia* of the Seville aristocracy were of eight- or nine-hundred *fanegas* (480–540 hectares) of arable and two-hundred or more *aranzadas* (73.4 hectares) of vines or olive-groves. Some enclosed pasture, or *dehesa*, was set aside for plough-oxen on predominantly arable estates. The labour-force was normally paid in cash and much of it was hired for particular seasonal tasks, such as ploughing and harvesting, on the basis of contracts which detailed conditions of work, the days and hours to be worked and the methods of payment. Contracts with *gañanes*, or workers on arable properties, specified the area to be covered, in the case of ploughing. The olive-harvesters were known as *cogedores* and were often women, organised into squads under a *cuadrillero*. Whole families sometimes went harvesting and ages might range from fifteen (or even twelve) to sixty. Normally, they arrived in the Seville area during the octave either before or after All Saints' Day and any who left early had to be replaced at the expense of the defaulter. The teams of olive-harvesters generally came from Extremadura, to the north. Target quantities were set of olives to be picked and if these were not achieved the deficit generally had to be made up in the following year.[26]

No figures for the relative numbers of *latifundia* and smaller estates are available for Seville. In Carmona, on the other hand, quite detailed information on rural property-ownership is provided by the tax-returns (*padrones*) of 1508–20. It has already been noted that over forty-one per cent of the *vecinos* of Carmona owned some olives or vines and the great majority of these were small properties. In the *padrones* of 1508–11, 293 owners of olive-groves had less than five *aranzadas* (1.84 hectares) each, while eighty-six had more. In the case of vineyards, the figures were 418 with less than five *aranzadas* and only fourteen with more. The picture with arable land is very different, however. According to notarial documents and *padrones*, most of the arable in the *vega*, the fertile area south of Carmona, was in the hands of ecclesiastics, convents, charitable institutions, officials of the royal government or noblemen. The majority of these came from outside Carmona and rented their lands to *colonos* (similar to Roman *coloni*) or share-croppers (*aparceros*) who were *vecinos* of Carmona. According to the *padrones* of 1508–11, nearly all the owners of arable who were citizens of Carmona were either town councillors or their relatives. However, they too had an 'absentee' attitude to their lands, generally cultivating them not directly but through share-croppers. Slightly later figures, from the 1535 *padrón*, give some idea of the predominance which had been achieved by outsiders as absentee landlords of the arable of Carmona. In that year, outsiders received 18 730 *fanegas* of wheat and barley as rent, while *vecinos* received only 7172½ *fanegas*. Thus over seventy per cent of cereal rents in Carmona in that year went to absentee outsiders.[27]

SOCIAL AND POLITICAL STRUCTURE

It will become clear later that land-holding in the neighbouring kingdom of Córdoba was similarly organised, but the reasons why this situation developed cannot be understood without reference to the political structure of western Andalusia as it developed after the Reconquest. The distribution of political power in the region between the Crown and local influences depended for the rest of the medieval period on the decisions taken in the early days by Ferdinand III and Alfonso X.

As a basic principle, the Crown rewarded those who had helped in the military campaigns, not only with lands, but also, in some cases, with jurisdiction over towns and villages in the area. The remaining territory continued to be directly subject to the Crown. These royal lands were called *realengo*, while those granted to nobles or ecclesiastical corporations were known as *señoríos*. The legal and historical development of the concept of *señorío* in the Crown of Castile is of considerable importance and interest. It depended on the acceptance in all Castilian law-codes of the principle, in family law, that a father had the right to undisputed supremacy over his son. The Visigothic *Fuero Juzgo*, which became the charter (*fuero*) of the royal towns of Andalusia after the Reconquest, gave children no property rights while their parents were alive, though the parents had the right to punish them in the event of a 'great offence or great dishonour'.[28] Alfonso X's *Siete Partidas*, which owed much to the laws of Justinian, justified the father's power and lordship (*poder et señorío*) over his son by reference to the superiority implicit in the original act of conception and to the debt which the son owed to his father because he would one day inherit his property.[29] This principle was easily extended from the family to society as a whole. Since late Roman times, Spanish society had been divided, like that of most of western Europe, into two basic categories – the nobles, who had wealth and power, and the peasants, who of right had little or none. Churches and monasteries, which owned extensive lands, were treated as *seniores*, or part of the nobility.

The manner in which Andalusia was reconquered ensured that the majority of the population would be dependent from the start on the small military group which carried out the essential military activity. When the Christian settlers arrived from the north in towns such as Córdoba and Seville, they found the land already allocated to various noblemen or to ecclesiastical corporations, such as cathedrals or military orders, particularly the Templars and the knights of Calatrava. Two kinds of *señorío* may be distinguished in late medieval Andalusia. One of these is the contemporary Castilian version of the well-known 'feudal' relationship between the lord and his vassal. As elsewhere, a man might become the *vasallo* of a *señor* in order to obtain military and legal protection, in return for his personal service. By the fifteenth century, vassals of this kind were generally rewarded by the payment of retainers, known as *acostamientos*, by their lords. It was possible for a subject to enter into this kind of arrangement with the king and some Andalusian nobles became *vasallos del Rey*, which meant that the king had the first call on their services in time of war and that they were more committed to him than his other subjects. Leading nobles also had *vasallos* to whom they paid *acostamientos* and such links were an important part of politics in the region.[30]

The vast majority of Andalusians, including those who lived in areas of *señorío*, were not, however, *vasallos* in this sense. In the central Middle Ages, the southward movement of conquest and resettlement had produced the concept of 'territorial lordship', in which when land was granted to a lord by the king its inhabitants automatically became that lord's vassals, although they had no personal feudal ties with him. In the later period, territorial lordship was commonly replaced, at least in the south, by 'jurisdictional lordship', whereby the conditions under which the inhabitants held or worked their lands remained unaltered when a *señorío* was created. Instead, the lord simply replaced the Crown as the local authority in administration and justice. The lord might be granted a specific number of *vasallos* when he received his *señorío*, but these would only be a minority of its population, like the *vasallos del Rey* in *realengo*. In these circumstances, it is clear that those who worked the land in a *señorío* did not necessarily owe feudal services and dues to its lord, but whether they were legally 'free' or not, their status was extremely low. Roman law, enshrined in the *Partidas*, equated those who settled on the land, the *pobladores*, with serfs (*siervos*), though this applied to *realengo* as well as *señorío*.

However, if Roman law strengthened the power of the lord over his jurisdictional vassals, its primary purpose in Castile was to establish the supremacy of the royal prerogative. One of the main features of medieval Castilian legislation was the perpetual conflict between laws which strengthened the royal government and those which conceded extensive powers to lords. Roman law was a two-edged weapon in the hands of the king, because while it guaranteed his sovereignty over the kingdom, this very fact allowed him effectively to give away large parts of his inheritance in *señorío* to nobles, while at the same time protesting that he was preserving his kingdom in entail (*mayorazgo*) for his heirs. The Cortes, representing the nobility, the Church and burgesses, tried on many occasions, notably in 1442, to limit grants of *señorío* to cases of 'great and urgent necessity', but the royal jurists countered their laws with others, such as the regalist *Ordenamiento* of Alcalá in 1348, which reaffirmed the statement in the *Partidas* that the king was free to grant any centre of population or castle to an ecclesiastical corporation or private individual, as long as he reserved the right to make peace and war in the territory concerned and provided that its inhabitants had the right of appeal to his supreme courts.[31]

The powers which a lord was granted when he received a *señorío* were always precisely defined in the document concerned. Under the Trastámaras, grants were made in accordance with the king's claim to absolute sovereignty over the whole kingdom. The *Partidas* asserted that the monarch's title was of divine origin and gave him the mission of administering justice throughout the realm and of commanding its armies. Because the title was hereditary, the kingdom partook of the character of private property. However, the old laws, which preceded the *Partidas*, still limited his power. The sovereign could change *fueros* if it was in the interest of the kingdom to do so, but this did not alter the fact that he had to swear, after receiving the allegiance of the *procuradores* of the Cortes, to observe the older versions.[32] The royal claim to 'civil and criminal jurisdiction in all the cities and towns of his kingdoms and lordships' meant that a lord could never consider himself entirely free, within his *señorío*, of the royal law and its officers. The Crown insisted that just as nobles had right of access to the king's supreme tribunal, the royal council (*concejo real*), so should the inhabitants of *señoríos*, though their cases were to be heard in the first instance by the local magistrates, the *alcaldes de su fuero*, appointed by the lord according to the provisions of the local charter.[33] The Crown reserved to itself, however, the hearing in the first instance of certain types of case, as an attribute of royal sovereignty. These were murder, rape, the breaking of treaties, the burning of houses, damage to highways, treason (*traición*), treachery (*aleve*), challenges or threats (*rieptos*) and cases involving widows, orphans and people in extreme poverty (*personas miserables*). The *Partidas* had included the forgery of money and the royal seal in this list of offences, but they were omitted by Montalvo, perhaps in error.[34]

The standard formula by which the Crown granted a jurisdictional lordship to a nobleman in the later Middle Ages referred to 'civil and criminal, high and low jurisdiction, *mero y mixto imperio*'. The Latin phrase came from Roman law, in which *imperium merum* was the complete power of a magistrate to settle criminal cases, called 'justice of blood' in Castilian, according to the sixteenth-century commentator Gregorio López. *Imperium mixtum* was the equivalent jurisdiction in civil cases. Apart from seignorial vassals' right of appeal to the royal tribunals, there was another limitation on the *mero y mixto imperio* which the lord received with the grant of a jurisdictional lordship. This was the right of royal officials to enter the *señorío* at any time, without the lord's permission, and administer justice in the king's name, if the Crown had any reason to believe that there was an inadequacy (*mengua*) in the justice given by the lord or his agents. This could be done even without a previous complaint by a litigant to the Crown. A lord was also forbidden to give sanctuary to those fleeing from royal justice, though the enforcement of this law, like so many others, depended on the strength of the Crown's resolution at any given moment.[35] The Crown could grant *señorios* without jurisdiction, but this became increasingly rare in the fifteenth century.

The delegation of administrative powers by the Crown to *señores* was authorised by the *Partidas*. The most important of these powers was the right to appoint magistrates and other officials in the same way as the king or the local community named them in royal towns. A typical fifteenth-century case was the grant to Don Diego López Pacheco, second marquis of Villena, of the *señorio* of Serón and Tijola (Almería) by the Catholic Monarchs, after the conquest of Granada, with the power to name the magistrates (*justicia*), the *escribanos*, or notaries, and the constables (*alguaciles*) of the two towns.[36]

It was also possible for lords to obtain some share of taxation revenue in their *señorios* which would otherwise have gone to the Crown. As in the case of jurisdiction, the Cortes fought to prevent this alienation of part of the royal patrimony. It was agreed that certain regalian rights, including some *tributos* and the coining of money, could not be alienated, but the Cortes admitted that the king could in other cases give the benefit of his rents to a private individual or delegate the power of collection to a lord. The difference between these concessions and an outright alienation was not in practice very great.[37] The Cortes' claim to control such grants was based on the law which forbade their proclamation without that assembly's consent.[38] However, just as the Cortes failed to stop the grant of *señorios*, so it also proved incapable of preventing the transfer of royal revenues, with complete legality, to private individuals. The conditions of such alienations were complex and reflected the chaotic state of the royal finances in the fifteenth century. In the case of some taxes, both the revenues and the power of collection remained with the Crown, while in other cases the lord was given power to collect on behalf of the Crown, and in others again, the revenue itself was granted to the lord as well. As an additional complication, it was also possible for a lord to obtain the revenue of a tax without a royal grant, by 'prescriptive right'. The concept of immemorial possession was received into Castile in its Roman law form. It was defined as one hundred years of 'quiet and peaceful possession without any contradiction'. In this way an individual could obtain a normal attribute of the sovereign, such as the power to collect a tax or even the possession of a whole *señorío*.[39]

When the Crown divided the reconquered lands of the kingdoms of Seville and Córdoba into *realengo* and *señorío*, it retained control of the main towns, notably Córdoba, Ecija, Carmona, Seville and Jerez de la Frontera. Each of these was given extensive lands, which, in the cases of Seville and Córdoba, contained other lesser towns and villages which were made subject to the new city councils. These outlying areas were known as the *tierra* or *término* of the town concerned. That of Seville was by far the largest. It originally stretched for about 240 km, both from north to south and from east to west, and it contained about 135 towns and villages. The majority of these had been lost by the end of the fifteenth century, but sixty still remained subject to Seville council. In the case of Córdoba, the delineation of the *alfoz*, or *tierra*, began at the order of Ferdinand III on 10 March 1241, concentrating on the southern boundary, which was still a frontier zone and to remain so for a considerable period. The precise positions of the seven boundary-marks (*mojones*) which were then established cannot be discovered, but they spread from the Córdoba–Andújar road in a rough semi-circle to a point west of the Guadajoz. The area covered was approximately half of the modern province and all of it was subject to Córdoba's *fuero* as *realengo*.[40]

Almost at once, however, the alienation of land began and, as a result of this process, the territory which remained subject to Córdoba in the early years of the Catholic Monarchs was only a small proportion of that granted by Ferdinand III in 1241. While the castles of Almodóvar del Río, Chillón, Obejo and Santa Eufemia and the towns, castles and lands, including silver-mines, of Gahete (from 1466 Belalcázar) and Pedroche were given to Córdoba in 1242, other territory was given to the military order of Calatrava, which had played a prominent part in the Reconquest. In the later thirteenth century, Córdoba made several gains. In 1264 it received Posadas (del Rey), which was constituted a town (*villa*) at the same time, and in the following year Santaella was added. Sancho IV incorporated Baena, Luque and Zuheros into Córdoba's *término* in 1293.[41] Nonetheless, the practice of alienating towns from the royal jurisdiction, having become established in the early days, caused a gradual decline in the number of towns included in the *tierra*. The process was not absolutely irreversible. In 1258, for example, Alfonso X restored to Córdoba the town of Cabra, which had been granted by Ferdinand III to his uncle, Don Rodrigo Alfonso de León, *adelantado de la frontera* (governor of the frontier).[42] However, there was a pronounced general trend towards the dismemberment of the royal patrimony. In the long run, Cabra was no exception. For some time it was in the hands of the order of Calatrava, then, in 1342, it was returned to Córdoba by Alfonso XI. The Trastámaras alienated it yet again and in 1439 it was given by John II to Diego Fernández de Córdoba, third lord of Baena.

The will of Gonzalo Fernández de Córdoba, first lord of Aguilar in the house of Córdoba, dated 15 December 1379, indicates the extent of the losses that Córdoba had already sustained by then. The former royal possessions which were included in the family estates were the *villas* of Aguilar and Priego and the *lugares* (lesser places) of Castillo Anzur, Montilla and Cañete.[43] In addition, Villafranca was given to the order of Calatrava in 1377, Baena was alienated by Henry II in 1386 and Zuheros by John II.[44] During the fourteenth century, Santa Eufemia was lost as well. However, it was in the fifteenth century that Córdoba experienced its greatest difficulties in preserving its *término*. Despite his promise, at the Cortes of Valladolid in 1442, to keep the royal patrimony intact, John II granted two of Córdoba's subject towns, Gahete and Hinojosa, to the master of the military order of Alcántara, Don Gutierre de Sotomayor. Henry IV gave Fuente Obejuna and Belmez to the master of Calatrava, Don Pedro Girón. Both succeeded in making these grants into personal possessions, which could be inherited by their families.[45]

Córdoba council had previously caused the king to abandon an attempt to grant Fuente Obejuna and Belmez to Don Gutierre de Sotomayor and in 1465 it was able, as a result of the exigencies of the civil war in Castile, to persuade Henry to revoke the grant to Don Pedro Girón, but in 1468, Fernán Gómez de Guzmán, *comendador mayor* (chief commander) of Calatrava, seized the two towns while Córdoba was distracted by internal disturbances. In April 1476, Fuente Obejuna returned to Córdoba's jurisdiction after a revolt in which the *comendador mayor* was murdered. It remained in Córdoba's hands until 1557, when it was sold by the Crown to Don Leopoldo de Austria, bishop of Córdoba. However, the order of Calatrava did not give up without a fight and Córdoba's possession was contested in a series of legal actions in secular and ecclesiastical courts which ended in a compromise, arrived at by the two parties on 6 October 1513, whereby Fuente Obejuna remained subject to Córdoba, but the order received compensation of 30 000 ducats, to be paid half by the Crown, which was by this time administering the goods of the order of Calatrava in any case, and half by Córdoba itself.[46]

Despite these losses, Córdoba retained control over many places during the reign of the Catholic Monarchs. The royal possessions may be divided into three main areas, the valley of the Guadalquivir, the Sierra and the north, and the Campiña. In the river valley, Córdoba had jurisdiction over Hornachuelos, Peñaflor, Posadas, Almodóvar del Río, Alcolea, Pedro Abad, Adamuz, Montoro and Aldea (now Villa) del Río. North of the valley, the remaining royal possessions were Santa María de Trassierra, Obejo, Fuente Obejuna, Alcaracejos, Pozoblanco, Torremilano (now, with the seignorial quarter, Torrefranca, known as Dos Torres), Añora, Pedroche (then known as Villa Pedroche), Villanueva de Córdoba (known as the *lugar* of Enzina until 1499) and Torrecampo. South of the Guadalquivir, Córdoba's *tierra* included Bujalance, Castro del Río, Castro Viejo (now a depopulated site near Bujalance), Villar, La Rambla and Santaella.

Some of the *señoríos* in late medieval Andalusia were in the possession of the Castilian military orders – Santiago, Calatrava, Alcántara and St John – which had large holdings elsewhere in the kingdom. However, western Andalusia was not a great source of strength to the orders, in comparison with areas which had been conquered earlier, such as Calatrava's territory in La Mancha and Santiago's empire on the Portuguese frontier to the north of Seville. Apart from Fuente Obejuna, which was lost in 1476, and Belmez, the only major possessions of the order of Calatrava in the kingdom of Córdoba were its commandery at Córdoba itself, including arable lands, and another at Villafranca de Córdoba, after 1377. The other orders, Santiago, Alcántara and St John, had no possessions at all in the kingdom of Córdoba.[47]

Another possible beneficiary of alienations from the royal patrimony was the Church, but, like the military orders, the dioceses of Seville and Córdoba were not generously treated by the Crown, in terms of *señoríos*, indeed the bishops of Córdoba had no major possessions at all. The town of Lucena had been lost in the late fourteenth century and in the 1490s bishop Iñigo Manrique sold the fortress of Toledillo to Don Luis Portocarrero, lord of Palma. In 1497, the Crown tried to make Portocarrero hand the castle back to the Church, but apparently without success.[48]

It is clear that royal grants of Andalusian *señoríos* mainly benefited the secular nobility.[49] The leading noble family in the kingdom of

Córdoba, in both social and economic terms, was the house of Fernández de Córdoba, which arrived from Galicia with the conquering armies in 1236. By the late fifteenth century, it had fragmented into a series of separate lines, but two of the senior ones had attained a position in the upper nobility of the Crown of Castile as a whole. The more powerful of these was the original line, known by the fifteenth century as the house of Aguilar, which had acquired a group of *señoríos* to the south of Córdoba, consisting of Cañete de las Torres, Aguilar, Priego, Monturque, Castillo Anzur, La Puente de Don Gonzalo (now Puente Genil), Montilla, Santa Cruz, Duernas and Carcabuey, the last three being obtained by purchase or exchange. The other line of the Fernández de Córdoba which may be included in the highest category is the house of Baena, which was the third branch of the family to become a separate lineage, acquiring the *señorío* of Baena from Henry II in 1386. By Ferdinand and Isabella's reign, it had also obtained permission to populate Doña Mencía, from John II in 1420, and had received the *señoríos* of Rute, Zambra, Iznájar as a viscounty and Cabra as a county. These possessions, significantly, formed a broad, continuous band, running from north to south across the southern end of the modern province of Córdoba.

Beneath the level of the upper nobility, which had more than regional importance, there was a middle category of noble families with *señoríos*. Two of these were branches of the Fernández de Córdoba. The first to break away from the house of Aguilar acquired in the late fourteenth century a *señorío* which consisted of Lucena and Espejo in the south and Chillón, on the northernmost fringe of Córdoba's influence. This family was known in the fifteenth century by the title of *alcaide de los donceles* (governor of the royal pages) which the head of the house had acquired in the 1370s. The possessions of the fourth branch of the Fernández de Córdoba – Montemayor and Alcaudete – were less scattered, but still did not form a complete 'empire', like those of Baena and, to a lesser extent, Aguilar. There were however two medium-sized *señoríos* in the north which were complete blocks of territory. In addition to their numerous possessions in the modern province of Badajoz, the Sotomayor had a band of territory which stretched south from Belalcázar to Espiel. Adjoining this was the *señorío* of the Mexía, which covered the north-eastern corner of the modern province of Córdoba and contained Santa Eufemia, El Viso, El Guijo and, from 1487, the castle of Madroñiz, on the border between the lands of Belalcázar and Santa Eufemia. The Méndez de Sotomayor, who were an old-established Córdoba family, quite separate from the Sotomayor of Belalcázar, had a *señorío* in the valley of the Guadalquivir, consisting of El Carpio and Morente. Also in the river valley was the *señorío* of the Portocarrero, which was based on Palma del Río and included Fuente del Alamo and La Puebla de los Infantes.

There were also seven minor *señoríos*, each consisting of one small town or village, to the south of Córdoba. Five of these belonged to descendants of the Fernández de Córdoba, one of them legitimate, the others not. The legitimate line was the house of Guadalcázar, and the others held the lordship of Belmonte, a now-depopulated place near Bujalance, Zuheros, Fuencubierta and the *cortijo* (farmstead) of El Fontanar. The other minor *señoríos* belonged to two families which had arrived in Córdoba with the reconquering armies. The Venegas received Luque from Henry II in 1374, while the De los Ríos received Fernán Núñez at the same time. A minor branch of the De los Ríos owned Las Ascalonias in the fifteenth century. At the bottom of the scale, however, it is sometimes difficult to decide which families should be included in the category of *señores*, because the difference between a village and a large farm is not always easy to distinguish at this distance.

The role of the Crown in assembling the estates of the nobility in the kingdom of Córdoba was clearly crucial. Of the forty-three *señoríos* which the nobility of the kingdom of Córdoba had obtained by 1474 (not all of them actually within that kingdom), twenty-seven were royal grants, the rest being acquired by purchase, marriage, exchange, or other means. In addition, a number of places in the second category had previously been granted by the Crown to other families. This fact is important, because it shows how power became concentrated in fewer hands in the late Middle Ages. Between 1369, when Henry II seized the throne, and the accession of Ferdinand and Isabella in 1474, the transfer of existing *señoríos* from another family to one of those mentioned above accounted for the great majority of the royal grants made in the period. Jurisdiction went with nearly all grants after 1300 and even if an earlier grant had not included it, this was generally remedied later.

The relative generosity of the various Castilian kings between Sancho IV and Henry IV is of some interest. The most enthusiastic grantors of *señoríos* were Henry II and John II with seven and Henry IV with five. The next highest number was Alfonso XI's total of three, with Sancho IV, John I and Henry III making one grant each. It is also noticeable that nearly all the leading families in the Cordoban nobility in the late fifteenth century had first come to the region under Ferdinand III or Alfonso X. The only exceptions were the Portocarrero, who married into the Genoese Bocanegra family, which had gained its *señorío* in the mid-fourteenth century, the Mexía, who married into an old Córdoba family, the Carrillo, during John II's reign, and the Sotomayor. The Sotomayor empire, to the north of Córdoba, was developed by Don Gutierre de Sotomayor, who succeeded his uncle as master of the order of Alcántara in 1432. Gutierre carried out a series of complicated political manoeuvres during the civil wars of John II's reign, but in return for a momentary show of loyalty to the king at a time when Córdoba council was supporting his dissident son, he was rewarded in 1445 with the lordship of two of Córdoba's towns, Hinojosa and Gahete, the latter becoming a county under the name of Belalcázar in 1466. Between 1445 and the end of John II's reign, he received sixteen more *señoríos*, including Villaharta and Espiel in Córdoba's territory, but an attempt to give him Fuente Obejuna and Belmez in 1450 was thwarted by Córdoba council's resistance. Nonetheless, Gutierre was able to leave a fine inheritance to his son Alfonso.

The shortage of new arrivals in the Cordoban aristocracy between the thirteenth and the fifteenth centuries was matched by a distinct lack of departures. Families such as the De los Ríos and Venegas, who were among the *conquistadores* of Córdoba, obtained *señoríos* comparatively late and failed to expand their holdings, so that an early arrival in the area was no guarantee of a place in the first rank after 1400, but on the other hand there was no family which lost this rank once it had been gained. The reasons for this remarkable stability will be discussed later, but it is now time to examine the internal structure of government in the royal town of Córdoba.

2

The structure of urban government

THE CITY COUNCIL'S OFFICIALS

Given that a political structure had to be built from nothing in the newly reconquered city and *tierra* of Córdoba, it was inevitable that the new government would owe much to previous experience in circumstances of this kind. In the early thirteenth century, the prevailing wisdom was that each town should be governed by what was called an 'open council' (*concejo abierto*), that is, an assembly of all the male householders (*vecinos*) to discuss their common concerns and make decisions. The *fuero* of Usagre (Badajoz) and Cáceres, for example, envisaged such meetings taking place after mass on Sundays.[1] Magistrates were appointed by the king, sometimes after election by the *vecinos*, to represent his overall authority, but there was no provision for the setting-up of citizens as councillors to make decisions on behalf of their fellows. This definition of the council was never superseded in any Castilian town subject directly to the Crown and documents were still addressed by Ferdinand and Isabella firstly to the *concejo* and only then to any other officials who might represent or govern it.

Much of the interest in the governmental structure of late medieval Córdoba centres around the office of *jurado*. As far as the major Andalusian towns are concerned, it seems probable, as Hipólito Sancho argues in the case of Jerez, that the *concejo abierto* never operated. Instead, they were divided into parishes, for governmental as well as ecclesiastical purposes, and in each parish a citizen was sworn (*jurado*) to represent his fellows and govern the town in conjunction with the king's magistrates. It appears that from the earliest times Córdoba's chief magistrate and constable were not elected but appointed by the king.[2] The ancestors of the late medieval *jurados*, however, appear for the first time in a document of 22 October 1258, which speaks of a representative of each parish (*collación*) who took part in the government of the town.[3] Another document, from Ferdinand IV's reign

24

(9 January 1296) refers to the duties of the *jurados* in keeping order in their parishes and in guarding the city walls, but the first clear description of *jurados* as they were to operate in the late fifteenth century is to be found in a document of 1320. Here Alfonso XI indicates that they were the spokesmen of their parishes and the king's agents, with the duty of informing him about the way in which the town was being governed.[4] There were two *jurados* for each of the fifteen parishes, these being conveniently divided into two groups. The former Medina contained, under Christian rule, the parishes of St Mary (the Cathedral), St John, All Saints', St Dominic, St Saviour, St Michael, St Nicholas 'de la Villa' and St Bartholomew. The Ajarquía to the east contained the parishes of St Mary Magdalene, St Lawrence, St Marina, St Andrew, St Peter, St James and St Nicholas 'del Ajarquía'.

The definition of the role of the *jurados* in the early fourteenth century coincided with the introduction to the city of a permanent council, whose members were known as *regidores*. The exact date of their introduction to Córdoba is not known, but the new council was the result of a policy carried out on a wide scale by Alfonso XI. Under the new system, the magistrates (*alcaldes mayores*) continued to be appointed by the Crown, but they were joined by twenty-four *regidores*, nominated by the Crown, who were commonly known, from their number, as *veinticuatros*. A council of similar size and type was introduced to Seville at about the same time.

The magistrates placed over the towns by the king were naturally assisted by officers to enforce the law and the post of *alguacil mayor* (chief constable) was established in Córdoba, as in other royal towns, in the thirteenth century. However, the simple structure of two magistrates, a chief constable, a council of *regidores* and two *jurados* from each parish was not regarded as adequate for the successful government of the town and extra officials were soon added. In late fifteenth-century Córdoba, there was an *alcalde de la justicia*, who heard criminal cases in daily audience at the public prison. There were *alcaldes ordinarios* for civil cases in the first instance. The *alguacil mayor* of Córdoba was provided with a deputy, the *alguacil menor*, and together they led a force of *alguaciles de espada*, or parish constables, one of whom was allocated to each parish.[5]

The orderly conduct of public and private life in Castile depended on the recording of transactions by *escribanos públicos* (public scribes). Public business in royal towns was placed in the hands of these *escribanos* by the *Siete Partidas* of Alfonso X, and by the mid-fifteenth century it was established by ordinance that there were to be twenty-four *escribanos públicos* in Córdoba.[6] Their duties were various. They were required to record legal proceedings before the magistrates, and gradually new tasks were given to them, as royal officials proliferated in the town. The *escribanos* of Córdoba, as a body, were required to provide one of their number to work in each of the city's parishes. The proceedings of the meetings of the *regidores* were recorded by a member of that council entitled the *escribano del concejo*. He normally appointed a deputy from among the *escribanos públicos*, who actually composed the records of council acts which are now one of the main sources of information about the government of medieval Castilian towns.

By the late fifteenth century, the public authorities in Córdoba had acquired a large staff of officials, ranging from the *alférez*, or town standard-bearer, whose duty it was to lead the town's forces into battle, to the council messenger and the town-crier. The most exalted of these officials was the *procurador mayor del concejo*, the council proctor, who represented that body whenever one man was required to speak in its name. The *regidores* also named two of their number, in addition to the *procurador mayor*, as proctors whenever the Crown summoned the Cortes, or parliament. Córdoba was one of the seventeen Castilian towns represented in this assembly, probably because it was the capital of the kingdom of the same name.

The council employed a number of other officials to help expedite its business. The most important of these were lawyers (*letrados*), who played a crucial role in many council decisions, a town-crier to publicise royal and municipal measures, trumpeters and drummers to accompany the council troops and perform on ceremonial occasions, a messenger (*correo*), a chaplain and an official to supervise the council porters (*fiel de la portería*).

Some of these minor officials helped to enforce the law. One of them was the *alguacil de las entregas*, a constable who appears to have been responsible for the collection of *entregas*, the payments required to settle debts or other legal cases.[7] Goods and cash collected in this way were stored in the council meeting-house, though in 1498 the Crown told the council to provide a special building for the purpose, and representatives were sent to examine the working of such a house in Seville.[8] There was a municipal gaol for offenders sentenced by the local magistrates. A *fiel* (literally a faithful or reliable man) was appointed by the council to supervise its running from the official point of view, while the interests of the prisoners were supposedly defended by an official who was chosen each year by the *regidores* from outside the council to be their representative, that is, the *procurador de la cárcel*.[9]

The council's property in rents and land, the *propios*, was supervised and administered by the council's *mayordomo*. This office was included in the original *fuero* and its holder had overall responsibility for the public accounts, with which he was assisted by the public accountant (*contador del concejo*). He was also helped by a collector of funds (*cobrador de la cuenta pública*).

In addition to the *mayordomo* and his staff, there were other officials to supervise public works, trade and agriculture. For public works, the council provided two clerks (*alarifes*) and a collector of funds. It also appointed two *mayordomos de las calles*, who were responsible for the cleanliness of the streets. The staff of the custom-house (*casa de la aduana*) was also provided largely by the council. It consisted of an *alcalde* and a porter, who were supervised by a *fiel* on behalf of the council. Other *fieles* performed a similar task for the various trades of the town. They and the *veedores* (examiners) were responsible for checking the weights and measures used by traders and for supervising the sale of salt, flour and fish, the trades of tanning and dye and cloth manufacture and the work of silversmiths.[10]

As will become clear later, Córdoba council was heavily involved in disputes over land boundaries. It employed a *fiel de los cortijos* to supervise the boundaries of farms, with the help of *medidores de tierras*, who carried out the actual measurement of the lands in question. When the council became involved in legal action over boundaries, it appointed a *procurador de términos* to take charge of its dealings with lawyers.

THE 'CORREGIDOR'

The arrangements made by Alfonso XI for the government of royal towns by *alcaldes mayores* and councils of *regidores*, helped by *jurados* and *escribanos*, did not prove to be definitive. As so often, later changes took the form of additions to the structure of government rather than the replacement of existing parts. By far the most significant change which took place between the mid-fourteenth century and the beginning of Ferdinand and Isabella's reign was the introduction of the *corregidor* (or *asistente*) as the Crown's representative with overall control of the government of its towns.

The idea of a magistrate with powers to supervise the actions of his colleagues in the locality had already found a place in Castilian practice before the Trastámara line seized the throne. In Andalusia, the *adelantado mayor* (chief governor) heard appeals against the verdicts of the *alcaldes mayores* in towns such as Córdoba. However, the new dynasty soon concluded that the major royal towns needed to be supervised more closely and the post of *corregidor* ('corrector' of abuses) was created. John I's 1383 legislation on the subject described the *corregidor* as an arbitrator, who was to be sent by the king to towns where the existing officials had proved unsatisfactory. He was to stay only as long as it took to rectify the situation and his salary was to be paid by the local community whose misdemeanours had caused him to be sent. The law also stated that a *corregidor* would only be sent if requested by the town concerned, but this notion never bore much relation to reality.[11]

Probably because of their temporary nature, little information is available about the early appointments of *corregidores*. However, it is clear that the reign of Henry III (1390–1406) was the important period for the development of the office.[12] The first known *corregidor* of Seville (in this town, the *Corregidor* was known as the *asistente* after 1459) was appointed in 1406. Two men held the office in that year, Dr Juan Alonso de Toro and Dr Pedro Sánchez del Castillo. They were succeeded by Dr Luis Sánchez de Badajoz in 1407, but thereafter no appointment is known until 1417.[13] According to Mitre Fernández, the first *corregidor* in Córdoba was Sánchez del Castillo, who served from 1402 until his appointment to the same office in Seville. He was replaced in Córdoba by Sánchez de Badajoz, who also moved later to Seville.[14] Information on succeeding *corregidores* in Córdoba is not available until 1452, but it is probable that appointments were intermittent, as in other towns in the region. Nearly all the early *corregidores* in Andalusia were lawyers from the royal administration and law-courts, suggesting that the Crown was still concerned to use the *corregidor* as a means of controlling the towns more closely. When a *corregidor* was appointed, he was given the supreme position in the government of the town concerned and no *alcaldes mayores* were chosen under the local ordinances during his period of office. As soon as he was withdrawn by the Crown, the local *alcaldes mayores* were restored. In John II's reign (1406–54), the alternation between the two systems could be fairly frequent.

The king had another resource if he was dissatisfied with the government of one of his towns. This was to appoint a *pesquisidor* (investigator) who generally came, like the *corregidor*, from the royal administration, to examine the situation in a local community and either make a report to the king or take action in his name, as appropriate. The *procuradores* at the Cortes of Burgos in 1430 asked the king to appoint *pesquisidores* to examine the conduct of *corregidores* and ensure that they did not abuse their powers.[15] John II gave an evasive reply, but gradually the idea was put into practice. There had been *pesquisidores* before this date, but they had been appointed, like judges with special commissions from the Crown, to investigate a specific problem.

In the mid-fifteenth century, it seems that *corregidores* were still appointed to Córdoba from time to time. They were servants of the Crown, such as Gómez de Avila, who was a *guarda real*, a member of the Crown's elite military corps, and Dr Alonso de Paz, who was a judge (*oidor*) in the high court, the *audiencia*. Unlike the practice in some towns, it was not customary in Córdoba for the local magistrates and constable to be suspended during the *corregidor*'s term of office. Thus noblemen such as the *alcalde mayor*, Don Alonso de Aguilar, continued to govern the town, more or less regardless of royal officials sent in from outside.[16]

This state of affairs changed drastically after Ferdinand and Isabella's visit to the area in 1477. Until then, the existing arrangements for the government of Andalusia had perforce to continue, because the Monarchs were preoccupied with the invasion from Portugal on behalf of Isabella's rival for the Castilian throne, Henry IV's daughter Joanna, known as 'La Beltraneja'. The region was left in the hands of the local magnates, many of whom were in varying degrees favourable to Joanna's cause. Once free, at least temporarily, of the Portuguese threat, Isabella went to Andalusia. When she arrived in Seville, in July 1477, she deprived the duke of Medina Sidonia of the governorship of the royal castles (*reales alcázares*), the dockyards (*atarazanas*) and the castle of Triana, and established *corregidores* on a regular basis. After the queen had been joined by her husband, they adjourned to Jerez and, on 20 October, provided the town with its first *corregidor* appointed directly by the Crown, and not by a magnate, since 1456.[17]

In the case of Córdoba, a *corregidor* was introduced before Ferdinand and Isabella's visit to Andalusia. During 1476, Diego de Merlo, a *guarda real* and member of the royal council, became *corregidor* of Córdoba. At first he was accepted by Don Alonso de Aguilar, who was anxious to lose any reputation he may have acquired for being favourable to Joanna's cause. However, Merlo's attempts to mediate in a long-standing dispute between Don Alonso and the count of Cabra quickly led to a breakdown in relations, and Isabella apparently suffered the embarrassment of having to ask Don Alonso to release her *corregidor* from prison. In July and September of 1477, there are references in royal documents to Diego Osorio, the *maestresala* (literally, head-waiter), a senior courtier, as *corregidor*, but for the sake of establishing her authority in Córdoba, the queen felt bound to restore Merlo to his post. Once the gesture had been made, however, the continuing need for good relations with Don Alonso became paramount and on 7 November, Merlo was transferred, in what might be seen as promotion, to the office of *asistente* of Seville. He was succeeded in Córdoba by Francisco de Valdés, a permanent member (*contino*) of the royal household.[18] At the same time, the *alcázar* (castle) and the tower at the south end of the bridge over the Guadalquivir, known as the Calahorra, were removed from the charge of the *alguacil mayor*, the count of Cabra, and entrusted to the *corregidor*.

Under Ferdinand and Isabella, there were few periods during which Córdoba had no *corregidor*. In October 1496, Francisco de Bobadilla died in office. The council of *regidores* held an emergency meeting and decided that as the permanent *alcalde mayor*, Don Alonso de Aguilar, and *alguacil mayor*, the count of Cabra, were still under suspension, and the *corregidor*'s officials had resigned as soon as he died, it was essential that the council should elect 'officials and ministers of justice and ordinary jurisdiction'. The existing officials in Córdoba's *tierra* were told to remain at their posts until the Monarchs' will was known. These arrangements seem to have worked satisfactorily until the Crown appointed Alfonso Enríquez as *corregidor*, after three months had elapsed.[19]

Between 1500 and 1516, there were three more breaks in the succession of *corregidores* and *pesquisidores*. In June 1506, Diego López Dávalos abandoned his post as *corregidor* at a time when the town was facing famine and disorder. To deal with this situation, the marquis of Priego, son of Don Alonso de Aguilar, and the count of Cabra, took up their offices as *alcalde mayor* and *alguacil mayor*, until the Crown provided a new *corregidor*, Don Diego Osorio, after two months had elapsed. A year later, the nobles returned, after they and the rest of the council had objected to the terms of the document renewing Osorio's appointment, and controlled the town from August until December, when new documents arrived. On the third occasion, the nobles intervened in doubtful circumstances in the summer of 1508 and the royal authority had to be restored by an army of veterans from the Italian campaigns, commanded by Ferdinand himself. The system seems to have functioned smoothly thereafter.[20]

At this stage it would be useful to examine the role of the *corregidor* in normal conditions – if such a phrase may ever be used – in the reign of the Catholic Monarchs. The first point to notice is that the time spent by a *corregidor* in any one town was generally strictly limited. The laws of Zamora established in 1433 that a *corregidor* was to have no more than one term in a town and that this might not last more than two years, with the requirement that it be renewed after one. This was still the law under Ferdinand and Isabella, although Juan de Robles remained for many years in another Andalusian town, Jerez de la Frontera.[21] In Córdoba, it was normal in this period for more than one renewal to be granted to *corregidores*. This applied in the cases of Francisco de Valdés, Francisco de Bobadilla, Alfonso Enríquez, Diego López Dávalos and Fernando Duque de Estrada.[22]

One of the first concerns of the Cortes under John II was to secure adequate legal means of checking on the conduct of *corregidores* in office, to prevent the abuse of their wide powers. At Toledo in 1436, the Cortes obtained a pronouncement from the king to the effect that *corregidores* would be subject to the requirement laid down in the *Partidas*, that officials had to supply financial guarantees, made by *fiadores*, when they entered office, that they would indemnify any who were proved to have just claims against them. Also, when the *corregidor* came to the end of his term, he had to devote fifty days to the satisfaction of those who had complaints against his administration.[23] This procedure became known as the *toma de residencia* and under the Catholic Monarchs it was carried out by a royal official of the same type as the *corregidor* himself, known either as a *juez de residencia* (judge of residence) or as a *pesquisidor*. *Tomas de residencia* were supposed to take place at the end of each two-year term, but although they occurred often, they did not precisely follow this pattern. In Córdoba, *pesquisas* or *tomas de residencia* are known to have taken place in 1480, 1490, 1494, 1495, 1499, 1500 and 1514. The lack of documentation on Córdoba in the 1480s may explain the long gap between investigations in that decade, but the failure of the Crown to provide *jueces de residencia* in the early years of the sixteenth century is well documented.

The provision of guarantees by *corregidores* and *pesquisidores* caused dissension on occasions. When Alfonso Enríquez was first received in

February 1497, he offered the last third of his first year's salary as a security for himself and his officials. This was no great concession, as the law stipulated that the last third of the year's salary was not to be paid in any case until the *residencia* had been carried out. The council insisted that the officials give their own guarantees and three *veinticuatros*, two *jurados* and one of the council's lawyers agreed to act as guarantors. This practice was later forbidden by the Crown, which required that all *fiadores* should be found outside the council, but in 1506 Diego Osorio had two *jurados* as his guarantors and in 1513 the Crown once again forbade such arrangements.[24] In 1500, the council raised the question of financial guarantees for *pesquisidores*, asking the new *corregidor*, Diego López Dávalos, to obtain such securities from the departing *pesquisidor*, Lic. de Porras, and his officials, or else seize his last four months' salary. Dávalos replied that he had no power to do this and the council received no satisfaction. Another attempt was made in 1514 to obtain guarantees from a *pesquisidor*, but to no avail. It is worth noting that, in both cases, the council later petitioned the Crown to allow the *pesquisidor* in question to remain in the town as *corregidor*, which suggests that no personal hostility was implied in the demand for guarantees.[25]

The clearest impression of the role which Ferdinand and Isabella envisaged for the *corregidor* in local government is to be found in the articles issued as a pragmatic at Seville in July 1500. This lengthy and comprehensive account of the duties of a *corregidor* consolidated past legislation, for example, the 1485 Seville ordinances recorded by Pulgar, and attempted to ensure that this official acted as far as possible in the same way as the Monarchs would have done, had they been present.[26] Priority was given to ensuring that the *corregidor* and his officials were entirely devoted to the royal interest and not either to their own or to that of the place which they were sent to govern. The salary of the *corregidor* was limited to the sum stated in his letter of appointment and he and his officials were confined to the tables of standard charges laid down by the Crown for their services to the public. When a *corregidor* was appointed, the existing *alcaldes mayores* and *alguacil mayor* were suspended without pay for his term of office. The *corregidor* then appointed his own officials, whom he brought in from outside. It was his responsibility to pay them out of the salary which the town gave him.[27]

The *corregidor* and his officials were forbidden to receive bribes in the form of gifts and promises and, indeed, they were not permitted to establish any personal connection with the inhabitants of the town concerned, or bring any of their own property, such as flocks, into its territory. They might not buy property or engage in trade within the area of their jurisdiction without specific royal permission. Their most important function, however, was the legal one and, in order to keep their justice as pure as possible, they were forbidden to act in law for private clients locally, though the *corregidor* was permitted to further, without receiving extra payment, the legal interests of his area as a whole. The officials appointed by the *corregidor* had to be natives (*naturales*) and residents (*vecinos y moradores*) of another place, and if they were related to the *corregidor* within the fourth degree of affinity, a royal licence was required for their appointment. To ensure that the fundamental duties of the *corregidor* as chief magistrate were efficiently performed, it was stipulated that either he or his *alcalde mayor* had to be fully qualified in civil and criminal law.

When the *corregidor* was first appointed, he had to visit the whole *término* of his town within sixty days of his arrival, without extra payment, and enforce the existing scale of charges for the services of *escribanos* and other officials. At the end of each year of his term, he had to give the Crown an account of the state of his town, including the problems which he had encountered and the steps which he had taken to solve them. Although he was free, within these limitations, to choose his officials, all such appointments had to be approved by the Crown, which reserved the right to replace his officials at any time. He was not permitted to take clothing or lodgings or any other gift or levy from the town to which he was appointed, and he and his officials were required to administer the legal and tax systems without profit to themselves.

The *corregidor* had a duty to investigate any circumstance, however small, which might affect the well-being and good government of the town and its territory. He had the power to alter or remove any local laws which he regarded as unsuitable, provided that he secured the agreement of the *regidores*, paying particular attention to the procedure followed in the election of officers, the prevention of fraud among public officials, the supply of food to the population at reasonable prices and the maintenance of public cleanliness in streets and slaughterhouses. He was especially asked to ensure that there was a suitable public gaol in the town and that the town council kept records of its own proceedings and stored the royal documents which it received. He was to defend the town against interference from ecclesiastical courts, curb the unlicensed building of towers on private houses and ensure that roads and bridges in the surrounding area were kept in good condition and that the taxes levied on travellers and their goods, including those raised by lords, had a sound legal basis and were properly collected. Strenuous efforts were to be made to secure the return of wrong-doers who took refuge from the royal justices in *señoríos* and, if these efforts were unsuccessful, the whereabouts of the offenders were to be reported to the Crown. The effect of this extraordinary code of instructions was to place the whole responsibility for the government of the town and its *tierra* on the *corregidor*. In order that local councils might be aware of the burden that the Crown had placed on their chief magistrate, each new *corregidor* had to produce the articles outlining his duties when he was received by the town.

The 1500 pragmatic also clarified the procedure to be followed in *tomas de residencia*. The inhabitants of the area concerned had first to be warned, by the *escribanos* who assisted the *juez de residencia* or *pesquisidor*, that the investigation was to take place. When it began, the *pesquisidor* was instructed to concern himself only with specific charges, not with vague denunciations, and to consider all evidence in favour of the *corregidor* as well as complaints against him. If a charge was substantiated, the *pesquisidor* was to give sentence, and the *corregidor* and other guilty parties had the right to appeal against his verdict to the royal council. The commission given to a *pesquisidor* was as all-embracing as that of the *corregidor* and was similarly phrased. He took over responsibility for the government of the town during the investigation and had the power to name officials to replace those of the *corregidor*, who were forced to remain in the town with their master, for as long as the investigation lasted, to answer any charges which might arise. The effectiveness of these safeguards will be apparent later, but it is clear from the legislation that the *corregidor* was intended to be the chief representative of the Crown's authority in royal towns.

OFFICE-HOLDING

The Crown did not, however, neglect other ways of influencing the government of the towns directly under its lordship, and one of the most important of these was control over the appointment of the towns' leading officials. By determining the balance between royal, or government, influence and local pressure in the appointment of each type of official, it is possible to gain some impression of the degree of political control which Ferdinand and Isabella could in practice exercise over their towns.

Until Alfonso XI introduced the council of *regidores* in the fourteenth century, the relationship between royal and local influences seems to have been quite simple. The king provided the *alcaldes mayores* and *alguacil mayor* and the parishes chose the *jurados* to represent them. When the *regidores* were introduced, however, the system changed. The magistrates were henceforth elected by this new permanent council, though the parishes retained their *jurados*. This did not, however, cause a shift in the balance towards local influence, because the *veinticuatros* were appointed for life by the Crown. As a result, Alfonso XI's measure did little or nothing to increase the vitality of local institutions and neither he nor his successors seem to have regarded such an aim as desirable. Nonetheless, there were complications in the appointment of *regidores* which merit study, and it is in any case important to understand the nature of the permanent councils which were such a vital part of urban government under the Catholic Monarchs.

A *veinticuatro* of Córdoba in the fifteenth century needed to have little fear of dismissal. Indeed, the Crown encouraged him to regard his office as a family possession, to be transmitted to his heir. Partly for this reason, the demand for offices of this kind seems to have exceeded the supply throughout the fifteenth century and not only in Andalusia. The number of *regidores* in Castilian towns had already gone beyond that fixed in their constitutions when John II declared in the Cortes of 1428 that the royal policy would in future be to return to the former number (*antiguo número*) of *regidores*, by not making further grants of offices beyond this number when their holders resigned or died.[28] This was made possible by the fact that the original offices (*oficios del número*) were always distinguished in official documents from the later additions, which were known as *oficios acrecentados*. However, in practice the king pursued the opposite policy and continued to expand town councils, as did his successor, Henry IV.

John II's statement of 1428, and a later revocation of grants of *oficios acrecentados* made by Henry IV at the Cortes of Ocaña in 1469, do however show that the Catholic Monarchs were not the first to tackle the problem. When they did so, at the Cortes of Toledo in 1480, they concentrated on the offices which had been added after 1440, thus implicitly blaming John II for the growth of the problem. Those who had received *oficios acrecentados* after that date were not allowed to

35

resign them to any other person and the Crown would not provide successors to the offices concerned.[29]

It is arguable that the situation in Córdoba was one of the main factors in provoking the Crown to act against *oficios acrecentados*. In theory, there had, of course, been a council of twenty-four *regidores* since the fourteenth century, but by 1469 the actual number had reached about seventy. In the last years of Henry IV's reign and in the early years of Ferdinand and Isabella, the council apparently grew each year, to reach a peak in 1480. In the surviving local documents, no fewer than ninety-five *regidores* are mentioned in that year and, according to a memorandum sent to the Crown in 1480, there were in fact ninety *oficios acrecentados*, which, when added to the original twenty-four, produce the remarkable total of 114.[30] Whether or not this particular case was responsible for the legislation which followed, there is no doubt that determined action was required and taken. Although Córdoba council at no stage returned to the *antiguo número* between 1480 and 1516, there was a gradual and steady fall in numbers, so that by 1515 the recorded total of *veinticuatros* had been reduced to thirty-four, leaving ten *oficios acrecentados* compared with ninety in 1480.

Despite this success, however, the demand for *veinticuatrías* was a force which Ferdinand and Isabella had to reckon with throughout their reign, and there is little doubt that the possibility of transmitting such an office to an heir, and thus establishing the family in a position of public influence and respectability for the future, was one of the main factors which created it. Councils of *regidores* were never intended to be democratic, and John II's legislation had allowed the hereditary transfer of offices. When he introduced a council of *veinticuatros* to Jerez de la Frontera in 1465, Henry IV explicitly acknowledged the hereditary principle.[31] John II had insisted, however, that the Crown should authorise each transfer individually and, in answer to Cortes complaints, had undertaken not to grant offices to a holder and his heir in the same document. Other limitations on royal grants of *regimientos* were that each beneficiary should hold only one office at a time and that he should reside in the town concerned, of which he had to be a native.[32] The procedure whereby an office-holder might resign his office to a chosen successor, applying afterwards to the Crown for ratification of this *renunciación*, seems to have been largely uncontrolled in the troubled years of the mid-fifteenth century. This meant that an *oficio acrecentado*, once created, was very hard to suppress. As early as 1428, John II declared to the Cortes that any *renunciación* which hindered the return of town councils to the *antiguo número* would henceforth be considered to have no legal force, but he had no power, or perhaps inclination, to take any action.[33]

Ferdinand and Isabella also realised that if the Crown could regain its control of resignations, the solution of the problem of proliferating offices would be brought nearer. The laws of Toledo thus contain a powerful statement of their intention to abolish hereditary office-holding altogether.[34] The preamble to the law concerned is a masterpiece of special pleading. In the first place, the practice of the Crown's granting letters of expectation (*cartas expectativas*) was rejected. These letters gave the recipient the right to the next vacancy in the town concerned, whichever it might be. In future, the Crown would only make provisions to specific offices and all previous grants of *cartas expectativas* which had not already been used were revoked. However, the law concentrated mainly on the principle of filling offices on a hereditary basis. The legislators expressed the view that the public service was too high a calling to be exercised by officials chosen in this way.

Both writings and experience [the Monarchs said] make us certain that many were good and had bad sons. Many were friends of God whose brothers were abhorred of Him. It would be a great error in thought to suppose that the gift or grace of governing well is derived from the father by the son or by one person from another.

If public office was open to all, the result would be higher standards, as 'all will exert themselves to practise goodness and virtues, to win the prize of honour'. In an argument which was probably less likely to appeal to those outside the legal and administrative circles of the Court, it was also stated that resignations to named beneficiaries were wrong because they limited the Crown's freedom to choose its own officials. It was also pointed out that in former times, 'when justice flourished, public offices were annual'. This was a somewhat unscrupulous argument, as it used the supposed golden age of local self-determination as a justification for a measure which was intended to increase royal control over appointments to council offices. The actual point of the law was very much simpler than the arguments used to justify it. A ninety-day period of grace was given to those who already had such grants, so that they might use them. After that, any attempt to do so would lead to loss of the office and confiscation of goods. Up to this time, many office-holders had obtained permission from the Crown in advance to resign their office to a named person, whenever they wished. In such cases, it was merely necessary, when the time came, to obtain royal confirmation of the transaction. No new licence was required.

In fact, the practice of resignation continued as before in the period after 1480, and the temptation to see the laws of Toledo as the beginning of a new era in the government of the royal towns should be firmly resisted. Indeed, the very same code included a law which implied that resignations were still permitted. It was stated that they would be considered valid if office-holders lived for at least twenty days after making them. This might require fine timing, but certainly did not make *renunciaciones* impossible.[35]

There is no doubt that resignations were normal in Córdoba after 1480. Between 1475 and 1515, the Crown is known to have granted sixteen faculties for future resignations of *veinticuatrías* to named beneficiaries and it is known when seven of these were used. In addition, thirty-two other resignations to particular individuals took place in this period. In twenty-one other cases, the Crown provided men who had not been named by the previous office-holders. These figures are incomplete, but they are sufficient to form the basis for general observations. They suggest that, on balance, the holder of an office was rather more likely than not to choose his own successor.

In view of this it is not surprising that the connection between the resignation of offices and the hereditary principle was very close. Thirty-four of the forty-eight recorded cases of resignation or faculty to resign a *veinticuatría* in Córdoba between 1475 and 1515 involved a transfer to the office-holder's son. In one case the beneficiary was the holder's father and there was one example of resignation to a brother and one to a nephew. Faculties for resignation in all cases involved sons. When the Crown provided a *veinticuatro* who had not been named by his predecessor in the office there was usually a particular reason. This was not stated in all of the twenty-one such provisions made to Córdoba offices between 1475 and 1515, but in ten of these cases the previous holder had died before he could resign, or obtain a royal faculty to resign, his office to a named individual. Up to 1480, such provisions might be made to a new *oficio acrecentado*, but afterwards this was not permitted.[36] In two cases the Crown used its discretion to restore *veinticuatros* who had favoured the Portuguese cause and in another case it restored a *veinticuatro* who had been removed, presumably because of his Jewish origins, after the riots of 1473.[37] Resignation, though, was still the normal way of transferring *veinticuatrías* after 1480, as before, even if the Crown might make its own provision in special cases. Faculties to resign expired with the office-holders who had obtained them and if they had not by then been used, the Crown was free to ignore them and make its own choice. This was also the case when officers were deprived after conviction of some offence.

It is a matter of some interest to discover what kind of man benefited from royal provisions to *veinticuatrías*, as it may be assumed that, after the *corregidor*, the Crown regarded the council of *regidores* as its main instrument for controlling local government. If royal nominees were to be placed in a town, this would be a likely place in which to find them. In fact, the practice of appointing Crown servants to *veinticuatrías* in Córdoba seems to have been relatively rare. Cristóbal Bermúdez, a captain of the royal guard under Henry IV, was a *regidor* of Córdoba until he lost his office for supporting the claim of Joanna to the Castilian throne. His successor, Diego Proaño, was certainly a full-time royal servant, as a magistrate at Court (*alcalde de la real casa y corte*), but his connection with Córdoba cannot be established.[38] These examples show that council posts might be used as rewards for royal servants, but most references to personal service to the Crown appear in documents ratifying resignations to relatives of previous holders. In these cases, local influence was almost certainly the stronger. There was a connection between Córdoba's council and the royal service, but most of the pressure for appointment to urban offices seems to have been local, with the Crown happy to allow this state of affairs to continue.

Although the council of *regidores* was the scene of the Crown's main effort to intervene in local appointments, there was some royal interest in controlling admission to other urban offices. Of these, the most ancient was that of *jurado*, which certainly did not escape the royal intervention experienced by the more recently created senior office. The problem of *oficios acrecentados* affected the *jurados* to a small extent, in that two extra *jurados* were added to St Mary's parish representation during the fifteenth century.[39]

Royal legislation tried to ensure that the *jurados* were effective representatives of their parishes by insisting that they had to live in or close to the parish concerned and might not appoint deputies to do their work for them.[40] However the main security for the representative character of the *jurados* was the right of the parishes to elect them, which was safeguarded in general by John II in 1432 and confirmed by the Catholic Monarchs in the specific case of Córdoba in 1484. The Córdoba privilege stated that when a *jurado* died in office, the citizens (*vecinos*) of his parish were to meet in the parish church and elect a replacement. These *vecinos* were the people included in the list of tax-payers (*padrón*) of the parish. The election was open, without lots or ballots, and took place in the presence of the other *jurados* of the city and the *corregidor*, if he wished to attend. The *vecinos'* choice had to be approved first of all by the other *jurados*, who then conducted the successful candidate to the council of *regidores* for their ratification. Once this had been obtained, the *corregidor* and the council administered the oath of office to the new *jurado* and instructed the constables to instal him in his parish.[41]

The details of fifteen such elections survive in Córdoba and they all took place after the previous *jurado* had died in office. Voting lists are available in two cases and the number on each is very small. Thirty-five *vecinos* are recorded as taking part in the election in the parish of St James in 1501, and sixty-five in a similar election in St Andrew's in 1510. The lists indicate that the voters consisted of a few *regidores* resident in the parishes concerned, some cloth-merchants (*traperos*), a range of tradesmen and artisans and a small number of tenant-farmers (*labradores*). Both elections seem to have been unanimous, which suggests that the selection in fact took place beforehand.[42]

Most *jurados*, nevertheless, between two-thirds and three-quarters in the period 1476–1515, were appointed by royal provision rather than local election, and in the majority of cases they were specifically named in their predecessors' resignations. As with *veinticuatrías*, the Crown exploited any unusual circumstances in order to make provisions. For example, three *jurados* who had been deprived of their offices for heresy were replaced directly by the Crown.[43] However, little use was made of *juraderías* as rewards for royal servants. One case in Córdoba was Alfonso Carrillo, a court servant who was made a *jurado* in 1479.[44]

There was also a heavy demand for *escribanías* and they were included in the legislation on *oficios acrecentados* in the laws of Toledo. According to the 1480 memorandum, there were in Córdoba in that year twenty-four *escribanos* of the *antiguo número* and twenty *oficios acrecentados* which had been added since 1440. By 1498, the total had been reduced to thirty-three, which meant that eleven of the *oficios acrecentados* had been suppressed. In 1501, eight *jurados* petitioned the council, asking that in its zeal for reform it should not suppress an *oficio del número*, but by 1503 the council had issued a directive that all surplus offices were to lapse at the death or resignation of their holders, until the number had been reduced to thirty, rather than twenty-four. The *escribanías* seem to have been stabilised thereafter at this compromise figure.[45]

According to the *fuero* of 1241, there should have been an annual election of an *escribano* in each parish. The practice did indeed continue in Ferdinand and Isabella's reign, but a fixed number of *escribanos* for the whole town had been added later and the power of provision to that body seems to have been invested for all practical purposes in the town council. Thus the eighteen resignations of *escribanías* in Córdoba which are recorded between 1493 and 1507 were ratified by the council, and only two of them received royal confirmation as well. Direct royal provision was also possible, but generally occurred in special circumstances, as with the other offices. Nine such provisions are recorded in Córdoba between 1484 and 1505, and in the six cases where details are provided, those being replaced were *escribanos* who had been burnt or reconciled by the Inquisition.[46] There was a dispute in 1496 between the royal *alcalde mayor* and the council, when an *escribano* was dismissed for dishonesty and the council provided his successor. The *alcalde* claimed the right of provision for the Crown, because it was a case of dismissal and not resignation. Eventually, the council candidate received a royal letter of provision, presented it to the *corregidor* and council and received the office again from their hands.[47] In this way, honour was satisfied, but the dispute serves to illustrate the delicate balance which had to be kept at all times between royal and local pretensions in the appointment of officials.

The other offices in the town were shared out between the Crown, the *alguacil mayor* and the representatives of the parishes. Direct nominations by the Crown were rare. Indeed, the only offices filled in this way were those of *fiel* and *portero* of the custom-house and *alférez*. The *alférez* was always a *veinticuatro* or a *jurado*, while the customs offices seem to have been used as rewards for royal servants. In 1475, the Crown gave the *fieldad* to the chronicler Gonzalo de Ayora, who was also a *veinticuatro* of Córdoba. He was frequently absent on royal business and when his son, who succeeded him in 1504, tried to follow the same practice, the council threatened to replace him. The office of *portero* in the custom-house was entirely honorary. In 1496 it was given to the royal steward (*repostero*), Rodrigo de Mesilla, and the town accepted his privilege without question.[48]

It has already been noted that the magistrates were either elected by the *veinticuatros* or appointed by the *corregidor*. The *alguacil menor* and the *alguacil de las entregas* were named by the *alguacil mayor*, but the vast majority of appointments were made by the town council. In some cases, the jobs went to members of the council itself, while in others the office-holders were sought outside. The council's *procurador mayor* was always a *veinticuatro*, as were proctors elected to the Cortes. Most of the officials, however, such as the lawyers, the chaplain, the musicians, the accountants, the *fieles*, the measurer of lands (*medidor de tierras*) and the *mayordomo*, came from outside the council. The appointment of some officials was disputed between the council and the *caballeros de premia*, who obtained their knightly rank on the basis of a wealth qualification. According to a council decree of 1496, the tradition was that the *alcaldes ordinarios*, the *alcalde de las dehesas* and the *alcalde de la aduana* should be elected annually by two *caballeros de premia* from each parish. The offices were to go round all the parishes in turn and each holder was to be restricted to a single term. However, the rights of the *caballeros de premia* were disputed, and in 1493 and 1498 the Crown had to intervene to protect their privilege against the attempts of the *corregidor* to take over the appointment of *alcaldes ordinarios*. The *caballeros de premia* seem to have been fighting a rearguard action for the former practice of electing magistrates locally.

Certain *fieldades*, notably those of the *almotacenazgo* and the council porters, became a battle-ground in the same way. A royal provision of 1480 supported the claim of the *caballeros* to make the election, but the council and *corregidor* obstinately insisted that the right belonged to them and continued to make the appointments throughout the region, although the *jurados* finally obtained a decision in favour of the *caballeros* from the Granada high court (*audiencia*) in 1515, after an action which lasted over twenty years.[49] Other *fieles*, supervising, for example, the tanneries and the sale of fish and flour, were elected by the *caballeros de premia* without interference. The *mayordomía de las calles*, an unpopular office because work on cleaning the streets had to be carried out at the office-holder's expense, was filled by the council and the parishes, acting jointly. Names were brought to the council by the *jurados* and the final choice was made by the *veinticuatros*. At the bottom of the scale were the *alcaldes* and *veedores* of the various trades, who were generally chosen by the practitioners (often known as *oficiales*) of the trade concerned from their own number, though the council might supervise the election, as with the silversmiths in 1498.[50]

Although a great many lesser posts in Córdoba were filled by nomination, the practice of drawing lots was also traditional and extensively employed. The council used lots to choose its *mayordomo, procurador mayor* and *contadores,* and also the *fieles* of the *almotacenazgo* and *portería.*[51] The *caballeros de premia* used the same method to choose the various *alcaldes,* but the appointment of the more important officials, such as the *letrados* (lawyers) was not left to chance in this way and lots were never used in direct royal appointments.

THE HERMANDAD

Alongside the internal structure of government in the royal towns, Ferdinand and Isabella set up a new and separate national organisation which was subject directly to the Crown and which was entrusted with the maintenance of order in the countryside between the major cities in which it was based. This new royal agency was known as the Santa Hermandad (Holy Brotherhood) and was an extension to the whole kingdom of the associations previously formed by local communities for the same purpose. The national Hermandad was set up at the Cortes of Madrigal in 1476 and all towns, including those under seignorial juris-diction, were required to swear allegiance to it. A permanent *junta* of royal servants and an annual assembly of representatives from the provinces (the *diputación general*) were the national organs of the Hermandad and, on a local level, the kingdom was divided into provinces, each with its chief town, or *cabeza de provincia.*[52] Córdoba was one of these chief towns and thus the council elected one of its members as *diputado general* when the *diputación* met. The Hermandad of the province was under the authority of two *alcaldes,* one representing the nobles (*hidalgos*) and the other the rest of the citizens. The latter was known sometimes as the *alcalde de los peones* or *pecheros,* in other words, commoners or tax-payers, and sometimes as the *alcalde de los caballeros,* or knights. The receiver of goods con-fiscated by Hermandad officers (the *receptor*) was a *veinticuatro* of Córdoba, chosen by the council. Each province of the Hermandad, including Córdoba, had its own prison, with a gaoler. The treasurer, who was subordinate to the *receptor,* worked in the same building. The *alcaldes* of the Hermandad were assisted in their duties by an *alguacil* and squads (*cuadrillas*) of men under *cuadrilleros.*[53]

The Hermandad was not established on a permanent basis in 1476, but had to be periodically extended. The first such extension was from 1478 to 1481. In the latter stages of the Granada campaign, the Hermandad was used to raise men and money for the Crown, thus avoiding the need to summon the Cortes. However, its basic function was always to keep order on the roads and in the countryside, and it was only possible to use it for military purposes as long as the royal armies were fighting on Castilian soil. After 1500, with the Crown's growing involvement in foreign campaigns, the Hermandad was once again entirely devoted to local peace-keeping. At first, the Monarchs dismantled all the national and provincial organisation, for example, the *junta general*, the *diputación general* and the provincial assemblies, leaving only the local *alcaldes* and *cuadrilleros*, but the provincial apparatus was quickly restored to provide an appeal mechanism and on this basis the Hermandad survived to be mocked by Cervantes.[54]

Although it was based in the towns, the Hermandad had no jurisdiction within them and it was not subject to the *corregidor* or the council, like the other magistrates and officials. It had charge of everywhere that was too thinly populated to have a council of its own. All places with fewer than fifty citizens were deemed to be *despoblados* (depopulated) or *yermos* (deserts) and placed under Hermandad jurisdiction, which also covered those convicted of crimes in the town who fled from royal justice to the countryside. Despite the fact that it had no part in urban politics, the Hermandad was inevitably distrusted by the other authorities in the town, and has a place in any survey of royal involvement in local government.

It is perhaps not surprising that the Crown should have been closely involved in the government of its own towns, both through the appointment of officials and in the person of the *corregidor*. What is more noteworthy is the scope still allowed for local influence even after Ferdinand and Isabella began their undoubtedly vigorous and fairly successful campaign to reform the town councils of Castile. The difference between the laws of Toledo and earlier legislation was not great. The same claim of overall royal sovereignty was expressed in both, and most of the policies which the Catholic Monarchs adopted were by no means original. However their legislation had greater bite and was better enforced. There is no doubt that the number of officials in Córdoba was drastically reduced, and even if the hereditary transfer of offices was not curbed, the effective establishment of *corregidores* in the town on a regular basis, for the first time, greatly strengthened royal control. Much still needed to be done, but it is undeniable that in 1516 all the major offices in Córdoba were more closely controlled by the Crown than they had been in 1474.

Before moving on to consider the procedures and activities of

Córdoba council in this period, it is worth noting one other feature. This is the virtually complete absence, in royal and municipal records, of reference to the sale of offices in the town. It is clear that the main motives behind the granting of municipal offices were the Crown's desire to reward its servants, and, more significantly, local families' desire for power and influence in their home district and their anxiety to preserve it for their descendants. Royal legislation scarcely mentions the purchase of offices, however, in marked contrast to practice in Castile under the Habsburgs, when sales were actively promoted by the Crown. One can only conclude that demand from local families was adequately catered for by royal grants and that the Crown either had not envisaged, or else did not need, the income which might have been gained from the sale of what the government was still content to give. The evidence which does exist for the sale of offices will be considered in later chapters, but it must be clear that such a practice would have contrasted sharply with the lofty principles for public office-holding which were set out in the laws of Toledo.[55]

COUNCIL PROCEDURES AND ACTIVITIES

Long before the *corregidor* was introduced to royal towns as the Crown's representative, a number of the sovereign's powers had been delegated to local councils. The Crown made provision for the conduct of these assemblies and the use which they made of the administrative, legal and financial resources which were entrusted to them.

Probably because they were anxious visibly to demonstrate the town council's independence of private influence, Ferdinand and Isabella, at the Cortes of Toledo in 1480, ordered all councils in royal towns to obtain a special meeting-house. This was to be done within two years of the publication of the law, on pain of removal for magistrates and *regidores* who failed to comply.[56] In Córdoba, a meeting-house is referred to as new in 1427, though in 1435 the council was meeting in the lodgings of the *corregidor*. The two regular weekly meetings of the council were on Tuesdays and Fridays until 1479, when the Tuesday meeting was moved to Wednesday. Other meetings were held as business required, Monday being a frequent choice, though in the early sixteenth century other days were equally common. Meetings were not normally held on Sundays or holidays, or in Lent, but there were exceptions, and when urgent measures were required, more than one meeting might take place in a day.[57]

45

If there was a *corregidor*, he had the right to preside at all meetings, but he frequently delegated the responsibility to his *alcalde mayor*, his *alguacil mayor* or some other deputy. Because he was an outsider, the *corregidor* was legally entitled to spend a third of the year away from his post, in order to attend to his own business. Before leaving for a lengthy period, he formally presented a deputy, usually one of his officials, to the council, to exercise his powers until his return. In many years, the lesser magistrates of Córdoba presided over far more meetings than the *corregidor*.

The way in which council proceedings were recorded by the *escribano del concejo* or his deputy inevitably creates the surviving impression of how they were conducted. Even with the same *escribano*, the method varied. Sometimes, documents were merely referred to, while at others they were fully transcribed, or else the originals were stitched into the book of acts. It was customary to record the names of the president and all those who attended the meeting, to summarise the discussion which took place, record the voting and set down all the decisions that were reached. However, the neatness of the surviving records indicates that they were composed after the meeting from notes and, indeed, a sheet of these notes, with corrections, survives in the book of acts for 1479. It covers the meetings from 25 to 27 July and contains lists of documents which had been received by the council or the *corregidor* and of the tasks which had been allocated to individual *veinticuatros*.[58] The Crown required councils to keep all royal documents which they received and the *corregidor* had to ensure that this was done, but the date of the earliest book of acts in Córdoba is not known. A loose sheet, giving an account of a meeting in December 1473, was stitched into the 1479 book, which is the oldest surviving, but this is not conclusive proof that books were not used at that stage. However, it is possible that they were introduced after the Monarchs' visit in 1477. The council also had a chest for the storage of privileges and other charters, in accordance with royal instructions. The keys were held by two different *veinticuatros*.[59]

Admission to council-meetings was tightly controlled by royal legislation. This was an inevitable consequence of the introduction of *regidores* and the laws of Palenzuela (1430), which limited entry to meetings to 'the *alcaldes* and *regidores* and the other people contained in the ordinances', merely confirmed this state of affairs. In Córdoba, these ordinances admitted the *jurados*, but they were only allowed to intervene in discussions if asked to do so by the magistrates and *regidores.* In 1503, a dispute arose over the presence of lawyers in council-meetings. A royal letter was received, forbidding them to attend, and both the *veinticuatros* and the *jurados* voted to appeal against it. Nevertheless, at the next meeting, on 11 October, Dr de Manos Albas and Bach. Alfonso Fernández de Baena, both lawyers, were ordered by the *corregidor* to leave the council-chamber or face a 50 000 *maravedís* fine. It appears that their advice had been required so frequently by the *veinticuatros* that they had virtually been coopted as permanent members of the council. They protested at their expulsion and threatened to appeal to the Crown, but the *corregidor* told them there was no procedure whereby they might do so as individuals. Nonetheless, the *corregidor* then asked the *veinticuatros* whether they regarded the lawyers as necessary to the council and was told that they were indispensable. After this, they continued to be called into virtually every meeting to help with specific problems, but although their opinions were noted and respected, they had no formal vote.[60]

Issues in council were decided by majority votes, with the presiding magistrate exercising a casting vote if necessary. Votes were generally given orally and frequently consisted of a statement of opinion, rather than a simple 'yes' or 'no'. Abstentions were common and so were proxy-votes. The latter enabled an absentee to participate by entrusting his vote to a colleague or to the chairman. If an action was agreed upon without a vote being taken, but a few of the *veinticuatros* were opposed to the decision, their dissent might be recorded in the book of acts in the phrase, 'Fulano no fue en esto' (N. did not agree with this). Sometimes a *regidor* or magistrate justified a particular vote or decision in writing and his reasons were recorded by an *escribano*, in some cases in the book of acts. This generally happened if there had been dissension over the issue in the council.[61]

Order was maintained in council-meetings by the presiding magistrate. In 1496, the *veinticuatros* and *jurados* were instructed by the *alcalde mayor* to remain in their seats throughout the meeting, so as to avoid violence. If trouble did occur, the offending parties, regardless of responsibility for starting the incident, were immediately confined to their houses and they and their 'relations and friends and servants' were forbidden to continue the quarrel. The effectiveness of such measures should become clear in due course.[62]

Although their votes, if taken at all, were not counted in any decision of the council, the *jurados* had the same power as the *veinticuatros* to make formal demands (*requerimientos*) to the presiding magistrate to allow a particular matter to be discussed or action taken. Problems might also be brought to the council's attention by means of petitions from citizens, either in groups or as individuals. When the matter concerned was discussed, the petitioners were allowed to attend the meeting and any other individual might be summoned if required to further council business. The acts for 1493 contain a note to the effect that a petitioner came to the council-house when there was no meeting and stated his business to a magistrate who was deputising for the *corregidor*.[63]

For a council-meeting to be held, there had to be a quorum of seven *regidores*, according to a royal provision of 1513, and this seems to have been enforced. In 1498, six *veinticuatros* were sent home by the magistrates as insufficient for a meeting. Attendance figures in the *actas* show that business was normally carried on by a limited section of the *regimiento* and a small following of *jurados*. Sometimes, no *jurados* at all attended. In 1479, when the council was nearing its peak membership of one hundred and fourteen *veinticuatros*, the most recorded at a single meeting were thirty-eight. In the same year, the highest attendance of *jurados* was twenty out of a possible thirty-two. A similar impression is given by the figures for the later years. The typical turnout for a meeting was between ten and twenty *veinticuatros* and fewer than ten *jurados*. Larger attendances were generally achieved when a *corregidor* was received or *procuradores* to the Cortes were elected.[64]

The *veinticuatros* were under oath to keep the proceedings of the council secret. In 1497, the *corregidor* required them to keep their oath on pain of six months' banishment from the town, and in 1500 the same demand was made of the *jurados*.[65]

What has been said up to now about office-holding and about the conduct of council-meetings may serve to illustrate the strong oligarchical tendencies in the government of Córdoba in this period. As a result, any group or institution which might counterbalance the influence of the *veinticuatros* assumed very great importance. The prime candidates, locally, for such a role were the *jurados*, as the survivors of an earlier and more representative political structure. In addition to attending council-meetings, the *jurados* of Córdoba assembled in a *cabildo* (chapter) of their own, with its acts recorded by one of their number. The surviving book for 1509–13 suggests that the *jurados*' meetings were less frequent than those of the full council and took place in the same chamber. The *jurados* had their own chest for funds, which seem to have consisted mainly of dues paid by new members when they were received by their colleagues. Each year, the *cabildo* elected one of its number as *alcalde,* to preside over its meetings, and another as *mayordomo* to take charge of its finances. Many royal documents were addressed directly to the *jurados* of Córdoba, some of them concerning their own affairs and others referring to more general matters, such as disputes between the *jurados* and the *veinticuatros* over the conduct of the town's business. One procedural difference from the full council was that the *jurados* fined any member who was absent from meetings without giving a reason. The fine was one *real*.[66]

A wide range of supervisory duties was delegated by the council to two *veinticuatros* and a *jurado* who were chosen by lots each month as *diputados del mes.* Their tasks were laid down in ordinances given by Henry IV in 1458, but they might be entrusted with extra commissions. For example, in 1493 they were given the task of publicising the laws of the Hermandad and in 1495 they were involved in tax-collecting. They also acquired the duty of hearing civil cases involving goods worth less than 3000 *mrs.* Apart from the *diputados del mes,* who were generally chosen for the whole year at one meeting, other members of the council might receive specific commissions to carry on official business. At the meeting on 27 July 1479, for example, the tasks allocated to commissions, which normally consisted of two *veinticuatros* and a *jurado,* included auditing the municipal accounts, examining weights and measures, collecting fines for failing to comply with the terms of private wills and investigating the affairs of the magistrates and of the cloth-dyers.[67]

THE 'TIERRA'

The scope of Córdoba town council's activities was not, of course, limited to the city itself. One of its most important roles was the control of its *tierra,* and this was exercised primarily through officials who were appointed or supervised by the council, but worked in outlying areas. Not all such appointments were in the hands of the council. Many of the towns in Córdoba's *tierra* had castles and fortresses and, throughout the reign of Ferdinand and Isabella, their governors (*alcaides*) were appointed by the Crown. Such cases in the period 1478–1513 include Castro del Río, Almodóvar del Río, Bujalance, Montoro, La Rambla and Hornachuelos.[68]

The structure of local government within the towns of the *tierra* seems to have been fairly rudimentary. There is only one indication in the Córdoba archives that any of these towns, apart from Córdoba itself, had a council of *regidores*. This is a reference to the *regimiento de la villa* in the 1511 ordinances of Montoro. If there were *regidores* in Montoro, it would seem likely that some of the larger towns in the *tierra*, such as Castro del Río and Bujalance, were similarly endowed, but in default of other evidence, it is more probable that the term merely referred to the officials of the town in general. It is known that the towns and villages of the *tierra* generally had councils which consisted, as in Torremilano and Montoro, of two *alcaldes*, an *alguacil*, two *jurados* and at least one *escribano*. However, the open council, consisting of *caballeros de premia*, or knights qualified by wealth, and the *peones*, who served the king on foot, still had a role on occasions. Thus while in Fuente Obejuna in 1496, entry to council meetings was restricted to the magistrates and *jurados*, the *escribano* and five representatives each of the *caballeros* and *peones*, in Montoro in 1511, the whole citizen body was summoned by bells to hear and approve the new municipal ordinances before they were submitted to the *corregidor* and council of Córdoba for ratification. Magistrates in the *tierra* of Córdoba were elected annually, and the city's 1483 ordinances forbade the extension of terms of office beyond one renewal of a year. Such extensions were only to be granted in response to a petition from the town concerned. There was some place for the local election of magistrates, at least in the larger towns. In Bujalance, the two *alcaldes*, the *alguacil* and his deputy were elected by the *caballeros de premia*, but Córdoba retained overall control of nominations in case of dispute. If magistrates were appointed directly by Córdoba, lots were used, containing the names of candidates proposed by the council of the town concerned.[69]

The provision of *escribanos* for the *tierra* was in general the responsibility of Córdoba. In nine cases, the resignation of the previous office-holder to a specific individual was ratified by the council. In 1497, for example, Fernando González de Badajoz, *escribano* of Castro, resigned his office to his 'lords', Córdoba council, and to his son, Rodrigo Yáñez. As with the *escribanías* in Córdoba itself, it was customary for the abilities of the candidate to be examined and there are five such cases recorded. On one occasion, an *escribano* died in office in La Rambla, without having named a successor. The council in Córdoba received petitions from two candidates for the post and when a vote was taken, the *veinticuatros* were equally divided between them. The last man to vote broke the deadlock by the simple expedient of going out of the council-chamber and examining the handwriting of the two candidates. Once, at least, in this period, the Crown intervened in the appointment of an *escribano* for the *tierra*, when one such official was suspended in Fuente Obejuna. The Crown took the opportunity to provide his successor, but within a few weeks the suspended *escribano* had gained another such office in the same town, by means of a resignation which was ratified by Córdoba council. In 1505, the council discussed the type of candidate which should be provided to *escribanías* in the *tierra* and decided that such offices should be confined to *vecinos* of the town concerned.[70]

All the royal possessions in the Córdoba area, except for Alcolea and Castro Viejo, were represented by two *jurados*. Their affairs were in the hands of the *cabildo de los jurados* in Córdoba, which had the power to appoint and remove them. Resignations were ratified by this *cabildo* and, if no specific person were named in the resignation, the *cabildo* was responsible for finding a suitable candidate. Thus in 1513, Andrés de Córdoba, *jurado* of St Marina, Córdoba, went to Montoro and chose Juan de Lorca to be *jurado* there. He was brought to Córdoba and sworn in at the *cabildo* of *jurados*. Often, *jurados* in the *tierra* resigned their offices into the hands of the *cabildo*, as with Alfonso Rodríguez of Torremilano in 1510 and another case in Posadas in 1511. *Jurados* in the *tierra* might also be deprived of their offices by their colleagues in Córdoba. This happened in 1510, when the *jurados* of Bujalance carried out a *pesquisa* on their own authority into the activities in the town of Córdoba's council and *corregidor*. Probably at the instigation of the authorities in Córdoba, the *cabildo* of *jurados* removed the officials in Bujalance, though one of them was restored in 1512.[71]

THE COUNCIL AND THE LAW

As elsewhere in medieval Europe, the law was essential to the expression and, in some cases, the resolution, of social and political conflicts. As a result, much of the energy of the authorities in Córdoba in this period was devoted to litigation, and it is therefore important to set Córdoba and its council in their proper legal context.

It has already been noted that the administration of justice in the region was one of the powers delegated to the local council by the Crown in the early days after the Reconquest. The majority of civil and criminal cases involving the inhabitants of Córdoba and its *tierra* were therefore settled by local magistrates. The hierarchy rose from the *alcaldes ordinarios*, through the courts of the *alcalde de la justicia*, to the *alcaldes mayores* and the *corregidor*, if there was one. This meant that actions which did not go beyond one appeal, which would clearly be the great majority, had no need ever to leave the boundaries of the town concerned. The right of the *alcaldes mayores* to hear first appeals in legal cases was enshrined in local ordinances and inherited by the *corregidor* when he swore to observe them. The appeal mechanism within the town might on occasions be by-passed, as in 1515, when a party appealed directly to the high court at Granada against his conviction by the *alcalde de la justicia*, and his appeal was admitted, but the Crown generally tried to leave most cases to the local magistrates.[72]

In 1480, the Crown confined civil cases involving goods worth 3000 *mrs* or less to the jurisdiction in which the supposed offence occurred, provided that it was more than eight leagues (about forty-five kilometres) from one of the high courts. Appeals in such cases were to be made to the council and justices of the town concerned, who then had to elect two deputies to hear them, after taking an oath to give good justice. In order that the matter should not be left entirely to amateurs, the judge who had given sentence in the first instance attended the hearing, but it should be remembered that the *alcaldes ordinarios* were themselves elected citizens and not necessarily qualified in law. This does not seem to have worried either legislators or the public. The former were more concerned with the efficiency of legal proceedings and the latter with their cost. The confinement of lesser cases to the locality would have found favour on both counts.

Córdoba seems not to have hurried to introduce this system of deputies to hear appeals. The first mention of the council's electing two of its members for this purpose is in 1498. At first, different *veinticuatros* were deputed each week, suggesting that business was fairly brisk, but after 1501 this duty was added to those of the deputies of the month. It may well be that after 1500 litigants became less satisfied with amateur judges, as there are signs of a growing demand for appeals, even in minor cases, to be heard in the high court. It is probable that these courts were becoming more efficient and the establishment of the *audiencia* in Ciudad Real and then Granada certainly made this kind of justice more accessible to Córdoba than it had been when the only such court was in Valladolid. In any event, the Monarchs found it necessary in 1500 to confirm the right of Córdoba's own magistrates to hear minor appeals and at the same time gave one litigant, Pedro Páez, the right to have his appeal heard by the magistrates and not the council's deputies. By 1514, matters had reached a stage at which the Crown permitted the *audiencia* at Granada to hear any appeals involving cases over goods worth 3000 *mrs* or less which reached it from Córdoba, despite what was said in the laws of Toledo, if they concerned the interpretation of the town's ordinances.[73]

Once a case left Córdoba's magistrates, it entered an appeal system which had developed piecemeal since the thirteenth century, or earlier, and was still evolving in the time of Ferdinand and Isabella. Throughout all the changes, the final court of appeal continued to be the royal council (*concejo real*), which consisted of clergy, nobles and secular lawyers. In order to deal with the select cases which rose as high as this in the legal structure, the Catholic Monarchs ensured that the council was provided with eight or nine lawyers, in addition to a basic quota of three *caballeros*, all under the presidency of a bishop. However, this was not the main business of the royal council and towards the end of the fourteenth century the duty of hearing appeals was given to special judges, known as *oidores* (lit. 'hearers'). At the Cortes of Toro in 1371, Henry II ordained that the seven *oidores* should give justice in the residence of the king and queen, but if the monarchs were away, cases should be heard in the house of the chancellor (*chanciller mayor*) or wherever the *chancillería* was working. Since 1200, if not before, the *chancillería* had been the department of the royal administration which housed the royal seal for use on letters and charters. Now, the *oidores* became a part of this department, so that the terms *audiencia* and *chancillería* were used indiscriminately to describe the tribunal. The old function of guarding the seal was retained, but the *chancillería* gradually developed into the appeal court of the kingdom.[74]

When a party in a civil case wanted to appeal against the sentence of a judge in a lower court, his representative (*procurador*) asked the *audiencia* to issue a summons (*real provisión de emplazamiento*), which would require all the documents of the case to be sent to the *audiencia* from the lower court. This summons was normally issued automatically. At the same time, the appellant would give his *procurador* power to represent him at the proving (*prueba*) of the case, during which the parties would bring forward their evidence, which consisted of documents and witnesses' depositions. If the *audiencia* took any steps to advance the case, it did so by means of a royal provision, issued in the Monarchs' names. When the hearing was completed, a group of *oidores* gave sentence (*sentencia de vista*). The document had to be signed by at least three of them. If an appeal was lodged immediately against this sentence, a review sentence was given, within four months of the date of the first sentence. Once this *sentencia de revista* had been given, or after the *sentencia de vista* if there was no appeal, the case was deemed to be completed (*pleito fenecido*) and a letter of execution (*carta ejecutoria*) was drawn up, which contained the definitive sentence. Cases which for some reason did not stay the course in the *audiencia* were either forgotten (*olvidados*) or stored away (*depositados*), in case they were ever revived. Appeals in criminal cases were heard by three *alcaldes*. According to royal dispositions of 1502, hearings were not to begin unless the *alcaldes* thought the appeals had some basis in law. The *alcaldes* were also entitled to demand information on cases from local magistrates, if they suspected that parties were unwilling to appear before them because of intimidation. In other respects, procedure in such cases was similar to that followed in civil hearings.[75]

In order to prosecute a case in the *audiencia*, a party had to appoint a *procurador* to represent him and engage advocates (*abogados*) to speak for him in court. Staff, such as *escribanos*, had to be paid by the litigant, through his *procurador*, and the client was also responsible for other legal costs, such as the collection of evidence from witnesses by *receptores* (receivers) outside the tribunal. However, the situation for Andalusian litigants was made easier in 1494, when a new *audiencia* was set up, on the model of the old, in Ciudad Real, to take care of all business from areas south of the Tagus. Its first president was Don Iñigo Manrique de Lara, bishop of Córdoba, and it dealt with most cases which went beyond Córdoba's local tribunals. It was transferred to Granada in 1505.[76]

The public authorities in Córdoba were heavily involved in hearings before the *audiencia*. In 1496, for example, the town was engaged in opposing the appeals of five lords at Ciudad Real. These were, Gonzalo Mexía, lord of Santa Eufemia, Don Alfonso Fernández de Córdoba, lord of Montemayor, Alfonso de los Ríos, lord of Fernán Núñez, Gonzalo de León, *veinticuatro* of Córdoba, and Fernando Yáñez de Badajoz. Other cases which came before the *audiencia* in the appeal stage involved the boundaries between Córdoba's lands at Castro del Río and those of the house of Aguilar at Carchena and the count of Cabra at Baena. The *chancillería* at Ciudad Real dealt at one stage with the dispute over Fuente Obejuna between Córdoba and the order of Calatrava. Boundary litigation was not, however, the only activity which involved Córdoba with the *audiencia*. The *alcaldes de los hijosdalgo* vindicated the claims to *hidalguía* of several of the town's citizens and the *chancillería* heard some appeals against the verdicts of Córdoba's magistrates. In 1495, Antón del Rosal appealed against his flogging, which had been ordered by the local magistrates. The *audiencia* demanded the documents of the case, but on this occasion Córdoba council was very reluctant to see the case leave its jurisdiction and decided to send to Ciudad Real a copy of its privilege, which stated that completed cases should not be taken outside the town's boundaries for further trial. The town's sensitivity seems to have been aroused when its opponents in law attempted to use the *audiencia* against it, as there were protests about infringements of the town's jurisdiction when private landowners brought actions in Ciudad Real, for example in 1496. On the other hand, the council was happy to use that tribunal to further its own interests. For example, a case in which a *jurado* in Torremilano was attacked in Añora was referred to Granada by the *corregidor* in 1506, with the council's consent, and in 1511, a dispute over the taxation of wine imported by the clergy of Córdoba was referred in the same way. More interesting, perhaps, is the use made by the Crown of the Granada *audiencia* for political rather than legal purposes, in the early sixteenth century. In 1506, the lawyers at Granada intervened to protect Pedro Fernández de Córdoba, brother of the *alcaide de los donceles*, in the governorship of the fortress of Castro del Río, which had been granted to him by the Crown against the wishes of Córdoba council.[77]

In order to pursue cases in the *audiencia*, it was necessary for a town to employ legal staff resident in Ciudad Real or, later, Granada. In 1495, for example, Córdoba sent a *jurado* as its representative to Ciudad Real to engage a *procurador* and a lawyer to carry on litigation there. They were appointed for a year and received a third of their salary in advance. Early in 1496, the town's lawyer transferred the council's business to one of his colleagues and only informed his employers of the fact afterwards. In June of that year, yet another lawyer was appointed. In addition to the *procurador*, who was resident in Ciudad Real and paid a retaining salary by Córdoba, the town would send another representative when summoned for the hearing of a particular case. For example, in 1496, Córdoba's *procurador de términos*, the official responsible for questions concerning boundaries, was summoned to Ciudad Real for a case involving an enclosure, which was in dispute between Córdoba and the council of Santaella.[78]

Before the *audiencias* were established as permanent appeal courts, the Crown used to appoint special judges, who were generally legally qualified members of the royal council, to go to the locality concerned and hear and judge the case in the king's name. This system continued after the Valladolid and Ciudad Real *chancillerías* had been set up, and the *oidores* from these tribunals sometimes performed such duties in the same way as the members of the royal council. These judges were given commissions to hear cases and were therefore called *jueces de comisión*. If they received a general commission to investigate all offences concerned with boundaries in a certain area, they might be known as *jueces de términos*.

Jueces de comisión were not prominent in Córdoba under the Catholic Monarchs, except in the more specific role of *jueces de términos*. Before 1480, the Crown had dealt with such questions by sending *jueces de comisión* to hear specific cases. Thus in 1457, Dr Diego Sánchez del Castillo was sent to deal with boundaries disputes between the council and Gonzalo Mexía, lord of Santa Eufemia. In 1477, the Crown appointed another *oidor*, Don Rodrigo Maldonado de Talavera, as *juez de términos* in the diocese of Córdoba. He delegated the commission to Lic. Diego de Rojas, who dealt with a number of cases in 1477–8. After this, such appointments were quite frequent. Lic. Sancho Sánchez de Montiel was in Córdoba between 1491 and 1499, Lic. Antonio de Cuéllar heard some cases in 1513–14 and Lic. Fernando Díaz de Lobón replaced him in the office between October 1514 and May 1515.[79]

While Montiel was in Córdoba, the Crown, apparently at his request, appointed Pedro Jiménez de Góngora, a citizen of Córdoba, as *juez de los cortijos* (judge of farms). He was first given a general responsibility, without any title, for ensuring that farms in the Córdoba area were properly marked. Córdoba council decided in January 1498 to appeal against the appointment, on the grounds that the *fieles* and judges were already at work to enforce royal legislation on land-use. The royal letter confirming Góngora's appointment stated that Montiel had asked for assistance because he was dissatisfied with the work of the existing boundary officials. Góngora was formally designated a judge in September 1498, but when he presented a royal letter ordering the *fieles* and *medidor* to work efficiently or else pay from their own pockets for the fencing to be done by others, the council protested to the Crown. This was to no avail, however, and after the *juez de términos* departed, Góngora replaced him in part, for example prosecuting Francisco Cabrera, a *veinticuatro* in 1504, for illegal enclosure. It is not surprising, therefore, that he was unpopular in council circles.[80]

In the administration of the legal system, Córdoba council acted as the intermediary between the Crown and the towns of the *tierra*. The royal judges and officials had the automatic right to enter Córdoba's *tierra* in the exercise of their functions, as in any *señorío*, but in March 1497 the council reiterated the principle that no royal letter, brought by a *juez de comisión*, might be received by a subordinate council in the *tierra* unless the judge's letters of credence had first been presented and approved in Córdoba. The Crown seems not to have accepted Córdoba's claim, however, as in 1502 La Rambla and Santaella successfully made a direct appeal to the Monarchs against the way in which their taxes (*alcabalas*) had been collected. They obtained royal judges to arbitrate, although, probably so as not to erode respect for Córdoba's authority, the choice of the judges was left to its *corregidor*.[81]

In most cases, the litigation of the towns in the *tierra* was undertaken by Córdoba council. If litigation was begun with the council's approval, Córdoba was prepared to pay the costs. In 1504, for example, the council paid a fine of 8000 *mrs* which had been imposed on Fuente Obejuna in a case over boundaries against the count of Belalcázar, and it also paid 4000 *mrs* towards Fuente Obejuna's expenses in the hearing. Such payments were apparently only made if the money could not be raised locally by a *repartimiento* of up to the maximum permitted quantity of 3000 *mrs*, collected from the citizens. Such fines could be a major burden on a small town. In 1493, for example, Córdoba told the *alcaldes* and *jurados* of Bujalance to raise by this method a fine of 15 000 *mrs* which had been imposed on the town for invading a *dehesa* which belonged to Córdoba. In cases where the authority of the council in outlying areas was in question, it naturally took a hard line and the same applied if a town started a legal action without the parent council's consent. In 1497, Fuente Obejuna was told, for this reason, that it would have to pay its own costs in a petition to the Crown about taxation. On other occasions, Córdoba's control over the *tierra* was exercised in a more beneficent way, as when the council, in 1497, sent two *veinticuatros* to arbitrate in a dispute over land between La Rambla and Santaella. In view of this evidence, it is perhaps not surprising that Córdoba's lordship over its *tierra* sometimes appeared more oppressive than that of lords in their *señoríos*.[82]

3

Royal taxation and municipal finance

There is little doubt that one of the main reasons for the Castilian Crown's anxiety to retain control over major towns, such as Córdoba, was the important contribution which they made to the royal finances. Without the taxation revenue which they produced, even the comparatively limited form of central government which existed in Castile in the late Middle Ages would have been impractical. The public finances of Córdoba in this period are therefore of interest for two main reasons. First, they illustrate the characteristics and the effectiveness of the royal taxation system and, secondly, they provide one of the best available indications of the distribution of wealth between public authorities and private individuals.

CASTILIAN ROYAL TAXES

In order to survey the many different taxes which affected Córdoba, it is best to adopt the scheme used by Ladero in his important study of Castilian royal finances in the fifteenth century.[1] This involves a division into direct and indirect taxation and, in addition, into ordinary and extraordinary revenues, although the latter distinction would not have been recognised by contemporaries. Two ordinary direct taxes were collected from the inhabitants of royal towns. One of these was the *moneda forera*, which had originally been an extraordinary aid, voted by the Cortes to the king 'in recognition of his royal lordship', as John II's *cuaderno* (book of instructions) for its collection described it. By the fifteenth century, it had become an ordinary tax of eight *maravedís* per head in Castile, Extremadura and the frontier regions and six *maravedís* in León, calculated in the old money, which was worth twice as much as the *maravedí* then current. It was collected every six years. The change in the status of this tax over the years indicates the problems encountered in distinguishing ordinary from extraordinary taxes. The other ordinary direct tax collected in Córdoba was the *tercias reales* (royal thirds), which was one of a number of royal taxes in the fifteenth century which were of ecclesiastical origin. The *tercias* were in fact two-ninths of the church tithe on cereals, wine, livestock and other agricultural products. They had been conceded to the Castilian Crown by the popes in the thirteenth century, on a temporary basis, to further the conquest of Muslim territory, but, as with so many Castilian taxes, they became permanent (in 1340) and in the fifteenth century they were collected with the *alcabala*, or sales-tax.[2]

Extraordinary direct taxation was important in the royal finances of the fifteenth century. It was voted to the king by the Cortes, as a survival of the vassal's aid and military service to his lord. Under Ferdinand and Isabella, no service (*servicio*) of this kind was voted by the Cortes between 1476 and 1500, but the money was raised instead by the *juntas de Hermandad*, following the same procedure. Each *servicio* was divided into the old-fashioned *monedas* and the later *pedidos*, but the principle on which these taxes were based was the same.[3]

The two main categories of ordinary indirect taxation were taxes on trade and taxes on transport. The main tax on trade was the *alcabala*, a ten per cent tax on all sales and other transactions, which by the fifteenth century was paid entirely by the seller, although originally it was divided equally between him and the buyer. The main tax on transport, the *almojarifazgo*, was important in Andalusia, where it was partly in the hands of local councils. Compared with this, the other customs and transport duties, such as *portazgo, rodas, barcaje* and *castellería*, were of minor importance, but this could not be said of the tax on the movement of livestock, the *servicio y montazgo*, which is not to be confused with the *servicios* voted by the Cortes. This *servicio* was a head-tax on the movement of animals, which replaced all other customs duties on such traffic. The *montazgo*, which was collected with it, was a tax on the use of pasture under royal jurisdiction. The *servicio* began in 1270 and the *montazgo* came under complete royal control in 1343.[4] The equivalent indirect tax to the Cortes and Hermandad *servicios* was the *sisa* or *imposición*, which was a one or three per cent tax on sales, which might be imposed in case of need, in addition to the *alcabala*. The earliest surviving reference to *sisas* comes from the reign of Sancho IV (1284–95) and they were extensively applied to foodstuffs under Ferdinand and Isabella.[5]

THE COLLECTION OF ROYAL TAXES

The royal administration in the fifteenth century was still inadequate to supervise the collection of taxes. The kingdoms of Castile were divided for tax purposes into *partidos*, which generally followed diocesan boundaries, but were sometimes less extensive in areas of great economic activity. The diocese of Córdoba was accordingly divided into four *partidos*. The Seville diocese consisted of three *partidos*, with others covering Jerez, Ecija and the county of Niebla. The last also included the Aljarafe and Ribera, in the kingdom of Seville. In each *partido*, the Crown appointed a chief collector (*recaudador mayor*) to supervise the collection of royal revenues, which he might delegate to subordinates (*recaudadores menores*), who would receive the taxes in four-monthly instalments from the local councils or other collecting agents.

Castilian subjects did not, generally speaking, pay their taxes directly to royal officials. Most of the king's revenues were farmed out to *arrendadores*, who paid him in advance a price that was fixed by auction and thereafter incurred all the risks and advantages. The weakness of the royal administration and the desirability of receiving the money in advance to meet required expenditure made this system both necessary and reasonably effective, from the Crown's point of view. The reserve price for each rent that was auctioned was fixed by the main royal financial agency, the *contaduría mayor de hacienda*, on the basis of information from previous tax-farmers. The conditions for the collection of rents were laid down in a separate *cuaderno* of instructions for each one. These *cuadernos* changed little after the reign of John II, though Henry IV and the Catholic Monarchs altered those for the collection of the *alcabala* and the *almojarifazgo sevillano*. Many rents were auctioned centrally, at the *estrado de las rentas*, which generally remained at Medina del Campo. Others were auctioned by the *escribanos de las rentas*, the tax-clerks in the different taxation areas. These officials were responsible for providing the *contadores* with information on the value of rents and also received one per cent of all those which they helped to auction.

When an auction was announced, bidders offered their bids until the *remate de la subasta*, that is, the sum acceptable to the royal financiers, was reached. After this first round, further bids (*pujas*) might be allowed under certain conditions, until the final round was arrived at and the rent was *rematada de todo remate*. The *contadores* encouraged bids by offering *prometidos*, that is, sums which the farmer might keep for himself. The original *arrendador* had a right to the *prometido* and part of the bids that followed. By the time the final *remate* was reached, the *prometidos* were frequently shared between the first *arrendador* and a number of major or minor speculators who had become associated with him in bids for the rent. Rights to farm rents, obtained in auctions, were often transferred later to others. Once a rent was *rematada*, the farmer was obliged to provide financial guarantors within ten to twenty days. These guarantees could be other financial benefits which the farmer received from the Crown, in the form, for example, of *raciones*, *quitaciones* and other types of salary. Such payments would be retained by the Crown to offset its losses if the *arrendador* failed to meet his obligations.

When arrangements had been made for the pricing and guaranteeing of the rent, the farmer received a letter authorising him to organise its collection, which required an army of *escribanos*, guards, collectors (*cogedores*) and other minor officials. Certain categories of people were excluded from farming taxes. These included all clerics and officials of the royal administration, powerful subjects (*personas poderosas*), especially in their own areas, commanders of military orders in their own *encomiendas* and governors (*alcaides*) of fortresses. All tax-farmers received the full formal protection of the Crown against interference with their work and the towns where they collected taxes were obliged to lodge them at reasonable prices. In certain circumstances, a farmer could fine those who obstructed him, but legal disputes arising out of the collection of rents were generally resolved by the local magistrates. Occasionally, a special judge might be appointed by the Crown to hear such cases and the highest appeal was to the *contadores mayores*. An *arrendador* could only summon a party to law in that party's place of residence or in the chief town with jurisdiction over it.

An alternative system for the collection of royal revenues existed, which might appear more suitable from the Crown's point of view. This was the naming of individuals known as *fieles* by the local council to collect the king's revenues. However, fifteenth-century Castilian kings did not find this a satisfactory way of raising taxes, because, unlike the *arrendador*, the *fiel* had insufficient financial interest in collecting the money, so that when *fieles* were at work, the Crown received only a small proportion of what was due. The salary of three per cent of taxes collected, which the *fieles* received, did not fire their enthusiasm and so this system was only resorted to when there was a delay in the appointment of a tax-farmer or if a particular difficulty arose with collection by the latter method. A farmer might claim his revenue for one or two years after the end of his farm and he was also entitled to ask for a discount (*suspensiones*) in cases where his rents had been legally or illegally taken by some overmighty subject (*persona poderosa*).

From 1495 onwards, another method came to be used for the collection of royal rents. This was the system known as *encabezamiento*, which involved the collection of rents, particularly *alcabalas* and *tercias*, by local councils, instead of *fieles* or *arrendadores*. Town councils had been trying for many years to take over the collection of the king's taxes. In doing so, they were in fact attempting to return to the situation which had obtained in the fourteenth century, when the towns, which then retained considerable political vitality, had achieved a stronger position in bargaining with the Crown. The creation of closed councils in the towns had had the effect of weakening this position and had resulted in the return of power over revenue collection to the Crown and its agents. By 1495, however, the *arrendamiento* system had run into difficulties, partly because of the expulsion of the Jews and the activities of the Inquisition, and the Catholic Monarchs were prepared to make agreements with the urban oligarchies for the latter to collect *alcabalas* and *tercias*, in return for an effective reduction in the burden of these taxes on local communities, caused by the fixing of levels of taxation for several years at a time and the scope given to the councils to decide how the overall total was to be raised.[6]

In theory, *servicios*, as direct taxes, were calculated on the basis of the wealth of individual tax-payers (*pecheros*). Collection of the aids voted to the Crown by the Cortes was left to the local councils and the total sum demanded was divided into two categories, *monedas* and *pedidos*. The *moneda* was the longer-established of the two and was equal to eight *maravedís* in Castile, Extremadura and the frontier regions and six *maravedís* in León. Thus in 1476, a contribution (*reparto*) of twelve *monedas* was asked for and this amounted to ninety-six *maravedís* per head. In order to pay the tax, an individual had to have goods valued at a previously fixed amount, though his bed, ordinary clothes, weapons and a pair of plough-oxen, if he had one, were excluded from the calculation. For the 1476 *servicio*, it was laid down that *pecheros* with goods valued at sixty *maravedís* or less, by this method, should pay only two *monedas* and that the full twelve should apply to those with 220 *mrs* or more. Leaving aside the ease with which the rich might conceal their wealth or obtain total exemption from *servicios*, the fact that a global sum was demanded of the kingdom and divided among the *partidos* meant that the tax could not in any case be collected on the basis of an assessment of individual wealth. Even in theory, the *pedidos* were not assessed like the *monedas* and, in practice, *servicios* in general were raised in whatever way the local councils found possible at the the time.

The municipalities showed little enthusiasm for collecting *servicios*, because they did not stand to gain from the revenue. Another problem was the high instance of exemptions, which the Cortes complained of, for example in 1442.[7] When *monedas* were collected, every place with more than thirty citizens resident within it (*vecinos y moradores*) had to appoint someone to compose a list (*padrón*) of tax-payers. This list had to be handed to the tax-collector within twelve days, so that he could collect the money and hand it over to the receiver of treasure within twenty days after that. When a tax-payer died, his widow and children continued to pay the tax, counting as one *pechero*. If his goods were divided after his death, more than one tax contribution (*pecho*) was formed. His orphan children became *pecheros* in their own right when they married. In 1451, it was established that land acquired between the granting of a *servicio* by the Cortes and the completion of the list of tax-payers was to count in the reckoning of wealth. However, the *padrones* were not revised for each *servicio*, but kept by the royal accountants (*contadores mayores*). Those produced in 1455–6 were used until 1476.

TAX EXEMPTIONS

Exemption from taxation was one of the main issues in Andalusian towns under the Catholic Monarchs, because while in Castile as a whole, certain social categories – the upper nobility, *hidalgos*, knights (*caballeros*), squires (*escuderos*) and noble ladies (*dueñas* and *doncellas*) – were automatically exempt, there was a theory that in Andalusia these exemptions did not apply. At the Cortes of 1451, it was stated that 'all pay taxes in common, "rich men" (*ricos omes*) in the same way as knights (*caballeros*), *hidalgos* and any others, which has always been customarily done for the common good and defence of that land'.[8] The exemption of clergy in major orders, priests, deacons and subdeacons, does not seem to have caused dispute, but that of *caballeros* was only admitted in Andalusia after some argument. In practice, three types of *caballero* were recognised as exempt from *monedas*. The first, the *caballero* who kept a horse and weapons continuously and served the king personally in war, was exempt not only from *monedas* but also from *pedidos* and other taxes, such as *moneda forera*, provided that he lived by the practice of arms and not by any 'low offices' and was ready to serve at any time until he reached the age of sixty. If they kept the weapons and horse, his widow and children could continue to claim these exemptions until the widow remarried and the children reached their majority. The second category of exemption was that of knights dubbed by the king in the field, who might follow a profession other than that of arms. In practice, the exemption of such knights from *monedas* was limited, so that this type of knighthood could not be used as a route for tax-payers who wanted to escape from their responsibilities. Any children they had before they were knighted continued to be *pecheros*, and the 1442 Cortes asked for the practice of granting such knighthoods by letter to be stopped. The Andalusian towns contained another type of knight, of whom much more will be heard later, known as the *caballero de premia* or *caballero de alarde*, who was exempt from *monedas* only. *Caballeros de premia*, as they were generally known in Córdoba, were ordinary citizens of any trade who reached a minimum wealth qualification and kept a horse and weapons for use by themselves or a substitute.[9]

Those with individual tax exemptions, who were known either as *exentos* or *excusados*, only in fact escaped the *monedas*. The possessors of these exemptions included a wide range of royal servants, not only at Court but also in the royal towns. In Córdoba, the Monarchs in 1478 confirmed, at the request of the *corregidor*, Francisco de Valdés, the exemptions granted by past kings to the *alcalde* and inhabitants of two castles, the Alcázar Viejo (Old Castle) and the Castillo Viejo de la Judería (Old Castle of the Jewry).[10] It appears that there were twenty-eight tradesmen's offices in these castles, which carried exemption from *monedas*, although those who held them were not knights. When the stone-mason Rodrigo de Torres died in 1497, he was succeeded by the man he himself had designated. One of the conditions laid down by the town council before it ratified this proceeding was that the new officer should not be a *caballero de premia*. The Alcázar franchise was not apparently intended to benefit those who were already exempt from *monedas*. In 1515, there was some dispute over the privileges of the inhabitants of the Alcázar Viejo, and a document in which the beneficiaries empowered two proctors to represent them at law reveals that in that year there were thirty-seven heads of household in the castle, one of them a widow. They included stone-cutters, masons, weavers, gardeners, shepherds, fishermen, tenant-farmers (*labradores*), book-copyists, a collier, a bird-catcher, a silk-mercer, a bonnet-maker and a surgeon.[11]

Various municipal officials obtained exemptions from *servicios*. It was assumed that *alcaldes* and *regidores* were exempt from all *pechos*, but concessions of this kind inevitably led to disputes over the status of the families and servants of beneficiaries. In 1496, Gonzalo Carrillo, *veinticuatro* of Córdoba, obtained confirmation of the exemption from *servicios* first granted by the Crown to his grandfather, which also applied to his children and servants. In the previous year, Doña Isabel de Tamayo, widow of the *alcalde mayor* Fernando de Narváez, had obtained a similar exemption. *Jurados* were generally exempt from all *servicios*, whether *monedas* or *pedidos*, though it was their responsibility to collect these taxes. However, it was laid down by the council that once an individual ceased to be a *jurado*, he should revert to the rank of *pechero* if this was his former status. Sons of *jurados* were not automatically entitled to exemptions and neither were *alguaciles*, even while in office, though *escribanos* probably were.[12]

Like *caballeros*, *hidalgos* were exempt from all *pechos*, in return for their personal military service, either on horseback or, in some cases, on foot. In order to become a *hidalgo*, a man had to prove to the *alcaldes de los fijosdalgo* at the *chancillería* that he resided in the same place as his father and grandfather and that they had not been tax-payers. If he succeeded in doing so, he obtained a letter of execution (*carta ejecutoria*) for presentation to the local council, which, in the case of Córdoba, then ordered the *jurados* to remove his name from the tax-list of his parish. The exemption from *servicios* applied to his wife, even if she was the daughter of tax-payers, as long as she remained married to him and preserved the chastity of marriage.[13]

Local councils were frequently called upon to decide whether certain individuals or groups should pay a particular *servicio*. Each demand from the Crown for money to be raised in this way led to a crop of disputes, in which councils tried to apply the general rules on exemption. For example, in 1495 Juan de Frías petitioned the council to exclude him from the tax-list on the grounds that he was a *hidalgo*. The criterion used by the council to decide the case was whether he had paid previous *servicios* or not. In the event, it was found that he had not, so that his exemption was allowed. Sometimes the Crown's authority was invoked, as when Commander Juan de Luna, *veinticuatro*, petitioned the Monarchs successfully on behalf of himself and the other knights of the military order of Santiago to order Córdoba council to exclude them from the *padrón*. This ruling was apparently based on the fact that the activities of the knights of military orders came in the same category as the personal military service of *hidalgos*.[14]

Another fruitful source of dispute was the status of those who claimed to be members of the households of *regidores* and other *caballeros*. If these claims were upheld by the council, the individuals concerned were deemed to have no independent legal existence, like wives and children of tax-payers, and were therefore not liable for *servicios*. This ruling was enforced by the town council in 1479, 1496 and 1501. Similar exemptions existed for those attached to monasteries and churches. This concession, which was confirmed by the Catholic Monarchs in 1478, paralleled that granted to the inhabitants of the royal *alcázares*, or castles, in towns such as Córdoba and Seville. In the case of the convent of St Clare, Córdoba, the local council controlled the fixed quota of exemptions on the foundation. Such an arrangement was probably typical. As with the franchises in the castles, beneficiaries had to be *pecheros* and not *caballeros de premia*. During the revolts in the kingdom of Granada in 1501, the council made the concession that the widows of those who died in action, whether *caballeros* or not, would be exempt from all *servicios*. It was apparently felt that they had already paid the ultimate war-service. Personal exemptions were also granted for various reasons. These sometimes emanated from the Crown, as when Isabel de León, a servant of the princess Isabella, received a grant from the king and queen for herself, her pharmacist husband and their children. In other cases they were granted by the local council. Córdoba council gave such exemptions to its town-criers, to a faithful lawyer in 1497 and to another individual for unspecified services to the town.[15]

THE HERMANDAD

When the Crown abandoned the use of *servicios* after 1476, it obtained direct tax revenues instead from the Hermandad organisation, which was reconstituted in 1478. For the next twenty years, *repartimientos* (allocations of contributions) were made in Castilian towns for the upkeep of this force, but after 1482 they were effectively used for the Granada war. While the Andalusian towns provided militia as well, the other towns of the kingdom contributed to the war effort mainly through the Hermandad levies of cash, animals and men. It was admitted by the Crown that the Hermandad *repartimientos* were a substitute for the Cortes *servicios* and when Castilian military activity spread outside the kingdom at the end of the fifteenth century, *servicios* reappeared. The similarity between the two levies is shown by the fact that the 1500 and 1502 *servicios* were collected using the same *padrones* as had been prepared for Hermandad *repartimientos*. As with *monedas*, there was a theoretical basis for calculating the contributions of each town, though for the Hermandad it was the size of population rather than individual wealth. The 1478 Hermandad laws stipulated that towns should maintain one *jinete*, a lightly armed horseman who rode with short stirrups in the Moorish style, for every hundred citizens and one man-at-arms for each 150. These terms applied to the basic annual contribution made by Castilian towns to the upkeep of the Hermandad. This money might be used for the Granada war, but it was not the same as the *repartimientos* raised specifically for that purpose, which were an additional burden on the towns. The basic Hermandad contribution was a subject for negotiation between the towns and the government, but *repartimientos*, like *servicios*, were specific sums requested by the Crown from individual towns. In Córdoba they were collected parish by parish, in the same way as *servicios*. The *jurados* and the parish *escribano* composed the tax-lists and each parish chose two representatives, one a *caballero de premia* and the other not, to hear complaints about the lists. Some attempt was made in the *repartimientos* to relate contributions to individual wealth, even if this was not done in the annual Hermandad contributions. In 1496, the council ordered that the *caballeros de premia* were to pay for the upkeep of two infantrymen (*peones*) each and that the contributions of poorer people were to be less.[16]

Exemptions from Hermandad *repartimientos* were similar to those from *servicios*, but according to the 1478 laws, those classified as *excusados* were not exempt from this tax. Local councils had the same discretion in deciding who should pay *repartimientos* as they did with *servicios*, and in 1496 Córdoba council called in the privileges of the town's *excusados*, apparently with a view to exempting them from the *repartimiento* of that year. Exemptions applied in any case to *regidores*, *jurados*, *hidalgos* and other *privilegiados* with personal grants from the Crown or the local council, the *escribanos* who composed the tax-lists, the parish *alguaciles* if they resided in their parishes, and the squires and households (*comensales*) of *caballeros*. The conditions for the exemption of the last were defined in 1496 for the purposes of the Hermandad *repartimientos*, but they probably applied equally to the *servicios*. Exemptions for squires (*escuderos*) and *comensales* were granted to those who received food, drink, straw and barley on a continuous basis from their lord and who owned no movable or immovable property. Those who owned flocks, land or buildings could not claim exemption. As with *servicios*, the basic criterion for deciding individual cases was whether the person concerned had paid the tax on previous occasions, but the *jurados* seem to have experienced difficulty in obtaining overall rulings from a council which was anxious to decide such matters on an *ad hoc* basis, a procedure which did not lend itself to consistency. When the *jurados* complained in the summer of 1496 about the lack of guidance, they only received, after some delay, an order to respect the exemptions of groups which were in any case fairly well-defined, such as *regidores* and *hidalgos*.[17]

VALUE OF DIRECT TAXES

Despite the importance to citizens of obtaining exemptions from direct taxation, for the sake of their social and financial well-being, much of the revenue required to pay *servicios* and Hermandad contributions came not from individual tax-payments but from impositions and loans. For example, almost as soon as the 1500 *servicio* had been voted by the Cortes, Córdoba council received permission to raise special indirect taxes to pay it. It was soon discovered that even these were insufficient and the council resorted to loans from wealthy citizens, from Genoese merchants and from those who had not served in the town's forces in the putting down of the Moorish revolts in the kingdom of Granada. Impositions, or *sisas*, were also permitted by the Crown for the payment of Hermandad levies in Córdoba. In 1496, the town's *caballeros de premia*, perhaps influenced by the council's desire to tax them more heavily than their less wealthy fellow-citizens, put pressure on the council to apply a royal letter which permitted the use of impositions for this purpose. In this case *sisas* were not applied for the payment of the *repartimiento* because they were already being used to raise the annual levy. The failure to use *sisas* to raise the 1495 *repartimiento* did not deter the Crown from suggesting the same procedure for the 1496 special levy, and on this occasion the council's initial reluctance was overcome when it was realised that after several months less than half the required amount had been raised. An imposition was placed on meat and fish, and when this proved inadequate forced loans from the *jurados* were resorted to. This mixture of *sisas* and loans was again used to finance the Hermandad in Córdoba in 1497 and 1498.[18]

The value of the *servicios* and Hermandad *repartimientos* raised in Córdoba may be measured either in the standard money of account, the *maravedí*, or in terms of the gold and silver currency. The latter is more useful for measuring the value of these taxes in terms of purchasing power. The available figures for *servicios* show how different are the results obtained if totals are given in, for example, gold Aragonese florins rather than *maravedís*. The most useful indication of the relative lack of importance of direct taxation under Ferdinand and Isabella is the fact that, in terms of florins, the Crown was obtaining less revenue in *servicios* from Córdoba in 1506 than in 1504, the latter figure being in turn lower than that for 1502. This trend could hardly be termed satisfactory for the Crown.[19] The annual contribution of Córdoba to the Hermandad seems to have been 2 050 000 *mrs* or 7735 florins. This sum was required each year up to 1498 and is similar to that required for the 1500 *servicio*, though later *servicios* were considerably larger.[20]

An important feature of the Castilian taxation system under the Catholic Monarchs was the survival of a large number of archaic taxes in addition to those which actually produced the greater part of the royal revenue. In the case of direct taxation, the *servicio* was the successor of the *moneda forera* and of the *cabeza del pecho* of Jews and Moors, which was a poll-tax on these communities. The *cabeza del pecho* appears among the municipal revenues in 1452–3 but was not collected after the death of John II. The *moneda forera* did survive, however, having become virtually an ordinary tax, which was farmed out by *partido*. Exemption from this tax followed the pattern of the later *monedas*, included in the *servicio*, which in fact originated with this older tax. Córdoba found it necessary to defend the exemption of *caballeros de premia* and their widows and children. The totals in florins for the *moneda forera* in the diocese of Córdoba show a sharp fall in the value of the tax between 1440 and 1488, and while the 1494 figures were much improved, the total for that year was still less than half of that for 1440.[21]

THE 'ALCABALA'

The most important indirect tax in Castile was the *alcabala*, which, with the *tercias reales* collected in cash rather than kind, amounted to eighty per cent of the royal revenues under Ferdinand and Isabella.[22] It appears to have originated as a Muslim municipal tax, forming part of the customs tax, the *almojarifazgo*, in Córdoba and Ecija and consisting of five per cent on the sale of certain products. This was the *veintena* (twentieth), which survived under that name in certain towns in the lordship of Arcos under the Catholic Monarchs. The *alcabala* is first referred to in surviving Castilian documents in 1101 and recurs intermittently up to 1303, in a local rather than a national context. In the early fourteenth century, the tax seems to have been under Cortes influence, being granted to the king in the same way as the *servicios*, but when Alfonso XI was granted the Castilian *alcabalas* in 1342 for his Algeciras campaign, he began to develop them as part of his effort to improve the state of the royal finances. His two main aims were to turn Cortes *servicios* into a regular source of revenue and to make the *alcabala* general and, if possible, permanent. In both cases he was reasonably successful, but while the *alcabala* did become a regalian right, it was not inalienable in terms of Roman law, as an exclusive attribute of royal sovereignty. Exemptions from the *alcabala* were extremely rare and were not granted to social categories as such. Even *hidalgos* did not escape and while some towns, especially those on or near the frontier with the Moors, obtained exemptions from the *alcabala* on agricultural and pastoral products, Córdoba was not among them. The clergy attempted to claim exemption, but the Crown counteracted this by stipulating in the 1465 *cuaderno* for the collection of the rent that, in transactions between laymen and clerics, the layman should pay the tax even if he was the buyer, although by the fifteenth century it was normally paid by the seller. The 1484 *cuaderno* put clerics under civil jurisdiction in cases involving *alcabalas*, in an attempt to curb evasion, but in 1491 the clergy achieved exemption for themselves as individuals and for their institutions, in transactions which did not involve trading for gain (*trato de mercadería*).[23]

In 1342, the *alcabala* rate was five per cent, but the Catholic Monarchs fixed it permanently at ten per cent. Nonetheless, it is worth noting that as late as the reign of Philip II, small villages often paid as little as three-and-a-half per cent, and it is probable that the rate of ten per cent was rarely reached in practice.[24] The tax also applied to exchanges of goods (*trueques*) and the tax payable in such cases was determined by an ordinary citizen (*hombre bueno*), named by the magistrate or judge responsible for litigation arising out of the *alcabala*. The tax was collected by means of farms and each *partido* might be divided into sections of rent (*miembros de renta*). This leads to the impression from the surviving material that there were many *alcabalas*, but while it is often useful to talk in this way when attempting to describe the immensely complicated structure for the collection of the tax in towns such as Córdoba, there was in fact only one *alcabala*, of which the taxes on different articles of consumption were parts.[25]

The procedure laid down in the royal *cuadernos* of 1429, 1462 and 1491 for the payment of the tax indicates the effort that was made to overcome the problems with which a fairly rudimentary governmental organisation was faced in trying to collect a sales-tax. The basic rule was that the *alcabala* was payable in the place of residence of the seller, though if an item was sold in one place and handed over to the buyer in another – and even stored in a third – the tax was generally paid where the article finally came to rest. If it could be proved that goods had been handed over at a place other than that of sale in order to avoid payment, those involved in the transaction were liable to a fine of four times the tax owed. When a farmer came to a tax-area to collect the *alcabala*, he had to announce his arrival and place of residence. Thereafter, sellers were supposed to notify their transactions to him within two days and pay the tax to the *arrendador* within three days after that, on pain of a fourfold fine. Buyers were also supposed to declare their purchases, but as the tax was not collected from them, they were not fined if they failed to do so. It was possible for a trader to make an agreement, known as an *iguala* or *avenencia*, with the farmer in advance, to pay him fixed sums at regular intervals. In these circumstances, the buyer was not obliged to make declarations to the tax-farmer. It was forbidden to move goods out of a town or village at night without the permission of the farmer, who had the power to station guards at the gates to make a compulsory examination of goods and register them. Within centres of population, the *arrendador* had the right to examine shop-keepers' books and to place guards at the sales-points of goods on which he collected tax. No goods might be moved from one town or village to another without licence from the *arrendador*. In transactions which involved a seller who was a citizen from outside the area, a cleric, a religious, a local council official or a powerful subject (*hombre poderoso*), the buyer had to report to the *arrendador* before the goods were handed over. If he knew that the seller had not paid the tax, he was obliged to keep the appropriate sum and pay it to the *arrendador* when required.[26]

Certain goods were exempt from *alcabala* according to the royal instructions. These included bread (but not grain), horses and mules, coins and precious metals, manuscripts and printed books, birds of prey, certain types of clothing, wood for the royal arsenal (*atarazanas*) of Seville, grain imported to Seville for sale by foreign merchants, captives and booty from the Moors, when first sold, goods received by the treasurers of the Crusade tax (*cruzada*) and goods transferred in dowries or in the division of an inheritance among heirs, including money to make one share equal another. In various parts of Castile, including the diocese of Córdoba, wayside inns (*ventas*) which existed to serve travellers in remote areas were also exempt from the *alcabala*. To avoid abuse, those within half a league (2.79 km) of a centre of population were excluded from this privilege.

The *alcabala* of Córdoba and its *tierra*, together with the *tercias*, were divided into four parts, the granary (*alhóndiga*), the major rents (*rentas mayores*) and minor rents (*rentas menores*), and the rents of the *tierra*. Before *arrendadores* could begin to collect *alcabalas* in Córdoba, they had to present their royal letters to the council and swear to observe the privileges, uses and customs of the town. In 1475, these were that the farmers should put offenders in the council prison and no other, and that they would employ only the local magistrates and police. They were forbidden to take prisoners more than five leagues (27.85 km) from Córdoba, they had to observe the privileges of *caballeros de premia* and those dubbed by the king, they were not allowed to collect taxes on dowries unless these had been committed as guarantees (*fianzas*) for payments, they might not summon offenders to the royal Court in the first instance and they were not to make an execution or sentence in cases which had already been judged by other magistrates.[27] When the farmers had sworn to observe these conditions, an announcement was made in the town that they would be available to receive offers from prospective farmers of the rents for individual products. By 1497, the further condition had been added to those of 1475, that the farmers were bound to observe custom in the collection of the tax on wine and farm it according to the conditions of past years.[28]

The possibility of introducing *fieles* to collect the *alcabalas* in place of the farmers gave the local council the opportunity to interfere in the gathering of indirect taxes. In 1496, after a complaint by the *regidor* Alfonso Carrillo, it was discovered that the *arrendadores* had failed to ensure that the lesser farmers of the *alcabala* were guaranteed financially, as they were required to do. The rent in question was the tax on fish, but the chief collector (*recaudador mayor*) admitted that there were others without guarantors. The *alcalde mayor* of Córdoba ordered an immediate investigation and it transpired that, in addition to the fish *alcabala*, the *almojarifazgo* on meat, which was counted as part of the *alcabala*, and the *alcabalas* of the butcheries and livestock, were not guaranteed. Furthermore, contrary to the terms of the 1491 *cuaderno*, which the Crown had drawn to Córdoba council's attention in 1493, the farmer of the meat *almojarifazgo* was the *recaudador mayor*, Alfonso de Castro, himself. There was already a *fiel* appointed by the council to supervise the butcheries, alongside the farmers, but both were without guarantors. The council named *cogedores* to collect all these rents and *fieles* to supervise them. Two fish-merchants were put in charge of the meat rents, while the fish *alcabala* was entrusted to two other individuals, one of them a lawyer. In addition, the council ordered that, in order to avoid frauds in the farming and guaranteeing of rents, the *recaudador* was not to sign the document of *arrendamiento* until all the money had been collected. Although there was sometimes difficulty with the guaranteeing of rents in future years, the council did not again find it necessary to put in *fieles*.[29]

The *recaudadores mayores* of the *alcabala* normally came from outside the area, but in some cases they built up connections with certain *partidos* over a number of years. Gonzalo de Monzón and Alonso de Castro, the latter a citizen of Segovia, were entrusted with the *alcabalas* of Córdoba from 1495 until 1500. Occupations of tax-farmers in this period included the sale of silk, cloth and spices. It was not a question of one farmer for each product, but rather of major farms being shared, while several of the lesser commodities were often allocated to one person.[30]

The method of collection varied according to the nature of the product. The taxation of grain was ensured by limiting sale to certain points. In towns with a central granary (*alhóndiga*), including Córdoba, grain might not be sold elsewhere and the 1491 *cuaderno* required all towns without an *alhóndiga* to build one. Various measures were taken by the Crown to make the job of the tax-collector easier. The sale of grain on the roads or in the fields was forbidden, so that it had to be brought into the town. In each large town, entry was restricted to three gates, while in towns without walls certain streets were designated for this purpose. In Córdoba in 1495, the *arrendador* was collecting the tax when the grain came through the gates and not at the point of sale. To counteract this and oblige its own citizens, the council was returning much of the payment to the citizens on the pretext that the grain was for consumption by the owner and his household and not for resale. To simplify the situation, the *arrendador*, Alonso de Jaén, agreed to collect the *alcabala* only at the *alhóndiga* and, if necessary, obtain a declaration from an *escribano*, witnessed by a private citizen, to the effect that a transaction had taken place. This declaration would then be deposited with the local magistrates to forestall council interference.[31]

The sale of meat was controlled in a very similar way. The *cuadernos* permitted *arrendadores* to weigh meat on their own balances in the town butcheries (*carnicerías*), so as to calculate the value of the tax payable and check that butchers gave an adequate account of the livestock and meat which they bought or owned. Butchers in Córdoba and Seville were required by the 1462 *cuaderno* to register the flocks which they owned. All butchers had to pay the *alcabala* on the animals which they cut up. If these belonged to the council or to private citizens, it was up to the parties concerned to ensure that the butchers were not out of pocket. There were three butcheries in Córdoba, in the parishes of St Mary, St Andrew and St Saviour.[32]

The *alcabala* on products which involved a large number of traders required other arrangements for collection. The 1429 and 1462 *cuadernos*, for example, laid down that all those involved in the cloth trade – merchants (*mercaderes* or *traperos*), old-clothes sellers (*aljabibes*) and shop-keepers (*tenderos*) – had to register and seal all the gold or woollen cloth which passed through their hands. An attempt was made to limit the points at which cloth might be sold in towns. The silk-exchange (*alcaicería*) was to be used if the town possessed one, as Córdoba did. The 1429 *cuaderno* authorised the sale of cloth, additionally, in the Calle de la Feria, during the two annual fairs, at the beginning of Lent (*Carnestolendas*) and in May. A royal provision of 1510 stipulated that the weavers and fullers of Córdoba should register their cloth for the purpose of paying the *alcabala*.[33]

In several other cases, traders took advantage of a system, permitted in the *cuadernos*, of making individual agreements with the *arrendador* for the payment of the *alcabala* on the products used in their trade. Such agreements were normally made for one year, during which the trader would make two tax-payments, based on an estimate of his turnover. These agreements were made before public *escribanos* and many of them survive. The tax on a particular product might involve several different trades. For example, the *alcabala* on animal hides (*corambre*) included tanners, boot-makers (*borceguineros*), shoe-makers, strap- or harness-makers (*zapateros de correa*) and wine-skin makers. The iron *alcabala* covered blacksmiths, wool-carders, locksmiths, tankard-makers and coppersmiths. The tax on linen and wool was also collected by this method. Payment was generally agreed in *maravedís*, but occasionally in gold ducats or silver *reales*. Some traders paying the hides *alcabala* also gave a sample of their craft to the *arrendador*, such as a pair of boots or shoes.[34]

The tax on some products was collected at the town gates. One of these was wine, which had to be imported through one of three specified gates so that the *arrendador* or his agents could register it and collect the tax later on this basis. Wine for domestic consumption was by definition excluded from the reckoning for what was in fact a sales-tax. The *arrendador* was permitted by the *cuadernos* to enter *bodegas* at any time and examine their contents, and also to supervise the vessels that were used for storing and selling wine. Those who wished to retail wine had to give notice of the fact to the *arrendador* so that he might supervise the sale. There is evidence that the farm of the wine *alcabala* was sub-let to local inhabitants for the collection in the *tierra*, for example in the vine-growing area around Santa María de Trassierra.[35]

The *escribanos* were a vital part of the collection of the *alcabala* on property-sales and transactions, excluding those concerned with dowries and inheritance. They had to show their records of transactions to the *arrendador* on demand so that the tax might be collected, though this royal disposition of 1461 did not appear in the *cuadernos*.[36]

As soon as the *encabezamiento* system was introduced for the collection of *alcabalas* and *tercias*, in 1495, it was adopted in the *partidos* of Córdoba. Ladero has evidence of its use in this area in 1498, 1499 and 1503 (the last in the *tierra*), and local evidence indicates the existence of such arrangements in 1497 (in the *tierra* only) and from 1500 until at least 1511. *Encabezamientos* seem, in fact, to have become the normal method of collecting the *alcabala* and *tercias* after 1500.[37] It appears that in the early days the town was reluctant to adopt the new system. In 1499, no less a person than Diego de Muela, a royal accountant (*contador mayor*), came to Córdoba to discuss with the council the merits of the *encabezamiento*,

and speak of the advantage that comes from it to the city and how [the city] receives great benefit from it and how in this Their Highnesses show [the city] great favour in it, and he gave many reasons for it all.[38]

It appears from other references that in the early years only four commodities, bread, wine, meat and fruit, were involved. It is probable, therefore, that Muela was discussing the inclusion of other articles. In April 1502, the council voted in favour of an *encabezamiento* covering the *alcabala* on fruit, olive-oil, hides, game and firewood, iron, earthenware, honey, wax and cochineal (*grana*), wood, esparto grass, gold and silver, and a conglomeration of rents including glovers, shoe-makers, leather-dressers, saddlers, clog-makers and pedlars. The whole *alcabala* and *aymojarifazgo* of the four *partidos* of Córdoba and also the *alcabala* of its *tierra*, were included in this arrangement. The document in which the *encabezamiento* was announced to the people of Córdoba added that,

all those persons and traders may give, for each of the abovementioned rents, the prices which they paid for them individually (*por menudo*), either in *encabezamiento* or *arrendamiento*, in the past year of 1501, for this present year and for the five following years, without any increase being made in them for all these six years, and all the officials and traders in each office [trade] have to oblige themselves on their own behalf for the total of each of . . . their rents and offices and not on behalf of any other, and this obligation and disclosure (*averiguación*) of price has to be done before the lord *corregidor* of this city and certain *veinticuatros* and *jurados* deputed for it, with the said treasurer. So that all of the abovementioned who wish to benefit from this grant shall find the said gentlemen, the *corregidor* and deputies and treasurer, in the council-house on each of the days following, from three hours after midday onwards, until with God's help this business is completed.[39]

The document makes it clear that the *encabezamiento* of 1502 was not compulsory for traders and there is evidence in the notarial archives that some declined to take part. In April 1502, a large number of carpenters and shoe-makers agreed before *escribanos* to pay a certain sum for that year and the five succeeding years as the *alcabala* on hides and wood. In addition, thirty tanners gave power to seven of their number to negotiate their contribution to the *alcabala* on hides with the council. However, it is known that thirteen shoe-makers refused to take part in the *encabezamiento* and continued to pay their tax on individual transactions, which they now declared to the council instead of the *arrendadores*.

The *encabezamiento*, because it took no account of the rise or fall of prices and variations in the ability of citizens to pay tax at the agreed level, might work to the disadvantage either of the Crown or of the towns. Each side was concerned that it should not lose by committing itself to a global sum for several years in advance. The royal point of view appears in an undated Simancas document of the early sixteenth century.

It will be a very good thing to collect the rents by *encabezamiento*, but it must be with such moderation that the *encabezamiento* is not made either perpetual or for a long period, because the king would lose all the growth and increase which there might be in the rents; therefore to put the increase in doubt would be an unreasonable thing, as through the increase in the population, expenses and outlay grow, from which it follows that trade and commerce must grow and as a consequence the duties of the *alcabala* must increase and grow also.[40]

Towns, on the other hand, sometimes found that they were unable to meet the demands to which they had committed themselves. In 1496 and 1497, there were riots and protests in Castro del Río and Fuente Obejuna over the limited *encabezamiento* then in force. Attempts by towns in Córdoba's *tierra* to by-pass the town in negotiating with the Crown over their tax assessments caused considerable friction, though the Crown did eventually allow Castro to negotiate in this way with the royal accountants.[41] Córdoba itself also complained to the Crown about the assessment of the meat rent in the 1502 *encabezamiento*, but nothing was done and the arrangement was continued indefinitely on royal initiative.[42]

'TERCIAS REALES'

The *tercias reales*, although a direct tax, were collected with the *alcabala* and came within the same arrangements, including *encabezamientos*. According to the earliest *cuaderno* for their collection, that of 1412, the connection with the remainder of the ecclesiastical tithe was retained and disputes in a particular place were heard by churchmen, but they had to resolve them in accordance with criteria laid down by the Crown. According to John II's 1433 *cuaderno*, each local council had to appoint an official to make a list (*padrón*) of contributors, which had to be signed by the parish priest. The goods concerned had to be kept at the disposal of the tax-farmer from the beginning of the tax-year, at Ascensiontide, until the following April. If they were claimed within this period, but the tax-payer could not produce them, the farmer might collect the equivalent amount in cash, based on the highest price of the season for wine, grain and livestock. The rate of *tercia*, which applied only to these agricultural products, was one *fanega* per *cahiz* (one-twelfth) of grain, one head in ten of livestock and one *cántara* or *arroba* in twelve of wine, though in the last case the rate was actually one-sixth for red wine and one-eighth for white. The farmer was liable for any losses after the goods had been collected. He endeavoured to avoid these by putting the goods in store, but he had to pay rent for the warehouses and to pay guards. The inevitable disputes over the lists of contributions normally went before ecclesiastical judges, though the farmer could ask the Crown for a *pesquisidor*.[43]

TAXES ON MOVEMENT OF GOODS

By far the most important tax on the movement of goods in Andalusia was the *almojarifazgo*, which was basically a royal rent, though, in both Seville and Córdoba, that part of it which was collected in the *tierra* had been granted to the local council, which collected it for its own use. The *almojarifazgo* of the city of Córdoba, known as the *almojarifazgo castellano*, was collected in the same farms as the *alcabala* and the *tercias* of the area. It also included what was known as the 'old *alcabala*' (*alcabala vieja*), which was a five per cent levy on the price of pack-animals (*acemilas*), payable by the buyer.[44]

The older taxes on the movement of goods which survived in the fifteenth century, the *portazgo, roda, barcaje, castillería*, and so on, had by this time become part of the municipal rather than the royal finances in Córdoba, as in many other royal and seignorial towns.[45] *Rodas* and *barcajes* appear in the municipal accounts, but citizens of Córdoba were exempt from *portazgo* within its boundaries. The *portazgo* was, however, collected from the citizens of other towns who travelled in the area. Its accounts were included with those of the *almojarifazgo*.[46]

The *servicio* and *montazgo* were collected in the late fifteenth century on the basis of a *cuaderno* from before 1438, in the case of the former, while the latter was collected by use and custom. The *servicio* was raised in accordance with a fixed scale of charges, while the *montazgo* rate varied from region to region. In Córdoba, it was two head per thousand. A document to record the receipt of tax and to register flocks entering or leaving *dehesas* (grazing-grounds) or traversing passes cost six *maravedís*. Those who kept their flocks within the area of which they were citizens, or who returned home with them each night, were not liable to tax. Animals which were kept in fenced pasture 'to breed and fatten' were put into a category known as *ganado merchaniego*, for which there were special charges, unless they were bought by a butcher for these purposes, in which case they continued to be considered as *ganado cabañil*. The distinction between these two kinds of flock did not apply to pigs. Generally speaking, all flocks moving about the kingdom were under royal protection and no other lord could usurp the *servicio*. Transhumant flocks which crossed the passes (*puertos*) were under the control of the council of the Mesta and had to follow fixed routes, going through passes at which the taxes were paid. The *servicio* was paid on all the animals in the flock and the *montazgo* was, for convenience, paid at the same time, for the use of pasture on the flock's journey from north of the *puertos* to the grazing-grounds of Extramadura, and during its time there. Flocks which returned north by a different route from that by which they had entered the grazing areas were liable to confiscation as *descaminados* (diverted).[47]

There was a third category of flock known as *ganado travesío*, which stayed within one region and did not migrate from north to south. The diocese of Córdoba was a recognised area for such grazing. All flocks of this type, going to pastures outside their own *término*, had to be counted first before an *escribano público*, and their owners had to obtain the licence of the tax-farmer or the local justices before leaving. The tax was paid on departure from the pasture and all flocks which were outside their own area on June 24 were counted, and paid the tax wherever they were on that day. Despite the problems involved in collecting the *montazgo*, this was one of the most efficiently collected of the Castilian rents in the late fifteenth century, because it was in the interest of the Crown, the tax-farmers and the Mesta to ensure that the money came in. However, it produced no more than two per cent of the royal revenues and Córdoba, like many other royal and seignorial towns, made strenuous efforts to avoid its citizens' having to pay. Sancho IV had given Córdoba a privilege in 1288, whereby the town might use the revenue from the *montazgo* for the repair of its walls and castles, but in the late fifteenth century the government made various attempts to collect the tax directly in Córdoba's *tierra*. The town opposed these attempts in the *audiencia* and in 1502, the farmer of the *alcabala*, Juan de Lorca, found that his collector, Alonso Pérez de Castro, was obstructed by Córdoba's council and its officials when he tried to collect the *montazgo* in its *tierra*.[48]

THE TAX BURDEN

The tax burden which rested on Córdoba and its *tierra* in the fifteenth and early sixteenth centuries can be calculated with a fair degree of accuracy as a result of Ladero's researches and the use of some additional local material. It is not possible to produce detailed figures for the level of royal taxation in a particular town in a particular year, because statistics for this purpose, using the same criteria for all taxes, are not available. However, the figures which do exist give an adequate general indication of the level at which the town was taxed by the Crown, if it is borne in mind that in Castile as a whole, in the fifteenth century, *alcabalas* and *tercias* provided eighty per cent of royal revenues, customs-dues (in Andalusia, the *almojarifazgo*) produced ten to twelve per cent and the *servicio* and *montazgo* two per cent. These percentages do not, however, include direct taxation in the form of Cortes *servicios* or Hermandad *repartimientos*.[49]

Approximate figures are offered for the value of royal taxation in Córdoba in various years between 1430 and 1502. The totals are given in Aragonese florins, in an attempt to indicate their real value, at least in monetary terms. They cover the *partidos* of Córdoba and its *tierra*, and consist of the known figures for the *alcabala*, *tercias reales* and *almojarifazgo castellano*, with ten per cent added to cover the minor royal taxes for which no detailed figures are available. *Servicios* and Hermandad *repartimientos* have been excluded from the reckoning, as have *tercias reales* collected in kind rather than cash. In 1430, a year chosen as typical of John II's reign, Córdoba paid the Crown the equivalent of 44 000 florins in tax. In 1465, the florin value of royal taxation, at the beginning of the civil war in Castile under Henry IV, was 48 000. The figure in 1480, the year of the Cortes of Toledo, was very little different, at 48 500. Despite Ferdinand and Isabella's efforts to improve the efficiency of the machinery for tax-collection, the yield from Córdoba and its *tierra* had in fact fallen in real terms, by 1490, to 39 000 florins. There was an improvement, to 42 400 florins, by 1494, but by 1502 the results of the new policies, including the introduction of the *encabezamiento* on a regular basis, had become visible, and the tax-yield increased to 60 600 florins. The reason for the fall in revenue from these taxes between 1480 and 1490 was the effect of the Granada war, which seems to have reduced indirect tax-yield in Córdoba and district. For the years 1478–98, the total of 7735 florins for the annual Hermandad contributions should be added to the figures already given. After the *servicio* was restored, in 1500, the Hermandad levies disappeared from the reckoning.

MUNICIPAL FINANCES

Royal town councils, such as that of Córdoba, had certain financial resources which they could call their own. All taxation revenue from the town naturally belonged to the Crown, but the local council was made responsible for collecting some of it and was permitted to use part of the result as public funds. It would clearly be anachronistic to divide the wealth and productive capacity of the Castilian economy in this period into 'public' and 'private' sectors, but nonetheless, a comparison between the resources of the Córdoba town council and those of some leading magnates in the region does provide an indication of the political, as well as the economic, strength of the two groups. Unfortunately for any attempt to study public finance in Córdoba and district, the only complete set of municipal accounts which survive from this period are those from Midsummer 1452 to Midsummer 1453, which are to be found in a legal document of the early sixteenth century. Partial accounts for 1478–9 survive in the *actas capitulares*.[50] This information, with other scattered material, indicates the main types of financial resource which were left at the disposal of the local council. These were ordinary taxes of various kinds, income from publicly owned lands and buildings, the fines imposed by municipal magistrates, exceptional levies on foodstuffs and other major commodities (*sisas*) and extraordinary direct taxation (*repartimientos*).

The most lucrative municipal tax in the Córdoba accounts for 1452–3 and 1478–9 was the *almojarifazgo*. This was a tax of Muslim origin, which consisted of duties on goods entering or leaving a centre of population. In the fifteenth century, it survived in the south of Spain and had, in many cases, been alienated by the Crown to local councils or secular lords. The *almojarifazgo castellano* in Córdoba, however, remained in royal hands.[51] It covered all goods entering the diocese of Córdoba for trading purposes, but citizens of Córdoba itself did not have to pay the tax within the city's jurisdiction.[52] According to the *cuaderno* for 1455–61, all goods had to enter or leave Córdoba by one of four gates – La Puente, Sevilla, El Rincón and Plasencia. At these points and in the custom-house, the farmers of the *almojarifazgo*, who were known as *almojarifes*, kept guards and collectors. Only migrant flocks were exempt from the tax and they were subject to other duties. The *almojarifazgo castellano* also covered river traffic between Córdoba and Seville. Goods might only be loaded or unloaded at the Córdoba jetties (*muelles*) if the *almojarifes* or their officials were present, or if an inventory of the goods had been made for tax purposes. However, although the main *almojarifazgo* in Córdoba itself was still in royal hands, the tax collected in the *tierra* was allowed to the local council. Thus, whereas the annual yield for Córdoba in 1448–50 was 7527 florins, the income recorded in the municipal accounts for 1452–3 was only 817 florins. Nonetheless, in the domestic budget of Córdoba council, this was an important quantity.[53]

The *actas capitulares* contain references to the collection of the *almojarifazgo* in the *tierra*. The council enforced the set charges, imprisoned defaulters in the town gaol, assisted the farmers when they met difficulties in outlying areas, such as La Rambla, and, in 1493, instructed its lawyers to investigate the collection of the tax on fish in Santaella, at the request of the local *almojarife*.[54] In terms of gold, the value of the rent in the 1478–9 accounts was much lower than it had been in 1452–3, because in the intervening period the equivalents in *maravedís* of gold and silver coins had risen sharply.[55] However, Córdoba's income from the *almojarifazgo* in its *tierra* probably fell in this period by the same proportion as the part of the tax which remained in royal hands. The decline was part of a general trend affecting Castilian public finances.

Another tax on the movement of goods and also flocks which appears in Córdoba's accounts for 1452–3 is the *roda*. This was one of a group of taxes on internal trade which included the *portazgo*, *barcaje*, *castillería* and others.[56] It appears to have assumed some importance in the Córdoba area because it affected sheep-rearing. In some documents, the *roda* is referred to in the same context as the *portazgo* and taxes on the use of passes (*pasaje*).

According to the 1452–3 accounts, a tax was collected to pay for a watch (*velas*) to be kept on the Guadalquivir above and below Córdoba, on the agricultural land to the south of the city, and in the Pedroche, with a separate arrangement for Fuente Obejuna. The method of collection is not known, but it appears that the tax was of diminishing importance, as the yield seems to have fallen from 144 florins in 1452–3 to a mere 1.66 florins in 1479. By this time, only one farmer of the rent is mentioned, whereas in the earlier accounts it was apparently collected in five parts. In July 1503, the *actas* state that the rent would no longer be collected, as the *velas* had ceased. The last farmer of the rent was probably Fernando Ruiz de Guadalupe, in 1503, as in September of that year a royal letter was received, forbidding the rent for *velas* in Córdoba and its *tierra*.[57]

Although it is not mentioned in the 1452–3 accounts, the 1435 ordinances state that Córdoba council farmed as a rent the *almotacenazgo*, a traditional Andalusian office, inherited originally from the Muslims, which involved the supervision of the city's markets, including weights and measures. The rent was collected in the form of duties for the use of the royal units of measure (*peso del Rey*) by non-citizens, fines for using false measures and for selling adulterated food, and duties on the import of various commodities by non-citizens. The duty payable by traders for the checking of their measures by municipal officials was also included in the *almotacenazgo*.[58]

Fines imposed by local magistrates were also a source of income for the town. These were not, however, paid directly into public funds, because the council did not employ the kind of bureaucracy which would be needed to collect them. Instead, it took the easier and cheaper route of farming the fines like taxes, thus assuring itself of a steady income without having to maintain an expensive municipal establishment. Two categories of fine appear in the 1452–3 accounts. There were the *penas de ordenanzas*, which were penalties for infringing the local ordinances, and the *penas de corredores*, which covered trading offences committed by brokers, especially those who dealt in livestock (*corredores de bestias*). Other material in Córdoba indicates the existence of further types of penalty, which were also farmed. These involved usurers, the playing of games, such as cards and darts, which were forbidden by the Crown, the illegal export of horses from Córdoba's jurisdiction, the illegal import of wine to the district and irregularities in the conduct of the butcheries.[59]

According to the notarial records, the *penas de ordenanzas* were rented to a single farmer for the city and the *tierra*, on an annual basis. He then sub-let the rent in the *tierra* to citizens of the individual towns. This system seems to have been followed, at least, in 1477, 1487, 1496, 1497, 1501 and 1512. However, 1512 was the last occasion on which the rent was farmed in this way. A surviving contract between the farmer, Francisco de Montilla, and a citizen of Montoro defines the penalties concerned as those for breaking the city's ordinances on the removal of bark from trees (perhaps cork-oaks) for export, and on the export of hides. In June 1513, the council voted that the rent should not be farmed in 1513–14 and on 11 September 1514, Pedro Fernández de Estrada presented a royal letter which forbade such a procedure in the case of this rent. In several of the contracts for *penas de ordenanzas*, the penalties for playing the prohibited games such as cards and darts were included in the same farm, though in others, before 1496, they seem to have been separate.[60]

The remaining types of penalty seem to have been farmed in the same way, but the isolated contracts which survive do not permit an assessment of the value of these rents as a whole to the municipal finances. While the prices paid by the farmers were inevitably arbitrary, they were offered on the basis of an anticipated yield, agreed between the farmer and the regular offender, like any other tax. As a help in the making of predictions, there were fixed fines for some offences. For example, the fine for each offence of importing Castilian wine to Córdoba without a council licence was 6000 *mrs*, reduced to 3000 *mrs* in 1496. The fine was divided, in accordance with normal contemporary practice, into three equal parts, one of which went to the accuser, one to the judge and one to council funds.[61]

Certain other minor rents contributed to the income of Córdoba council. One of these was the rent of the water-carriers (*aguadores*) and another the *meaja*, an obsolete coin worth half a *maravedí*, which was payable on each piece of cloth imported to Córdoba by non-citizens. The latter was not raised after 1502. Two taxes on the Moorish inhabitants of Córdoba were also included in the municipal income. One of these was the poll-tax (*cabeza del pecho de los Moros*) and the other was a duty on the meat sold to the Moorish community. The method used for collecting these taxes is not known, but it is probable that they were farmed, like the other municipal rents.

Apart from taxation, Córdoba council's main regular source of income was the letting of publicly owned land and buildings. By no means all the land in public ownership was let. The Crown automatically held uncultivated high ground (*montes reales*) for the use of all citizens and also, with the town council as its agent, kept lower uncultivated lands (*baldíos*) as public grazing for citizens' flocks. These lands might not be rented by private individuals. However, the council did gain considerable revenue from letting some of the pastures which it owned to individual tenants. These pastures were known as *dehesas*, because they were 'defended', or fenced in, and only the flocks of the owner or his tenant might use their grazing. In 1452-3, the council let seven such enclosures and the half-share which it owned in another. They produced, according to the accounts, more than a fifth of the council's income for the year. Later material shows that Córdoba owned at least seven other enclosures, which were not normally let to private citizens. The town's possession of these lands was by no means undisturbed. In 1489, the council gained from the *audiencia* of Valladolid a *carta ejecutoria* giving it possession of the *dehesa* of Navas del Moro. In 1517, it attempted to regain the *dehesa* of Trassierra, which had been seized by a local *jurado*. Almost all the references to publicly owned enclosures in local material concern measures taken by the council to defend its possessions or prevent the misuse of the lands. As an exceptional measure to raise money to send messengers to Court, the council let the *dehesa* of Navas del Moro in 1493, first to some citizens of Córdoba and then to a citizen of Villafranca. In 1500, the *dehesa* of Dos Hermanos was let to a private citizen, after having been restored to Córdoba in the previous year. Also in 1499, the town was allowed by the Crown to make a new enclosure near Las Casillas, out of lands which had been recently restored to public ownership.[62]

While *dehesas* provided most of Córdoba's income from land, there is some evidence from 1495 that the council also gained some revenue in the form of corn paid as rent for the use of public arable land. Such payments were known as *terrazgos*. In January of that year, the royal council ordered Córdoba, by letter, to permit its citizens to sow with corn up to fifty *fanegas* (about thirty-two hectares) of land which had recently been restored to the town's possession in Carchena. The town's *procurador*, or representative, was duly despatched to the place in question to discover how much land was in fact available for this purpose and in July he sent a deputy to collect the *terrazgos*.[63]

Córdoba council also gained some income from buildings which it owned, both in the city and in the *tierra*. All these properties were let in return for more or less permanent quit-rents (*censos*), bringing in no more than one hundred *maravedís* a year, in most cases. The buildings concerned were bread-ovens in Córdoba and in various towns of the *tierra*, and combined houses and shops in Córdoba. Six of these were used as pharmacies. These publicly owned shops, known as *alcaicerías*, were a Muslim legacy and, as will become clear later, were partly devoted to the sale of textiles. The town's income from buildings was, however, tiny in comparison with the rent obtained from letting *dehesas*.[64]

It is clearly important to attempt to provide figures for the municipal income and expenditure of Córdoba in this period. Those available are unfortunately no more than fragmentary. In 1452–3, the council's income was 2674 florins, but its expenditure was 3009 florins, giving a deficit of 335 florins. There is no record of income and expenditure in subsequent years until 1500–1, when a surplus of 797 florins is recorded. This seems to have been exceptional for the period as, in 1503–4, income amounted to 3435 florins and expenditure to 3360 florins, giving a surplus of 75 florins. In 1506–7, there was a surplus of 311 florins, after which no such figures are recorded.[65] It would be interesting to know how the large increase in income between 1479 (2244 florins) and 1503–4 (3435 florins) was achieved. Details of how revenue was raised in this period are not available, but a document of 1470 indicates clearly how the council was accustomed to tackle the problem of increasing its income.[66] The method used was to place impositions on everything 'which is generally bought and sold, except on bread'. The impositions were farmed under the supervision of a commission of the council, consisting of four *veinticuatros* and two *jurados*, and covered butcheries, livestock, fish, wine, cloth, clothing, fruit and hides, in both the city and the countryside, and oil and property transactions in the *tierra* alone.

The detailed instructions laid down for collection indicate the similarity between the impositions, or *sisas*, and the *alcabala*. The tax was collected by the seller's giving less of the product for the original price. Thus a wine-seller would give seven *azumbres* for the price of an *arroba*, which was equivalent to a tax of twelve-and-a-half per cent. It was the seller's responsibility to pay the tax and this was done each Friday, when importers of goods through the town gates handed over a tax of five per cent to the tax-farmer. In this way, the imposition affected goods at two stages, import and sale. With fish, for example, whether fresh or salted, there was an import duty of six per cent in the city and five per cent in the *tierra*, and, in addition, as with meat, the value of three ounces per pound sold was paid to the farmer. As with the *alcabala* and the *almojarifazgo*, the farmer was entitled to place guards at the gates to ensure that the duty was paid. An effort was made to ensure that the unloading and sale of goods was supervised by the tax-farmer and his men. The most elaborate of the council's instructions were devoted to the prevention of abuses in the import and sale of wine. The quantity counted as a load for tax purposes was twelve *arrobas* for a pack-mule (*acemila*) and eight for an ass, and it was forbidden to pile more wine-skins on to an animal in order to reduce the number of loads on which tax would be charged. The restrictions on import by night or by forbidden gates applied to the imposition as well as the *alcabala*. The five per cent duty applied to nearly all commodities, although the conditions for taxing cloth were much more complicated. The *escribano* of the commission for collecting the imposition received one per cent of the money collected and it appears that this was the practice with the other municipal rents as well. Impositions of this kind were raised whenever towns could not meet their commitments in any other way. Like the Crown, local councils preferred indirect to direct taxation as a way of raising large amounts of revenue, though *repartimientos* were sometimes made in the *tierra*.

Inevitably, much of the money which the council collected in taxes and rents was spent on the salaries of municipal officials. Of these, the most prominent was naturally the *corregidor*, who under Ferdinand and Isabella received 500 *mrs* a day, though there was a shortlived reduction to 400 *mrs* in the 1490s. The normal figure brought his salary to 687 florins per annum and made it much the largest item in the municipal pay-roll. In addition, the *corregidor* received one hundred *mrs* a day as governor (*teniente*) of the fortress of the Calahorra. Compared with this sum, the amount paid to *veinticuatros*, *jurados* and other officials was insignificant. By Ferdinand and Isabella's reign, each *veinticuatro* in Córdoba received a salary of 3000 *mrs*, with an addition of 1000 *mrs* per annum, which were described as *castellanías*. These were in fact another form of salary, as very few *veinticuatros* had duties concerned with fortresses and those who did received separate payment. The burden of *regidores*' salaries clearly reached its heaviest in about 1480 and then decreased as the number of these officials fell by more than half. Between 1495 and 1514, a number of minutes refer to the council's reluctance to pay salaries to absentee *veinticuatros*. This attitude was completely justified by legislation, but the Crown insisted on making exceptions. The offenders were generally distinguished citizens, such as the count of Palma, the *alcaide de los donceles*, the 'Great Captain' and the lord of El Carpio.[67] *Jurados* received no supplement to their salary, but this rose from 3000 *mrs* per annum in 1479 to 4000 *mrs* in 1510.[68]

All other municipal officials received a salary from the council, except for magistrates and constables who were nominated by the *corregidor*. Locally elected *alcaldes*, on the other hand, did receive salaries from the council. The 1452–3 accounts show how much the council saved if it did not have to pay a *corregidor*. In that year, the municipal pay-roll came to 898 florins, but this included only twenty-six *regidores* and no *corregidor*. In view of the known size of the council in the late fifteenth century, it is possible to estimate that more than 2600 florins a year were spent on salaries in those years. Of this, about 700 florins went to the *corregidor*, half being contributed by the town and half by the *tierra*. Salaries and expenses paid by the council to lawyers and to messengers sent to Court or elsewhere on public business have not been included in this reckoning, though both were regular items of expenditure in the municipal budget. Legal costs, if any, are not included in the 1452–3 accounts, but the *actas capitulares* show that expenditure on lawyers and trials in the *audiencia* between 1493 and 1515 amounted to about a hundred or two hundred florins per annum, depending on the number of cases in which the town was engaged. In addition, between 1491 and 1499 and in 1513–15, the town had to pay 250 *mrs* a day in salary to a judge of boundaries. This amounted to 344 florins per annum.

Payments to messengers sent on council business also varied from year to year, ranging from about seventy florins in 1479 to 436 florins in 1496, though the normal level of expenditure was around ninety florins per annum. As a Cortes town, Córdoba had from time to time to find salaries for its two representatives to that assembly. The expense was only sporadic but could be considerable. In the early sixteenth century, the proctors were paid about a ducat a day (350 *mrs* in 1506 and 375 *mrs* in 1515). They always returned to Córdoba with royal letters ordering the council to reimburse them, but they often received an advance payment to help with expenses.[69]

Part of the municipal income was placed in a special fund for public works, known as the *propios de los labores*. This was used for the upkeep of fountains, roads and bridges in Córdoba and its *tierra*. The fund was entrusted to the *veinticuatro* Egas Venegas, and an *escribano* was delegated to assist him. The precise source of the money for this fund is not known, as the taxes set aside in the early stages after the Reconquest for use on fortifications cannot have been important by the late fifteenth century.[70] The sums involved were quite considerable. In 1479, 550 florins were spent on fortifications and in 1497, 765 florins were devoted to the repair of bridges in the *tierra*. The council put such work out to tender and then paid the wages of the craftsmen and labourers and for the materials used. In the early years of the sixteenth century, the public works fund was in a healthy state. A surplus of 721 florins was held by Egas Venegas from the year 1502–3, and in 1503–4 a further 690 florins were obtained. The surplus for 1503–4 was 599 florins and in 1504–5, the year before Venegas' death, another 847 florins were raised. The works fund was not the only source of money for these purposes. In 1499, for example, the road from Córdoba to Trassierra was in need of repair and all owners of property adjoining it were required to contribute to the work or pay a fine of 5000 *mrs*. The principle of demanding contributions from those most likely to benefit from the project was also used to help finance the largest scheme undertaken in this period by Córdoba council. This was the construction of a new bridge across the Guadalquivir at Montoro. In 1498, a plan was approved by the council for the building of the bridge in four years, at a cost of 2906 florins. As this sum was nearly equal to the council's entire income for the year and as this income was already committed to expenses such as salaries and litigation, it was inevitable that money would be required from elsewhere. A fixed sum was to be obtained from the public works fund for each of the four years, but this was expected to produce only a quarter of the money required. The *almojarifazgo* of the *tierra* was to be used on this project, despite the other calls on the municipal revenues, and the penalties for the illegal export of flocks from the Pedroche area were to be used in a similar way. However, it was thought that nearly half the money would come from property-owners on Córdoba's lands in the area, that is, the inhabitants of Bujalance, Pedro Abad, Aldea del Río and Montoro itself. Hopes were expressed by the proponents of the scheme that contributions might also be obtained from neighbouring landowners outside Córdoba's jurisdiction, such as the bishop and Cathedral chapter, Don Alonso de Aguilar, who held the lordship of Cañete, and the lord of El Carpio and Morente, but the council very wisely put no cash value on such help. In the event, the scheme quickly ran into difficulties and the bridge, although it was eventually constructed, was a drain on the town's resources for many years, but the 1498 plan does indicate fairly clearly the way in which large public projects were tackled in royal towns at the end of the fifteenth century.[71]

While Córdoba council's financial position in the reign of Ferdinand and Isabella was by no means entirely gloomy, a glance at the figures for approximate annual income from royal and municipal rents is enough to show the small scale of the funds at the local council's disposal. The clearest sign of the weakness of public finance, both royal and municipal, was the ever-growing dependence on temporary taxes raised on basic products, particularly foodstuffs. The use of these impositions was made necessary by the fact that no satisfactory way had been found, either by the Crown or by local councils, of tapping the resources of the wealthiest citizens. The main flaw of the Castilian taxation system, along with many others, in the late Middle Ages, was that the most powerful subjects, who were often also the most wealthy, instead of making a larger contribution than their fellows to the king's income, made no direct contribution at all. In addition, there was in practice no way of relating the contributions of those who did pay taxes to their wealth.

PRIVATE WEALTH

Efforts to assess the wealth of seignorial families in the Córdoba area have only been made fairly recently. So far, there are two full studies of Cordoban noble houses. These are the works by Cabrera on the county of Belalcázar and its lords, the Sotomayor, and Quintanilla on the house of Aguilar and Priego. Information on other families still has to be sought in fragmentary notarial records, which so often fail to describe property in entail (*mayorazgo*), generally the most important of a noble family's possessions.[72] In view of the lack of such records for the Córdoba area, it is necessary to use the published accounts of the lordships of the dukes of Medina Sidonia in the early sixteenth century.[73] The most significant feature of these accounts, which concern territories covering most of the modern province of Huelva and much of that of Seville, is the colossal size of the income which they record. In 1509, 1510, and 1511, this came to over ten million *maravedís*, or 37 735 florins, a figure comparable with the amount gained by the Crown from the *alcabalas* of the diocese of Córdoba and the equivalent of about four per cent of the entire royal income from the kingdom. According to these accounts, the main sources of the dukes' income were, in order of importance, customs duties (particularly the *almojarifazgo*), rent from *dehesas* in ducal ownership, which were mainly used as pasture, the rent of the butcheries of the towns of the *señorío* and the rent of public offices in these towns. The ducal administration was virtually a mirror-image of the regime in towns such as Córdoba and the dukes were almost completely successful in replacing the Crown in the lives of the inhabitants of their lordships. However, their control did not generally take the form of specifically seignorial tributes, such as the costs of the lord's administration of justice, or of the use of his balances to weigh provisions. In 1509, these sources produced only 25 000 out of over ten million *maravedís*, and that in only one or two towns. The largest cash contribution to the income of the duke in that year was revenue from royal taxes which had been diverted into the ducal coffers.

Ideally, annual income is not the only guide to the value of an estate, but it is impossible to discover the capital value, either of the dukes of Medina Sidonia's estates or of any other, except for the possessions of the leading family of the area, the house of Aguilar, which seems to have had wealth virtually on a par with that of the second family of Andalusia, the Ponce de León, if not of the dukes of Medina Sidonia themselves. Don Alonso de Aguilar's will, dated 1498, contains no valuation of the Aguilar *mayorazgo*, which contained the bulk of the family's holdings, but it states that Don Alonso's wife, Doña Catalina Pacheco, brought a dowry worth 22 000 florins and that a total of 56 000 florins was paid by this couple for the three daughters. Even without the *mayorazgo*, the Aguilar goods were valued in 1498 at 110 000 florins. There is, however, a fuller valuation from the end of the period. When, in 1518, Doña Catalina Fernández de Córdoba, daughter of the first marquis of Priego, married Lorenzo Suárez de Figueroa, she took with her the whole *mayorazgo* of the house of Aguilar as her dowry. The properties and rents in question were valued at 670 924 florins (eighteen million *maravedís*). Unfortunately, there are no surviving accounts to provide further details.[74] The main rivals of the house of Aguilar, the counts of Cabra, possessed in Baena the largest and most valuable town in the kingdom of Córdoba, outside the capital itself. An indication of the town's economic vitality is the assessment of its *alcabala* at 6037 florins in the farm of 1493–5, according to a document of 1497. This figure is comparable with the duke of Medina Sidonia's income from the *alcabala* of his whole *señorío* in 1509–11.[75]

Apart from the house of Aguilar, the best-documented lordship which has so far been surveyed is the county of Belalcázar.[76] The information in question is to be found in the Osuna section of the Archivo Histórico Nacional, and mainly in an inventory of the goods left at his death in 1464 by the second lord of Gahete (known as Belalcázar after 1466), Don Alonso de Sotomayor. This does not give the family's income from rents or the relative values of its different possessions, but it does show the main sources of the Sotomayor's wealth.

The most important properties which came to the family with the lordship of Gahete and Hinojosa, though not without violent resistance from their previous owner, Córdoba council, were the *dehesas* of Madroñiz, north of Gahete, Madroñicejo, which adjoined it, El Hinojoso and Torrecatalina, west and north of Hinojosa, and six other smaller properties between Hinojosa and Gahete. In addition, the Sotomayor had, by 1464, purchased another *dehesa* in the same area, from two citizens of Córdoba. *Dehesas* were large areas of enclosed land which were generally used partly as pasture and partly as arable land. Thus they produced cash income for their owners in return for the letting of grazing and also grain, in the form of *terrazgos* as rent for the use of arable, assessed at so many *fanegas* per *yugada* of land. Cash income from the largest *dehesa*, Madroñiz, seems to have been about 1000 florins per annum in the mid-fifteenth century, while one of the smaller properties, El Cachiporro, yielded 50 florins in 1458, and four others together raised 4500 florins. The letting of these lands for arable use seems normally to have produced a *terrazgo* of two *fanegas* of wheat or barley per *yugada*. In addition to the properties in the Córdoba area, the Sotomayor possessed many *dehesas* in the viscounty of La Puebla de Alcocer, in Extremadura, which gave a cash income from the letting of pasture of 3678 florins in 1454–5.[77] Unfortunately, as the surviving documents give no information about stock-breeding, which is known to have been an important family interest, it is impossible accurately to assess the Sotomayor's wealth, either in cash or in goods.

This brief survey of the wealth of a few leading noble families should indicate the relative weakness of public, as opposed to private, finance. The injustice of this state of affairs was manifest to contemporaries, including the town councils themselves. However, it was only when a cash crisis of some magnitude occurred that a body such as the *regimiento* of Córdoba would discuss the distribution and taxation of wealth in society as a whole. Even when such discussions did take place, as when Córdoba council, in 1496, considered the possibility of relating direct tax contributions more closely to the wealth of individual citizens, they always stopped short of an attack on the real cause of the trouble, which was the concentration of wealth and influence in few hands. As the *veinticuatros* owed their own position to their success in a society organised in this way, this limitation was inevitable. Exemption from taxation continued to be regarded as the natural accompaniment to financial and social success, and all attempts to put information on private wealth in the hands of local authorities were steadfastly resisted. In these conditions, public finance inevitably remained weak in comparison with private wealth. All measures to remedy the situation failed because of the underlying assumptions about the nature of society which limited their scope. The fact was that rich men were prepared to contribute to the cost of those activities which were the public concern of the local community, but they refused to do so on a regular, or compulsory, basis by means of taxation. Instead, they offered loans or gifts when they felt so inclined and thus retained the fullest possible control over the disposal of their own wealth. The economic, political and social effects of this approach on Córdoba and its surrounding district will gradually become clear.

4
Córdoba in the regional economy

The economy of Córdoba and its territory has not, generally speaking, received nearly as much attention as that of neighbouring Seville or the well-known trade axis which connected Burgos with the Netherlands. One reason for the failure, until quite recently, to study the Cordoban material is the continuing preoccupation of many economic historians with the more spectacular manifestations of international trade. As a result of the belief, held by some, that the 'progress' of the European economy from a rural to an industrial base was caused in large measure by the development from the medieval period of towns and trade, economies such as that of western Andalusia have generally been studied only in terms of their part in the patterns of international commerce. Thus attention has been mainly focused on the ports of Málaga, Cádiz and Seville, which were used as trading stations by the Genoese, who dominated this sector of the economy from the thirteenth century onwards.[1] Whether such an evolutionary model is helpful or not in the study of economic development is a matter for debate, but in any case it is a fact which must be recognised that the late medieval Andalusian economy was primarily agrarian, particularly in the interior regions, such as Córdoba. In view of this, any investigation of the role of the city and its surrounding area in the production and marketing of commodities must begin with the organisation of agriculture.

GRAIN

Grain was and is the most basic of all agricultural products. It has been estimated that in the fifteenth century over sixty per cent of European food requirements were met by cereals, and in this general picture Andalusia figured as an exporting region.[2] As far as the production of grain is concerned, recent work by Ladero and González Jiménez now makes it possible to calculate, at least approximately, the amount produced in various years in the Andalusian dioceses.[3] The calculations for total harvests in the diocese of Córdoba, as for other parts of Andalusia, are based on the yield of the *tercias reales*, the two-ninths of the ecclesiastical tithe which had been collected by the Crown since the thirteenth century. The tithe on cereals was collected in kind and thus Ladero has been able, by multiplying the tax-yield by forty-five, to calculate the probable total volume of grain production in the diocese between 1486 and 1510.[4] As was customary in Andalusia until quite recently, the grain produced was *pan terciado*, that is, two-thirds wheat and one-third barley, the wheat being devoted to human consumption and the barley being reserved for the plough animals. There are, as usual, various difficulties with the figures, which are incomplete because the city parish of St Mary, with its large stocks of grain in the hands of the bishop and Cathedral chapter, is not included, and neither are some of the more important *señoríos*, in which the lords legally or illegally collected the tithe for themselves. Nonetheless, the figures do give some indication of general trends in the period. As might be expected in an area of dry climate but without the assistance of irrigation, there could be variations, sometimes of up to thirty-three per cent, between consecutive harvests. There was a ten or fifteen per cent increase in average yields between 1495 and 1502, with a relapse in 1510. Ladero suggests that in order to compensate for the areas excluded from the tax documents, ten or fifteen per cent should be added to his published figures.[5]

Approximate calculations of total yield are of limited interest without some information on the distribution of grain production and the amount produced per hectare. In order to estimate yields per hectare, Ladero works from the figures of Pierre Ponsot for the seventeenth century in western Andalusia, which are four or four-and-a-half to one for wheat and five or six to one for barley, increasing to five or six-and-a-half and ten or twelve to one, respectively, in the eighteenth century. The traditional measurement used in Castile for the weight and the capacity of grain, the *fanega*, had as its metric equivalents 55.5 litres or 44.3 kilograms. However, the *fanega* was also the name used to designate the area of land notionally required to produce that amount of grain, and was reckoned at about 0.4 Ha in the Toledo area and 0.6 Ha in Andalusia. On this basis, Ladero, following Ponsot, calculates the average yield in the kingdom of Seville in the late fifteenth century as about 11.1 to 12.5 Hl per hectare.[6] However, on the basis of an estimate from a royal document of 1489, which gives a twelve-fold yield for the neighbouring Campiña of Ecija, Ladero believes that the contemporary yield in the Córdoba Campiña was probably similar. Thus if, as was normal practice, one or one-and-a-half hectolitres of cereal were sown on each hectare, the yield would vary between twelve hectolitres and eighteen, which would be considerably higher than the yield in the kingdom of Seville as a whole. Such figures would, however, be applicable only in the Campiña and not in the less fertile Sierra.[7]

The area cultivated with grain in the late Middle Ages was probably about 32 000 to 48 000 Ha, with an equal area fallow, which is about half the area being used for grain in the province of Córdoba in the 1960s. According to the records of the *tercias reales*, about eighty per cent of this production came from the Campiña. By far the largest harvests, according to these figures, came from the southern towns, such as Castro del Río, Santaella, Hornachuelos and Montoro, which belonged to Córdoba, and Baena, Palma del Río and Montemayor in *señorío*. There was a smaller number of productive centres, such as Villapedroche, Fuente Obejuna and Belalcázar, in the Sierra. In order to go into greater detail, it is necessary to turn to the investigation which was undertaken for military purposes in September 1502, by the *corregidor* Diego López Dávalos on behalf of the Crown, of the grain-holdings of individuals. The investigation covered the royal towns of Castro del Río, La Rambla, Montoro, Adamuz, Bujalance, Pedro Abad, Santaella, Pozoblanco and Fuente Obejuna, as well as the parishes of Córdoba itself.

The resulting totals, which survive in Simancas and have been published by Ladero, are particularly valuable as a statistical indication of the extent to which the leading inhabitants of Córdoba lived from the production of the *tierra* and its inhabitants. The investigation ignored all holdings of less than ten *cahices* (sixty-six litres) of rent, but this leaves all the major figures in the reckoning, and in the process a useful indication is also given of the distribution of the richer citizens among the parishes. Easily the richest parish in terms of grain rent was St Mary's, which included the Cathedral. The bishop's table (*mesa*), or household, alone held 13 200 Hl of grain, the other Cathedral dignitaries, including the canons, held 21 000 Hl and other individuals in the parish held 7500 Hl. These included five *veinticuatros* and the widow of another, and all the others mentioned came from prominent office-holding families. The next wealthiest parish in terms of grain, with 13 000 Hl, was St Nicholas 'de la Villa'. Here the most important holdings were those of the marquis of Priego, who lived in this parish and kept part of his grain there. Others mentioned include three *veinticuatros*, the wives of two others, the wife of a *jurado* and another *jurado*. Next came St Peter with 7000 Hl, including the holdings of the Aguayo, De los Ríos and Cárcamo families, which all had offices in the town. Five other parishes, St Marina, St Saviour, St Mary Magdalene, All Saints' and St Dominic, produced totals ranging from 6500 Hl to 3500 Hl. The remaining parishes, St John, St Andrew, St Nicholas 'del Ajarquía', St Lawrence and St Michael, together mustered only eight per cent of the town's total stock. As Ladero observes, the investigation highlights the control exercised over the surrounding countryside by the politically dominant families of Córdoba. Apart from the bishop and chapter, only forty-eight corporations or individuals are recorded as holding more than fifty *cahices* (330 Hl) of grain, and it is clearly no accident that these individuals include members of office-holding families such as the Fernández de Córdoba, Méndez de Sotomayor, Venegas, Godoy, Hinestrosa, Páez de Castillejo, De los Ríos, Ponce de León, Argote, Carrillo, Cabrera, Narváez, Aguayo and Angulo.

Equally valuable are the results of this investigation in the *tierra*. Here, the *corregidor*'s officials, who acted in conjunction with the local magistrates and constable in each place, seem to have encountered considerable resistance. Seignorial towns were not visited at all and in *realengo* many inhabitants went away, leaving their relatives or servants to answer the investigators' questions. Nonetheless, the results give the best available indication of who received rent in grain in each of the nine places visited, how much they received, the types of farm which they had, their size and rent regime. The investigators were also to ask about the purchase of grain for resale, but, significantly, there are no answers to this question.

The full results have been published by Ladero, but in general terms they confirm those of the holdings in Córdoba itself. The difference is that the answers from the *término* also show those who failed to produce a surplus of grain. The most extreme case recorded is that of Pozoblanco, in the Sierra, where no one declared a surplus and there were no absentee landlords. In contrast, in Castro del Río, in the Campiña, thirty-two arable farms (*cortijos*), parcels and mills produced the massive total of 5871 Hl of grain in rent. Nearly all of this was delivered either to the Church or to the houses of private individuals in Córdoba. The importance of absentee landlords in the Campiña is illustrated by the fact that two such proprietors held 536 Hl of wheat and 182 Hl of barley in Bujalance. Five absentee landlords between them held 1449 Hl of wheat and 683 Hl of barley in Santaella. In contrast, even in these and other major centres of grain production, such as Adamuz, La Rambla and Fuente Obejuna, very few people actually had any grain to spare after paying their rent in kind and supplying their own needs. Ladero quotes the example of two peasants in Pedro Abad who produced a harvest of 140 *fanegas* (77.7 Hl), but after handing over forty-six *fanegas* in rent and allocating the necessary amounts for their own consumption and as seed-corn they were left with a surplus of only fifteen *fanegas*. The document suggests that many tenant-farmers in the Córdoba area were not even in this precarious state. In La Rambla, some declared that they were not producing enough to live on, and the tenants of the *cortijo* of Algallarín, near Adamuz, which was owned by the Jeronymite monastery of Valparaíso, answered that after paying the rent they did not have enough grain for food and seed and had to buy it elsewhere. If even tenant-farmers (*labradores*), who were by no means at the bottom of the rural hierarchy, were in such straits, it is not hard to imagine that much of the population of the Córdoba countryside in the early sixteenth century must have been on the verge of starvation at most times.

Although not designed for that purpose, the 1502 investigation does give some indication of the structure of land-holding. It is clear that the pattern of large-scale absentee landlordship, which has already been described in a general Andalusian context, applied in the Córdoba district and particularly in the Campiña. There were small landholders, especially in the *ruedos* which surrounded the towns of the *tierra*, but most peasants worked on other people's land. Some of those recorded in the 1502 investigation held public office in one of these towns and others are described as stewards for absentee landlords, but most were simply ordinary tax-payers. Fuente Obejuna was unusual in apparently having a more equitable distribution of land and no absentee landlords. In this area, it appears that far more peasants worked their own land.[8]

The conditions under which the arable land of the region was worked are best shown in contracts recorded in the notarial registers of the city itself, which include sub-lettings as well as the activities of absentee landlords. It was normal, but not inevitable, that a complete *cortijo* should be let to one person or group of people. Quarter- or third-shares were quite commonly let separately. The contracts were almost always *arrendamientos* for a period of years between three and eight, and the rent was generally fixed at a certain quantity, expressed in *cahices*, of *pan terciado*, to be delivered each year to the owner, generally at his or her house in Córdoba. The tenant was expected to pay the tithe on the grain concerned.[9] Somewhat exceptionally, the *alcaide de los donceles* in 1507 let a *cortijo* in the Campiña near Aguilarejo to Juan Prieto, a blacksmith, for a rent of 27 000 *mrs* in cash per annum for three years.[10] It is unfortunately rare for tenants' occupations to be mentioned in contracts, though it was common for consortia to rent farms from their landlords. There is also evidence of sub-letting for purposes of exploitation. In November 1485, for example, Alfón Beltrán, a citizen of the parish of St Lawrence, let to a fellow-citizen of the parish two *cahices* (14.4 Ha) of arable land which he had rented for three years from Juan de Cabra, in the Cortijo de la Almedilla. More interesting, perhaps, is a rare contract of February 1481, involving the letting of arable land in return for a perpetual *censo*, or ground-rent. Alfón Fernández, a stone-mason of the suburb of Torre Malmuerta, which was counted in the parish of St Marina, gave to a labourer, Rodrigo Alonso, and his wife, who lived in the same suburb, a piece of arable land with space for building one or more houses, in a site identified only by the adjoining properties, in return for a perpetual *censo* of 150 *mrs* per annum. The conditions were that Alonso was free to sell or otherwise dispose of the land, provided that he did not do so to 'a knight, or to a monastery, or to a powerful man', or without offering it back to the lord first. It is unclear whether this lord was someone other than the stone-mason, but it seems probable that he was and that the contract represents the sub-letting of property held for *censo* from an unnamed third party. This and the indication in the contract that a future sale of the *censo* by the tenant to another was envisaged, serve to illustrate the large measure of freedom of disposal which was allowed to those who held lands or other property by *censo*.[11]

WINE AND OLIVE OIL

Incomplete as the surviving figures for grain production may be, and clearly both tax-returns and investigations of the kind made in 1502 are highly susceptible to error, they are nonetheless better than any which are available for the other staples of Mediterranean agriculture, wine and olive oil. One important source for the location, if not the quantity, of wine production is the account of the tithes collected by the bishop of Córdoba in 1510, which is preserved in the Cathedral archive and has been published by Cabrera.[12] In that year, ten per cent of the bishop's rents, calculated in *maravedís*, came from wine, twelve per cent if only tithes are included.[13] The main alternative source of information on the location of vines is the notarial archive, but references in private contracts conflict, in some cases, with the bishop's lists. The reason for this discrepancy seems to be that the 1510 document only includes the sums still owing in rent on wine and not the full amount due. In addition, the notarial registers in Córdoba do not normally include contracts concerning seignorial towns.

The large totals ascribed to the city parishes once again indicate the extent to which Córdoba's citizens benefited from the production of the countryside. On the whole, the values recorded as owing to the bishop on wine in the different parishes correspond to the distribution of wealth in terms of grain-holdings. Once again, the largest total is that of the Cathedral parish of St Mary, followed by those of St Marina, St Mary Magdalene, St Peter, St Dominic and St Nicholas 'de la Villa'. The smaller totals are those of St John, St Saviour, St Nicholas 'del Ajarquía, and St James, the last having apparently been omitted from the grain investigation of 1502, as All Saints' was from the 1510 document. Notarial evidence suggests that the main areas of wine production in the *tierra* were in the river valley around Córdoba itself and Alcolea, in the Sierra round Trassierra, in Fuente Obejuna to the north and around Bujalance, La Rambla and Santaella in the Campiña. On the whole this impression is confirmed by the list of episcopal rents. Of the places just mentioned, large totals are ascribed to Trassierra, Fuente Obejuna and Bujalance and smaller amounts to Santaella, La Rambla and Alcolea. To supplement the notarial evidence, sizable totals are recorded for the seignorial towns of Fernán Núñez and Luque in the Campiña and Chillón far to the north. Additional royal towns mentioned include Almodóvar del Río, Montoro, Adamuz, Hornachuelos and the towns of the Pedroche.[14]

Unfortunately, the figures for olive oil in the 1510 document are even more fragmentary than those for wine, as it appears that the farmers of the rent had largely settled their accounts when the list was drawn up. About seven per cent of the bishop's rents in that year seem to have come from the proceeds of olive cultivation, and the main areas of production mentioned are Castro del Río, together with the neighbouring seignorial town of Espejo, Fernán Núñez, Posadas, Adamuz, Santaella and Hornachuelos, to which the notarial documents add La Rambla and the Sierra of Córdoba.[15]

As elsewhere in Andalusia, vines and olive-trees were commonly cultivated in the same properties, so that it is desirable to study the organisation of production of both commodities at the same time. There is no general survey of wine and oil holdings to match that for grain. Instead, references in notarial documents must be used. The normal unit of measurement for the area of vineyards and olive-groves was the *aranzada* (o.37 Ha), but the exact size of holdings was rarely included in contracts, which generally refer to *pedazos* (parcels) of vines or olive-trees. The contracts normally included buildings such as stores (*bodegas*) and houses for labourers, as well as presses for the grapes and olives. In contrast with arable land, vineyards and olive-groves were commonly let for one or two lives in return for a *censo*, or ground-rent, paid mostly in cash but partly in kind. Less frequently, lettings (*arrendamientos*) were made for between two and nine years, in return for an annual rent which was also paid mostly in cash but partly in kind.[16] The vineyards and olive-groves of the Córdoba area, which like those elsewhere were grouped in *pagos*, were often held by members of the upper echelons of local society. Thus the contracts already referred to involved properties held by Don Martín de Guzmán, the widow of the *veinticuatro* Gonzalo Yáñez de Godoy, Egas Venegas, who was lord of Luque, and Doña María de Sotomayor, the daughter of the lord of El Carpio. However, as Manuel González discovered in Carmona, this kind of property, unlike most arable lands, could still be found, in the late Middle Ages, in the hands of lesser men, including tradesmen and artisans.[17] Thus in 1483, Juan Rodríguez, a carpenter, let some vines in the Sierra of Córdoba for three years and there is considerable evidence of the ownership of vineyards, with power of free disposal, by shoe-makers, fruiterers and even labourers (*traba-jadores*).[18]

FRUIT AND VEGETABLES

It is also appropriate to consider briefly at this stage the cultivation of fruit, particularly oranges, lemons and pomegranates, and vegetables. Orchards and market-gardens, often irrigated (*huertas*), were mainly to be found in the valleys of the Guadalquivir and Guadajoz, and the largest concentration was naturally around, or even within, Córdoba itself and devoted to the supply of the urban market. These properties were let in a similar manner to that employed for vineyards and olive-groves, and *huertas* might be divided into very small sections or let to share-croppers. *Huertas* often formed part of properties which were primarily used for vines or olive-trees.[19]

THE URBAN MARKET

It is clear that, apart from the extraction of surplus agricultural production from the surrounding countryside, the disposal of surpluses was the essential feature of the regional economy. The Christians who reconquered Córdoba in the thirteenth century inherited a highly urbanised economy in which the central markets of the city dominated the sales and purchases of rural inhabitants. In Islamic Córdoba, the main commercial quarter was, as elsewhere, the *alcaicería* (in Arabic, *al-qaysariyya*). This term covered an area of shops and workshops for artisans and traders, which might be shut off from the rest of the city when required and which generally belonged to the ruler, who let the shops to individual tenants. Those who occupied the *alcaicería* itself were generally engaged in skilled and luxury trades. The rest of the Islamic market structure of the larger towns, such as Córdoba, consisted of a nearby square or squares where transactions not requiring permanent buildings might be carried out, and further markets close to the gates, where producers from the countryside might dispose of their surplus and acquire cash in order to pay taxes which were collected in specie and to make purchases for themselves if they were lucky enough to have any money to spare.[20]

Unfortunately, there is no surviving plan of Córdoba before 1811, but even at that date the Muslim influence on the layout of the city was still obvious. Town-planning as such was not part of the Islamic conception of urban life. Instead, life revolved round the central religious and trading quarter, in the Medina. Roads led directly from the town gates to this central area, which contained the Great Mosque and the main markets. Otherwise, there was no street-plan as such, and it is more than probable that late medieval Córdoba still presented a predominantly Muslim appearance. The Mosque had been little altered, at least from the outside, and apart from a few palaces, which were more like fortresses than their Renaissance and Baroque successors, and the parish churches, there were few buildings large or impressive enough to be distinguished from ordinary dwelling-houses, shops or workshops. The Islamic view of domestic architecture as providing refuges of peace and seclusion from the heat and bustle of the streets and squares had led to a profusion of blind alleys, which could be shut off in case of civil disturbance. Such features still existed and still had their uses in the late fifteenth century.

The Córdoba *alcaicería* occupied a more or less square block of about 2500 square metres, which survived in the late Middle Ages, immediately to the east of the mosque in the parish of St Mary. It had four main gates, which were shut at night, and probably consisted of about a hundred *tiendas* (shops or workshops), which were used both for the manufacture and for the sale of luxury goods. These *tiendas* probably did not contain living accommodation, other than for watchmen, although they are often referred to as *casas tiendas*. Cloth-merchants, silk-merchants, goldsmiths, shoe-makers, blacksmiths and many other traders and craftsmen were represented, each group having its own street or part of a street. This Islamic practice was reinforced by the 1435 municipal ordinances. The tenants held their shops in the *alcaicería* by annual rent. The sum of three *maravedís*, a peppercorn rent, had to be paid to the farmers of the rent in the first fortnight of January. However, the payment of this sum only guaranteed entry to an auction (*subasta*) which was held over the next four months. Only one tenant was allowed in each shop, except in the case of a father and son. Agreements by prospective tenants to keep their bids low seem to have been common.[21]

In the early stages after the Reconquest, the Crown retained a considerable direct interest in the urban economy, which was inherited from the former Muslim rulers. Some of this remained in the fifteenth century. For example, in addition to the *alcaicería*, the Crown possessed four cobblers' workshops, known as *realejos*, in various parts of the town, which were let annually for a cash rent of 1800 *mrs* and a chicken or fish, in the late fifteenth century. However, most other royal possessions of this kind were gradually given away to secular or ecclesiastical lords. As has already been noted, the limitation of sales-points for taxed goods was encouraged in order to facilitate collection, and a case in point is the grain market (*alhóndiga*), which remained in its traditional place, close to the *alcaicería* and the mosque. Grain was supposed to be brought there for taxation and sale, but the *alhóndiga* was apparently alienated for the first time to a nobleman as early as 1241. In 1261, Alfonso X granted thirty-three pottery workshops in the parish of St Mary to the Cathedral chapter. In the late fourteenth century, the alienation of the rents of the *alcaicería* began and in 1393 Henry III granted all the royal *tiendas* therein, together with the shops in the *corral* of the *alhóndiga*, to the brothers Alfonso and Ruy Méndez de Sotomayor, who were both *veinticuatros* of Córdoba. Among the additional concessions included in this grant was the *almotaclacía*, which was a rent paid by the tenants of shops in the *alcaicería*. Not all the shops were in royal hands, as some contracts for private sales exist, but most of the *alcaicería* remained in the Méndez de Sotomayor family throughout the fifteenth century, until on 30 December 1489, Don Alonso de Aguilar, head of the house of that name, bought half the shops, the rent of *almotaclacía*, and the *realejos*, together with a share of the *almojarifazgo*, for 350 000 *mrs*, from Luis Méndez de Sotomayor. A year later, he bought the rest from Luis's cousin, Gonzalo Méndez, for the same amount. For the purpose of a fictitious sale of these assets by Don Alonso to his son, Don Pedro Fernández de Córdoba, in 1497, they were valued at a million *maravedís*.[22]

A similar mixture of public control and private enterprise existed in the case of the meat markets. The traditional points for the slaughter of livestock and sale of meat, the *carnicerías*, were in the parishes of St Andrew, St Saviour and St Mary. An additional *carnicería* was opened in the parish of St Mary Magdalene in 1504, at a cost of 1245 *mrs* to council funds. The requirement that all meat should be sold at these fixed points was confirmed by the Crown in 1493. However, the town council engaged in a long battle to gain control over the slaughterhouse (*matadero*) in the Plaza de la Corredera, which belonged to the Cathedral. The ecclesiastics had begun a process in Church courts before 1489, in order to preserve their rights. Despite the diversion of the case to secular courts, the slaughterhouse remained in the Church's control, but the council was allowed to use it.[23]

Mention has already been made of the *almotacén*, the municipal official who was responsible for supervising markets and, in particular, weights and measures. The name is a transcription of the Arabic *muhtasib*, an official who, in the Islamic world and originally in Syria, had supervised the administration of the special law called *hisba* (calculation), which had been developed on Hellenistic models for the control of urban economic life. *Hisba* legislation became a part of Christian practice in the eleventh-century Reconquest, and by the twelfth century the *almotacén* had become the normal chief market official in the towns of Castile and León. In the process of transfer from one culture to another, he may have abandoned his Islamic links, but in some cases, at least, he acquired even more powers than his Muslim predecessors. In Andalusian towns such as Córdoba, the office of the *almotacenazgo* became after the Reconquest a municipal rent. In

Córdoba, it was alienated to the Méndez de Sotomayor and the lord of Luque, in the early fifteenth century, but by the Catholic Monarchs' period it had been returned to the council and was being administered by *fieles*. Apart from the charges for the use of the official measures, the *almotacenazgo* consisted largely of taxes on the importation of foodstuffs and manufactured goods by non-citizens.[24]

Any attempt to describe the full diversity of the urban economy of Córdoba would inevitably become a catalogue. Even if the Christian city was considerably smaller, both in area and in population, than its Muslim predecessor, it nonetheless retained a vast range of trades and crafts, many of them specialised and sophisticated. However, in order to appreciate the strengths and weaknesses of the economy of the whole region, it is necessary to examine the supply of certain basic commodities to the city.

SUPPLY OF BASIC COMMODITIES

Wine

Among agricultural staples, it has already become clear that wine production was a significant activity in the region and that vineyards were an important source of wealth, not only to the leaders of local society but also to quite humble traders and artisans. Licences issued by the council to individuals for the tax-free import of their own wine for private consumption or for some special occasion, such as a wedding, indicate the involvement in this activity of virtually all the *veinticuatros* and *jurados*, various monasteries and individual churchmen, merchants and artisans and inhabitants of the *tierra*. The frequency of these licences, which are recorded in the council acts, is greatest in the summer months, but there seems to have been no month in which the traffic stopped. However, while it is easy to show the importance of wine production in the area, it is not certain that the Córdoba district was self-sufficient. In 1479, the council discussed the illegal import of 'Castilian wine' and a commission was set up to investigate. In 1493, Pedro de Illescas was fined 5000 *mrs* for selling Castilian wine in Córdoba. Nonetheless, the fact that no special measures concerning wine were taken in the emergency period of the early sixteenth century suggests that the region was indeed largely self-sufficient.[25]

Until 1497, it seems that the town council made no attempt to regulate the wine trade, beyond those measures necessary to ensure the collection of taxes on import and sale. However, in January of that year, the council discussed the problem of 'regrating' or speculation in the retailing of wine. The *alcalde de la justicia*, Gonzalo Monzón, issued a *requerimiento* to the council to act and as a result the producers were asked, parish by parish, to state their views on the best way of marketing their wine. As so often, the discussions proved inconclusive, but from February 1497 onwards the licences granted by the council to producers to sell their wine in private taverns were recorded in the *actas capitulares*. Clearly, the wine-growing interest was a powerful one and this is shown by the prominence of *veinticuatros* and *jurados* among the recipients of tavern licences. As always, taverns remained a regular source of disorder among the urban population.[26]

Olive oil

The supply of olive oil, like that of wine, seems to have remained in the hands of producers, who sold their surplus in private outlets scattered throughout the city. Although a council licence was needed in order to construct an olive-mill, none was required in order to retail the oil and the few attempts at municipal regulation were limited to bans on export during the apparently small number of periods, such as 1503, 1507 and 1514, when supply failed to match demand, and to vain efforts to control prices. The producers claimed, when faced with price-controls, that there were ample supplies available, but although in 1514 one *veinticuatro* went so far as to propose that council members who owned olive-groves should leave the chamber when the subject was discussed, municipal regulation seems to have been largely ineffective.[27]

Salt

More successful efforts were made by the council to control the supply of salt to Córdoba. Although this traditional regalian right had been alienated to secular nobles by the fifteenth century, the concessionaries who held the salt-workings in Castro, Espejo and Aguilar, only the first of which was still a royal town, were not allowed to sell any of their production until the supply of the city had been assured, apart from seventy *cahices* (37.2 tonnes) which they might sell to cover the cost of production. According to the 1435 ordinances, all citizens of Córdoba who produced for the council's *fiel* a document certifying their citizenship, in the Plaza de la Corredera between 15 August and 30 September, might receive a quota of salt, according to their social rank. An *alcalde mayor* would receive twenty-four *fanegas*, a *veinticuatro* eighteen, a *jurado* twelve, a *caballero de premia* eight and an ordinary citizen or the widow of a *caballero de premia* four. In 1500, the Crown ordered the *corregidor* to investigate whether the system was still working satisfactorily. Unfortunately, the identity of the holders of the salt-workings in the later period is not revealed in the documents.[28]

Soap

As in other Andalusian towns, the production of soap in Córdoba was a monopoly in private hands, but under the supervision of the council. This was already the case when the 1435 ordinances were drawn up and the soap was made in special houses, the *casas de almona*, which were situated in the parish of St Peter in Córdoba and at various points in the *tierra*. In 1489, the Crown decreed that soap should be made and sold in the city, at a fixed price, by the monopoly-holders, who were to be authorised by the royal council. After this, the claim of the *veinticuatro* Juan de Sosa to a share in the monopoly was referred to that body. He appears to have lost his claim, as after Lic. de Aguila had been sent to investigate, the owners of the *casas de almona* were said to be Gonzalo Carrillo, Egas Venegas and Alfonso de Aguayo, all *veinticuatros*, and Doña Juana de Horosco. The owners did not exploit their holdings personally, but let them en bloc to another individual. In 1477 this was Antón Martínez, the son of the *jurado* of St Peter's, Martín Alonso, and in 1486, 1493, 1494, and 1495 it was another of Martín Alonso's sons, Pedro Fernández, who is described as a cloth-merchant (*trapero*). Lettings of *casas de almona* were normally for a period of one to three years, in return for a cash rent and an annual tribute, generally of chickens. The same applied to contracts for sub-letting such houses in the *tierra*. The monopolists were protected by the town council, with the support of the Crown, provided that they submitted to price-control. Negotiations were conducted between the council and the 'lords of the *almona*', not the tenants. In 1489, the Crown accepted the monopolists' rights, but stipulated that those who had charged more than the agreed price were to pay a levy to the town in compensation. In 1490, the council announced that soap was to be obtained only from these *almonas* and that the price was to be five *maravedís* a pound. After an investigation by the royal council, in 1493, the profit margin was fixed at one *maravedí* per pound. The *almonas* were supervised by the council, which also protected the monopolists from illegal competition. The council fixed the price of soap by means of an assay, in which the ingredients required to produce fifty-eight pounds of soap – one *arroba* of olive oil, one-third of a load of firewood, one *fanega* of ashes and one *fanega* of lime – were taken and priced. The resulting price was then set by the full council, to include the statutory profit margin. This procedure was meant to be carried out every four months. Most of the results survive between 1493 and 1514, indicating a variation in price per pound between 3.5 and 5.0 *mrs.*[29]

Fish

It is generally only in cases where a monopoly existed that prices were controlled by the council. The marketing of fish in Córdoba was in the hands of the fishermen themselves, who appear to have formed their own trading guild (*gremio*) for the retail of fish. The main issue in this period was the attempt by individual citizens to prevent the use of rivers and streams within their lands for this purpose. In 1478, the Crown ordered the justices of Córdoba to act against anyone who threatened the goods of its fishermen and in 1489 the council was ordered to maintain the guild's privileges. The royal policy was given further impetus when the judges of boundaries, Diego de Rojas and Lic. Sancho Sánchez de Montiel, whose main activities will be surveyed shortly, heard cases against Pedro de Porras in 1478 and Diego Fernández de Córdoba, *veinticuatro* of Córdoba and governor of the castle of Almodóvar del Río, in 1490, for closing fisheries to general use by the city's fishermen. In September 1493, the Crown went further and proposed to the council that a monopoly for the sale of fish should be introduced. Apparently in anticipation of resistance, the *alcalde mayor* was told to impose the new system if the council had not agreed to it within a week. In the event, the council voted against it by twenty to one, with two abstentions, among the *veinticuatros*, and four to none among the *jurados*, whose opinion was asked for once, on the grounds that a large number of citizens would be harmed if the system were changed and that the current price of nine *maravedís* a pound did not justify a monopoly. The scheme for Córdoba seems to have been quickly forgotten, but there was apparently a monopoly in Bujalance, at least, among the towns in the *tierra*. It was normally only at the beginning of Lent that the council attempted to regulate fish prices, so as to avoid profiteering in a time of special demand, and otherwise there were no controls. Fish might be imported via Seville to Córdoba by a royal privilege of 1440, confirmed in 1478, but the scale of the traffic is not known.[30]

Meat

Very great importance was attached by the council to the supply of meat to Córdoba. The method used in order to ensure that the markets always had enough meat to sell was to turn the supply (*abasto*) into a rent, which was farmed out to certain individuals, who might or might not be butchers themselves. The agreement would cover beef, pork and the meat of castrated goats, to be sold at a fixed price per pound, and would normally run from about Pentecost until the first of the three days preceding Ash Wednesday, known as *Carnestolendas*, in the following year. Summer and winter prices were generally included in the contract, changing over in May–June and November–December. It was normal for the council to fix a price for merino mutton in Lent.

It was the responsibility of the municipal market officials to check that the butchers' stalls were stocked for enough hours in the day and levy fines if they were not. The council might, in case of need, order the butchers to slaughter animals sooner than they had intended. At the time when the Crown was introducing *encabezamientos* for the *alcabala* to many Castilian towns, it proposed, in 1493, that Córdoba should make *abasto* agreements for meat over four or five years at a time, but the local council successfully rejected the proposal. One problem seems to have been the involvement of council members in *abasto* consortia. In 1498, Diego de Aguayo was one of the suppliers and in 1501 Alonso de los Ríos, lord of Fernán Núñez, followed suit. In 1502, the council decreed that *veinticuatros* and *jurados* should not contract for the meat supply, but very soon the arrangements collapsed. In the summer of 1502, the two contractors, Alfonso Fernández Malcome and Pedro Sillero, were arrested by the Inquisition and the council at first failed to find substitutes. It is interesting to note that during its attempts, it discovered that the cost of undertaking the supply was between 600 000 and 700 000 *mrs*. Egas Venegas offered to lend the council the money, if two publicly owned *dehesas* were given as securities, but the council was rescued by a group of butchers who signed a contract of the normal type in September 1502. The *dehesas* of Villalobos and La Bastida, which Egas Venegas had been hoping to take over, were apparently let by the council to butchers for the grazing of livestock for slaughter. On 17 October 1502, for example, the council agreed to pay six *maravedís* a pound for the meat produced in the *dehesa* of La Bastida, to a consortium of tenants led by Diego de Palma. The production of the property was estimated at 833 pounds of meat.[31]

SUPPLY PROBLEMS

Meat

The difficulties with the meat supply in 1502 began a period of severe problems in the supply of vital commodities, and in particular meat and grain, to the town. These years are worthy of detailed consideration, because they reveal the consequences for regional society of the distribution of political power and economic resources which has already been described. As far as meat is concerned, acute shortages seem to have begun in 1504. In August of that year, the council ordered all those within its jurisdiction who were rearing sheep for meat (*carneros*) to slaughter one-third of their stock at once, but not to sell the rest, on pain of a large fine to the royal exchequer. The export of livestock from Córdoba's territory was also banned. In 1505, however, the town's problems became even more acute, when no Córdoba butchers came forward to take on the *abasto* contract, and the council sent in desperation to other towns, such as Jaén, Ubeda, Baeza, Ecija and even Jerez, seeking suppliers. As a temporary expedient, various *veinticuatros* offered loans, as did the *corregidor* and one *jurado*. At the beginning of March, a group of cloth- and general merchants undertook the contract, but by the time arrangements were made for 1506, many of the town's flocks had died and the council failed to find a supplier. As it was at the same time struggling to find money to pay for grain imports, there seemed little hope that the 500 000 *mrs* for the year's meat could be found. The council petitioned the Crown to allow an imposition on wine to help repay loans for the purchase of meat. Livestock-owners were threatened with confiscation of goods, according to the quotas allocated to them earlier in royal levies of animals in wartime. In addition, to encourage stock-breeders to slaughter their animals, all taxes on the sale of cows and oxen were temporarily abolished. There were, however, repercussions. First, the tax-farmers naturally complained that the three meat rents were not being collected. Then the Crown reacted to complaints from Córdoba's butchers about the council's threats against them. The town was ordered to send a representative to Granada to discuss the matter with the *audiencia*. After this, an unhelpful letter arrived from Ferdinand, instructing the town to find suppliers, so that the meat rents might be collected once more. The council could only reply by pointing out the difficulties. There were similar problems in 1507 and the situation did not significantly improve until after 1510. The most important change in the later period was the direct sale of animals from private lands at the public markets in 1513. Those who by-passed the traditional monopoly of retailing in this way included several office-holders, such as Pedro de los Ríos and Cristóbal de Morales. In the following year, the financing of the meat supply was reformed, on royal orders. A fund of 460 000 *mrs* was to be devoted to this purpose and kept in a chest with keys held, one by the *corregidor*, one by the *veinticuatros* and one by the *jurados*. The money was to come half from the previous suppliers and half from the council. The council appointed deputies to supervise the working of the system and a group of butchers continued to supply the meat to the markets in the usual way.[32]

Grain

It is not possible to consider the problems of meat supply in Córdoba without also taking into account the question of cereals in the region. As should become clear when legislative and commercial measures on the subject are examined, the balance between pastoralism and cultivation was of vital importance to the development of Andalusian society and, indeed, to the fate of Spain as an imperial power in the sixteenth century.

In the light of Ibarra's important study, it has been taken as axiomatic that the Catholic Monarchs had a definite policy on grain, which was to regulate both prices, by means of fixed charges, and trading movements, by means of export controls and the construction of a network of public granaries, or *alhóndigas*. Ibarra provides ample evidence that such a policy was being implemented by the Crown by the early sixteenth century, but it is interesting to see what actually happened in an area such as Córdoba.[33] In contrast with the region round Jerez, Córdoba was not especially noted as an exporting area for grain. There are records of licence being granted to individuals for the export of grain consignments in 1479, but these are insignificant in comparison with the traffic out of Jerez.[34] As in other parts of Andalusia, the harvests in the Córdoba area in the last years of the fifteenth century seem to have been satisfactory, but in November 1502, the council began to take steps to protect its supplies from the holders of royal export licences. At this time, it followed up the September investigation of individual holdings, which has already been referred to, with a royal letter ordering 'lords of vassals' not to obstruct the flow of grain to Córdoba. In July 1504, the council appointed two *caballeros de premia* from each town in the *tierra* to patrol their local area in order to prevent the illegal export of grain. Such was the zeal of these guards that in 1505 the council agreed to return some consignments which had been incorrectly seized at Castro and Bujalance, from individuals who included Alfonso de Córdoba, lord of Zuheros.[35]

Before the emergency became general, in April 1506, extra supplies were obtained for Córdoba from seignorial towns which still had a surplus. The dependence of the town on private individuals, first in terms of grain shipments and later in cash, became ever more obvious and led to the paradoxical position in which the council was attempting to preserve the sale of grain as a process under public control, to which private interests were to be subordinated, and at the same time becoming totally dependent on those interests for the grain that was sold. Thus while shipments were arriving from seignorial towns, their lords were officially excluded from trading in grain because they held offices in Córdoba as well. The seriousness of the crisis ended this contradiction, however, as in April 1506, everyone who had grain was authorised to sell it, the avowed reason being the threat of disorder if this was not done. The council ordered that all remaining supplies should be brought to the council meeting-house and, when it became clear that no more was forthcoming locally, the Crown was petitioned for help. Eventually, 90 000 *fanegas* of wheat arrived from Sicily and 40 000 from France, but the council could not pay for the grain and was forced to ask Genoese merchants in Seville to buy it at the dockside, on behalf of Córdoba, with the council's publicly owned property as a security of reimbursement. The guarantee for the Sicilian shipment was the enormous sum of 10 000 ducats (3 750 000 *mrs*), which could only be supplied from the fortunes of the local magnates, who therefore had to advance both cash and securities. The grain was transported from Seville to Córdoba on carts, some of which seem to have been commandeered from various towns in the *tierra*.[36]

Complaints were regularly made in and to the council about the quality of the grain that was being shipped and there were threats of paying less if it did not improve, but of course nothing came of them. Ultimately, the success of the town's efforts to secure adequate supplies of the available foreign grain depended on the council's credit rating, and it soon became clear that this was not great. The Genoese let it be known that 'for greater security and their own good', they preferred to do business with private individuals rather than the council, when securities were required. Thus when the lords no longer had grain to supply, the town still depended on them for cash. As a temporary expedient, it was possible for the council to excuse itself from paying Francisco de Riberol for the Sicilian grain which the Genoese had supplied, on the grounds that this had been a transaction between private individuals, but ultimately the council was held responsible. In 1510, it agreed that its *mayordomo*, Luis de Valenzuela, should repay, from the fund which had been set up during the emergency to finance the import of grain, the sum of 300 000 *mrs*, which had been transferred to it from the money held by the *corregidor* for works on the fortifications of the Calahorra. The rest of the grain fund (*depósito*) was to be paid to the Genoese, Francisco de Riberol and Antonio de Sopranis, and supplemented from the bread *sisa* if necessary. After an agreement between the *corregidor* and the creditors, the letters of obligation which had been signed when the contract was first drawn up in 1506 were deposited with a Genoese, Domingo de Marín, and a Cordoban cloth-merchant, Juan García, until the debt was paid. Four years later, Antonio de Sopranis obtained a letter of execution from the royal council, ordering the *mayordomo* to produce 576 170 *mrs* which had been deposited with him by the *veinticuatro* Pedro Muñiz de Godoy. The *mayordomo* persuaded the council to reduce the amount to 332 170 *mrs* and, on 9 October 1514, the town pledged its property for the repayment of 315 915 *mrs*. There was little sign of a settlement, however.[37]

So far, in order to explain Córdoba's difficulties over grain supply in the early sixteenth century, it has been assumed that the cause of the problem was a series of bad harvests, between 1502 and 1507 in Córdoba and from a year later in the kingdom of Seville. It has also been assumed, by Ibarra and others, that the introduction by the Crown in 1502 of fixed prices, a *tasa*, of 110 *mrs* per *fanega* for wheat and 60 *mrs* for barley, was an attempt to halt price-rises which were caused, as usual, by shortages. However, the evidence for grain production in Córdoba and the rest of Andalusia, which has already been quoted, suggests that the cause of the supply problems in these years was not poor harvests but a failure to put grain on the market, possibly accompanied by a rising population, at least until the plague of 1507. It appears that the 1502 harvest was well up to the level of the 1490s in the kingdom of Córdoba, and Ladero suggests that it was the Crown's attempt to set grain prices at a lower and more stable level which initially created shortages. The intention may have been, as Ibarra thought, to help ensure cheaper grain for ordinary people and reduce the export traffic which the Crown itself had earlier fomented by issuing licences. Another motive was probably to obtain as much cheap grain as possible from Castile and Andalusia for military campaigns in Roussillon and Naples. The result of the 1502 *tasa* as applied in Córdoba has already been made plain and the local council was in no doubt as to the cause of the problem. In April 1503 it was openly stated that the low prices paid under the *tasa* were deterring those with surplus grain from sending it to the market and as the council was itself dominated by major grain-producers, it was in the best possible position to know. There is no record in Córdoba of prices as high as the 600 or 1000 *mrs* per *fanega* recorded in Seville in 1503–6, but the agreement for selling one-third of the Sicilian consignment in 1506 specified a price of 310 *mrs* per *fanega*, while the French wheat was sold at 260 *mrs* a *fanega*. When the official prices were first introduced to Córdoba in February 1503, they involved reductions in the prices fixed the previous November by the council, from 136 to 110 *mrs* a *fanega* for wheat and 68 to 60 *mrs* for barley. Almost immediately, though, the pragmatic of 1502 became irrelevant, and Ladero's summary of the causes of the problem cannot be bettered:

Certainly it will be difficult to find a better example of a cereal crisis in whose origin and development the maladroit application of political measures and speculative zeal played a larger part. As a result, when Isabella I died, Andalusia and the Crown of Castile as a whole were suffering from the worst general famine of the reign.[38]

PASTORALISM

One other factor is inescapable in explaining the problems of grain supply in Córdoba in the early sixteenth century, and this is the role of pastoralism in the regional economy. Increasing stress has been placed in recent work on the importance of stock-breeding in western Andalusia. Much effort was devoted to the raising of cattle, which not only contributed to meat supplies but also supported the leather crafts for which Córdoba had been famous since Muslim times, though unfortunately there are no detailed figures for cattle ownership. None-theless, even if the numbers of cattle were increasing and cow-hide was tending to replace sheep and goat leather in Cordoban goods, there is no doubt that the sheep was by far the most significant animal in the regional economy.[39]

Little can be said about pastoralism in late medieval Castile without reference to the Mesta, the national association of sheep-breeders which dominated this activity throughout the Crown of Castile. As a result of Klein's pioneering study, it has been natural to assume that the Castilian export trade in wool was conducted by means of migrating flocks, which moved between grazing grounds in the south, including the Córdoba area, and the northern fairs. If this were a true picture, it would suggest that grazing in the area was rented by outsiders for the use of transhumant flocks during the winter months. Klein draws a Mesta route along the Guadalquivir and then northwards through the Sierra Morena, more or less following the line of the modern road from Andalusia towards Madrid.[40]

In actual fact, Córdoba's connection with the Mesta seems to have been tenuous and hostile. There was at least one Mesta route (*cañada*) which crossed the northern part of Córdoba's *término* via Belalcázar, the valley of Alcudia, in the province of Ciudad Real, the Mochuelo pass and Villanueva de Córdoba, a town of the Pedroches. On 10 May 1490, the Crown gave the Mesta licence to build a bridge over the river Guadalmez, and further evidence of Mesta activity in the area may be found in the case brought by Gonzalo Mexía, lord of Santa Eufemia, against the Mesta shepherds, which reached the royal council. Mexía's hostility towards the Mesta was matched by that of the town council in Córdoba. In 1497, the *procurador mayor*, Alfonso Martínez de Angulo, stated in council that, 'this city never had a *mesta* and that it should not walk through her lands'. In 1510, the council took a copy of the Mesta ordinances, but it was again stated that the council had had no dealings with the Mesta for at least eighty years, in the area to the south of the castle of El Vacar and Adamuz, though its activity was permitted further north, for example in the Pedroches.[41]

However, it has recently been forcefully stated by Bishko that excessive concentration on the national Mesta has led to the neglect of local grazing interests, which, in Andalusia at least, were generally far more important to the local economy. In the case of Córdoba, there was no formal association of graziers in this period, but the interest was nonetheless extremely powerful and the examination of local material on pastoralism and its social and economic role in the area answers many of the questions which Bishko asks in his general survey.[42]

Although there are no general figures on stock ownership to match those for grain production, there is ample evidence of large-scale sheep-rearing in the area. In 1500, for example, Córdoba council began a case against the council of Cabeza del Buey (Badajoz), before a judge of commission, accusing twenty-three shepherds from that town of owing the *roda* and *portazgo* on 22 000 sheep and goats to Córdoba's tax-farmer, for 1499 and 1500. Similarly, a complaint from Juan de Lorca, the farmer of the *servicio* and *montazgo* of Córdoba diocese in 1502–6, revealed a large-scale traffic in flocks belonging to local graziers in the La Rambla area, which were being sent to pasture in Estepa and Ecija (Seville), Villamartín (Cádiz) and Ronda and Antequera (Málaga). This was apparently a regular practice and not one provoked by special circumstances, such as the 'dry year' of 1506. The demand for grazing was not only evident in the La Rambla area, but seems to have been a preoccupation in the Córdoba region throughout the period. It is unlikely that graziers would have laid themselves open unnecessarily to the payment of *servicio*, which was inevitable if they sent their stock out of Córdoba's territory, had there not been a shortage of grazing.[43]

The anxiety to increase the area available for livestock, and especially for sheep, showed itself particularly in the issue of enclosures, which seems to have dominated the activities of private landlords and the resulting litigation carried on by Córdoba council. The problem is highlighted by the series of documents which the Crown issued to protect public lands and limit the scope of private enclosers. The first salvo in the Catholic Monarchs' attack on the enclosers was a pragmatic, issued by the royal council in Córdoba on 28 September 1490, which forbade all inhabitants of the *tierra* of Córdoba to enclose more than a quarter of their lands and ordered them to allow all citizens and inhabitants (*vecinos y moradores*) of the city to exercise common rights on their land. These involved hunting birds and rabbits, fishing, picking asparagus and other plants, gleaning and gathering hay. A further document issued by the Crown in November 1490 mentioned explicitly the connection between enclosures and the rearing of flocks for the wool trade. It referred to complaints received by the royal council to the effect that, during the last thirty years, various inhabitants of Córdoba, who had persistently damaged cultivated lands with their flocks, had been buying the broken-down vineyards and olive-groves at a low price, clearing them of vines and olive-trees, and turning them into enclosed land, which they then expanded by illegally annexing commons. As an added refinement, they were said to have deliberately left gaps in their fences, in order to increase their income by using the town's ordinances to fine other stock-owners whose animals thus entered their 'property'. In view of this, the royal council decreed that the local ordinances on enclosures (*dehesas*) should be complied with, 'as though they were made and promulgated in Cortes'. All enclosures created without royal licence within the jurisdiction of Córdoba during the previous thirty years were to become common pasture again. Landholders were to permit the free exercise of all common rights in lands 'not being sown, or in pledge, or planted or worked'. Owners who illegally exacted penalties from inhabitants of Córdoba were liable at the first offence to lose the money which they had collected, which was to be divided equally between the victims and the upkeep of Córdoba's bridges and walls. For the second offence, the landholder was to lose all right to the property concerned. To reduce the damage done by livestock in culti-vated land, close seasons were established, during which all flocks were to be excluded. For this purpose, a flock was held to be four cows, oxen or other large beasts, ten pigs or fifty sheep or goats. Valuers (*apreciadores*) were to be appointed by the town to calculate the com-pensation which was to be paid to landholders.[44]

The penalties for illegal enclosures were modified in a royal pragmatic of Valladolid, 15 July 1492, which was published in Córdoba on 22 October of that year. No one might, in any case, enclose land without a royal privilege but the 1492 pragmatic changed the conditions under which such enclosures might be made. Citizens of Córdoba were now allowed to hold half their lands within its *término* as *dehesas*. Citizens of other towns who held lands in Córdoba were allowed to enclose a quarter, if they lived in the city and an eighth if they did not. Fencing was to be carried out by the *medidor* (measurer) in the company of *fieles* appointed by the local council. Fines for illegal enclosures were to be 1000 *mrs* for the first offence, half for the royal exchequer and half for the council's funds, while for the second offence the landholder would lose all right to enclose his land in the future. The pragmatic was intended to be the basis of a coordinated assault on a serious denial of common rights by landlords. It went on to deal with another method used by enclosers to enlarge their holdings, which was to enclose the uncultivated land (*baldíos*) included in the property and let it for gain. This practice was forbidden on pain of confiscation of the rent money from the lord and a fine of equal size for the tenant. Legal enclosures by individual royal privileges were still allowed, but all existing holders of such documents were ordered to send them to Court for examination within a hundred days of the publication of the pragmatic.

One clause in the 1492 pragmatic is of particular interest because it hints at royal support for large graziers. Enclosures of less than four *yugadas* (about 124 Ha) were forbidden, without special permission from the *fieles*, 'so that the land should not be closed to the grazing of flocks because of such small enclosures'. It appears that the Crown was content to see an extensive wool trade, but this does not necessarily imply support for the national Mesta. It is worth noting that the effort to protect the land from transhumant flocks, included in the 1490 pragmatic, was repeated in 1492 with the stipulation that owners of flocks or shepherds who interfered with private fenced pastures, uncultivated lands or commons were liable to a 1200 *maravedís* fine and damages to be assessed by the *fieles*. The movement of flocks was not included among common rights. The clearest indication that the Crown intended action to be taken against illegal enclosures is the instruction for the appointment of an *alcalde de las dehesas* (magistrate for enclosures) and two *fieles*, who were to inspect all the properties within Córdoba's boundaries twice a year and implement the pragmatic. The *corregidor* and *veinticuatros* were to ensure that these officials' sentences were carried out and that they were given the royal 'security and protection' for their work.[45]

An *alcalde de las dehesas* had existed in Córdoba as early as 1447, but there was clearly a revival of activity after 1492. According to a 1496 account, the official was elected at the beginning of each year by two *caballeros de premia* from each parish, and no one might serve more than one term of office. The elections were by lots, but, as in the case of other urban offices, it seems that the Crown attempted to interfere, for example appointing Arias Savariego to the post in 1512. After a revision of various local ordinances on office-holding in 1496, one of the two offices of *fiel* for measuring agricultural properties was reserved for the *veinticuatros*. They were to do the job, in turns, for one year at a time and there were to be no second chances until everyone had served a term.[46]

A strong indication that Córdoba's pastures were overcrowded in this period may be found in the local council's efforts to restrict the use of grazing within its boundaries by outsiders. According to a council decision of April 1495, such individuals had to keep the local ordinances on land-use and were not allowed to import flocks from seignorial lands.

These regulations originated in a letter from the royal council and were presented in greater detail in the ordinances for farms of 9 May 1499. In the new code, the quotas of stock which might be imported to Córdoba's grazing by farmers (*labradores*) who lived under seignorial jurisdiction were fixed at fifty sheep for each *yugada* rented, or five cows, fifty pigs or three mares. All livestock above these figures which was found on Córdoba's lands was to be subject to the *quinta de los ganados*, a levy of a fifth of the animals concerned. The local council's anxiety to protect its pastures from the flocks of other towns was also revealed in a reference, at a meeting in 1493, to the 'old ordinance' keeping strangers' flocks out of the city's grazing, on pain of unspecified fines (probably the *quinta*) and expulsion from Córdoba's territory. A similar concern was reflected in the repetition, in the ordinances of 1499, of a regulation from Henry IV's reign to the effect that holders of enclosures and farms in Córdoba's territory should not let the grazing to outsiders, though hay might be sold from licensed enclosures to feed the flocks of graziers in seignorial areas, during the winter. There was clearly an attempt to reduce the letting of grazing to outsiders in 1493, when the council decreed that current contracts, running into 1494, might stand, but that new ones should not be made. The issue was still, however, very much alive in 1514.[47]

BOUNDARIES DISPUTES

One of the best sources for information on tensions and difficulties in the countryside in this period is the collection of sentences by the *jueces de términos*, the 'judges of boundaries' who were sent to Córdoba by the Crown to deal with abuses in the ownership and use of the land. The sentences given by Lic. Diego de Rojas, Lic. Sancho Sánchez de Montiel, Lic. Antonio de Cuéllar and Lic. Fernando Díaz de Lobón, which cover the periods 1477–8, 1491–9, 1513–14 and 1514–15 respectively, survive in collected form, and some of the actual trials also remain. The main charges made in the trials were the illegal enclosure of uncultivated lands (*baldíos*), the blocking of public thoroughfares, on land or water, including the diversion of streams, the usurpation of commons and other royal lands, particularly on high ground (*montes*), the seizing of public fountains and fisheries and the illegal enclosure of private lands. The sentences for 236 cases survive and of these 146 were pronounced by Montiel. As might be expected with an enterprise sponsored by the Crown, the judges concentrated mainly on private usurpation of public property. Such offences led to over two hundred of the sentences.

The geographical distribution of the offences was fairly even throughout Córdoba's *tierra*. The cases are an important source of information on land-use and they indicate that pasture, in this case all enclosed, predominated in two main areas, first, the valley of the Guadalquivir and, secondly, in a band stretching westwards from the Pedroches to Fuente Obejuna, or in other words the Mesta route. Bishko has recently noted that in 1492 the Crown proposed, in response to complaints from the local *caballeros de premia*, that a municipal *mesta* should be set up in Córdoba. The suggestion was successfully rejected by the council, for reasons which should become clearer when the boundaries legislation of this period is studied in greater detail.[48]

First of all, though, it is necessary to show that there was some connection between enclosures and grazing. The royal document of 3 November 1490 referred to the conversion of arable enclosures to pastoral use and the boundaries litigation provides some specific evidence. In 1492, three cases heard by Montiel resulted in convictions for the illegal conversion of arable or other cultivated land into enclosed pasture. All three properties were near Córdoba and the charge in each case was the same. Commander Antonio de las Infantas and his predecessors over thirty years were said to have bought some fruit-orchards and vineyards in the Pago de los Arenales and turned them into enclosed pasture, so that all was 'level and depopulated', although other, adjoining vineyards 'are now populated'. Similarly, the late precentor (*chantre*) of the Cathedral, Pedro de Hoces, had bought some vineyards and olive-groves in the Pago de las Quemadas and turned them into pasture for wool production (as a *heredad de lana*), by uprooting the vines. The *veinticuatro* Pedro Muñiz de Godoy was convicted of uprooting olives and sowing arable land with grass in two properties, in order to let them as an enclosure. He was ordered to return the arable land to cultivation and replant the olive-grove, 'as the other olive-groves are kept in Córdoba, ... because a place where there are one or two or three olive-trees, sparse and separated, is not understood to be an olive-grove'. In each case, the penalty was the full exercise of common rights and the payment of legal costs.[49]

A number of cases involved the illegal letting of grazing and among those accused were the *veinticuatros* Francisco Cabrera and Pedro González de Hoces, who were convicted in 1512 and 1513, respectively, and Don Francisco de Benavides, lord of Guadalcázar, who was convicted in 1514. In his appeal to the royal council, Don Francisco made the interesting statement that the accusation had been brought against him by the stock-breeders (*criadores de ganados*) of Córdoba. This seems to lend substance to Bishko's theory that the refusal of Córdoba council to set up a local *mesta* was the result of resistance, on the part of the noble oligarchy which dominated the council, to the complaints of the many lesser men who had grazing interests in the area. In contrast, the Crown's support for the judges of boundaries was clearly seen as part of its general defence of the royal patrimony and attempt to regain what had been lost, which was initiated at the Cortes of Toledo in 1480.[50]

There is no doubt that the upper nobility was the prime target of the judges' activities, but the magnates were not alone. Although the initiative in bringing cases before the judges belonged to the council, its own members were not exempt from attack. One approach was to require holders of royal privileges for enclosures to produce the documents concerned for scrutiny. Such privileges had to be confirmed by each succeeding monarch if they were to remain valid. It appears that in its zeal to put the pragmatics of the 1490s into effect the council brought actions against those who did have legal titles to enclosures and gained virtually no satisfaction. In no surviving case was a privilege, once presented, found to be invalid, though Pedro González de Hoces failed to produce confirmation of a privilege for the *cortijo* of Fuencubierta, before Lic. Francisco Galíndez, a judge of commission, and thus lost the right to keep the land enclosed. Of the twenty-eight defences of privileges which survive, twenty-four were successful and the other four inconclusive. Among those involved were the bishop, seventeen *veinticuatros*, four *jurados* and two other members of office-holding families. In some cases, the actions brought by the town were welcomed by owners of enclosed land as opportunities to establish their rights and exclude those who attempted to use their lands as commons. The *jurado* Luis del Bañuelo, for example, protested against the violation of his *dehesa* of El Ochavillo. In his letter to the royal council, which brought about the vindication of his privilege by Montiel, he claimed that the estate had been in his family for more than a century, thus qualifying as a prescriptive right, but, more significantly, he mentioned that his fellow-citizens were using the laws of Toledo in order to put his rights in question. In several other cases, also, holders of enclosure privileges had them vindicated by the royal judges.[51]

Litigation of this kind indicates the ease with which the wealthy and influential could make use of the Crown's help to resist the implementation of its own laws. Nowhere can this more clearly be seen than in the relations between the great lords of the Córdoba region and the town council over the question of enclosures, and the individuals involved are of sufficient importance for some of the main cases to be examined one by one.

The house of Aguilar, in the persons of Don Alonso de Aguilar and his son, the marquis of Priego, came into conflict with Córdoba over its stock-breeding interests. The main dispute was over the *dehesa* of Carchena, south of Castro del Río. In 1494, the town brought a case before Montiel against Don Alonso de Aguilar for the illegal enclosure of the sheep-walk which separated Córdoba's lands from those of the seignorial towns of Aguilar, Baena and Cabra. Don Alonso claimed the land in question by prescriptive right, arguing that because of his long and peaceful possession Córdoba council could not bring an action against him under the laws of Toledo, but Montiel was not impressed and found in favour of the city on 21 August 1494, with costs payable by Don Alonso. Five days later, Don Alonso lodged an appeal, but on 1 October Montiel went ahead and placed the landmarks in accordance with his sentence. Don Alonso's proctor went round with him, appealing against each mark as it was placed. The appeal was heard by the *audiencia* of Ciudad Real in 1495, but was still in progress in 1503, by this time under the direction of Don Alonso's son, the marquis of Priego. Eventually, the appeal was turned down and Córdoba received a letter of execution from the *audiencia*, which upheld Montiel's judgement and ordered the marquis to pay the legal costs within nine days. The marquis did not pay until 1508 and the council took formal possession of the disputed lands on 10 October of that year. However, this was not the end of the story. According to a requirement presented to Córdoba council by the judge of boundaries, Lobón, on 22 February 1515, the inhabitants of the marquis's town of Montilla ignored all these proceedings, continuing, even after the 1505 letter from the *audiencia*, to build houses on Córdoba's land in the Castro area and to arrest citizens of Córdoba who attempted to enter it. Lobón accused the *veinticuatros* of Córdoba not only of failing to visit the city's boundaries regularly, as the law required, but even, in some unidentified cases, of actively obstructing the council's own boundaries officials, when they tried to arrest citizens of Montilla and Cabra who had entered Córdoba's lands illegally. The council expressed suitable horror at this suggestion and on the following day sent a commission to renew Montiel's boundary-marks, but this effort seems to have been equally ineffective, as Lic. Galíndez was still trying to enforce the 1505 *audiencia* verdict in 1516, and Córdoba made another attempt to obtain satisfaction by means of litigation in 1546.[52]

All the leading noble families were involved in litigation over boundaries, including the counts of Cabra, the lords of Alcaudete and the *alcaides de los donceles*. Among families with holdings to the north of Córdoba, the most prominent were the counts of Belalcázar, who have been fully studied by Cabrera, and Gonzalo Méxia, lord of Santa Eufemia, who had a long history of seignorial violence and conflicts with Córdoba council. As early as 1457, Méxia was convicted by Dr Diego Sánchez del Castillo, judge of boundaries for Henry IV, of usurping the lands of El Bercial, Los Robledillos, Las Valverdes and La Cañada de Toril, which were on the border between the lands of Córdoba and Santa Eufemia. Méxia was said to have defied an agreement with Córdoba council, by enclosing these lands and letting the grazing to mountain shepherds from elsewhere, who were apparently connected with the national Mesta. He was accused of illegally arresting citizens of Córdoba who entered these lands and of seizing a pasture for plough-oxen (*dehesa boyera*) which belonged to Torremilano, a royal town. Montiel heard the case against Méxia in 1493 and found in favour of the council, but Méxia appealed successfully to the Crown. When advising the council to appeal in its turn, the lawyer, Lic. Daza, proposed that its case should rest on three points. First, the town's views had not been heard by the Crown and, secondly, Montiel had given sentence in accordance with the laws of Toledo, which stated that all sentences given by the judges of John II and Henry IV should be implemented. Thirdly, he pointed out that the Crown had not seen the documents of the case heard by Castillo in 1457. In the event, Córdoba managed to restart the litigation and it was still in progress in 1500, but it appears that Méxia won another letter of execution against Córdoba in 1504. Yet another hearing took place at the *audiencia* of Granada in 1512 and the case was then no nearer a conclusion.[53]

The failure of Córdoba council to achieve the implementation of sentences against the upper nobility was often matched in cases involving lesser individuals. In the 268 cases which are documented in the municipal archive, including defences of enclosure privileges, whether instigated by the owner or the town, convictions were achieved in 228. Twenty-six actions failed completely, though all but two of these were successful defences of private enclosure privileges. Five cases were settled out of court and there were nine in which the surviving documents do not indicate the result. Appeals against conviction had to be made within thirty days, or else were not allowed, as in the case of Doña María Manuel, widow of Don Alvaro de Guzmán, in 1493. Thirty-seven such appeals are recorded in the surviving documents and it is clear that this resort was in effect confined to the upper echelons of local society. Those involved included three great lords, Don Alonso de Aguilar, the count of Cabra and the lord of Alcaudete, three lesser lords, Egas Venegas, lord of Luque, Alfonso de los Ríos, lord of Fernán Núñez, and Antonio de Córdoba, lord of Belmonte, one lord from another province, ten other *veinticuatros* and seven *jurados* of Córdoba, five members of office-holding families, two lawyers' families, four monasteries and the Cathedral chapter. Only two individuals did not fit into any of these categories. Boundaries were marked in accordance with the sentence, even when an appeal had been made, but defiance of such measures by seignorial vassals made this procedure rather futile. Violations of the judgements of boundary judges apparently occurred on a spectacular scale, as the prospect of ceaseless litigation stretching into the future apparently caused widespread cynicism in relation to the law. One specific example involved the inhabitants, both of the royal town of Bujalance and of Cañete, which belonged to the marquis of Priego. Montiel gave sentence in 1496 against both towns for the illegal sowing with crops of royal lands between the two towns, but when Lobón visited the area in 1515 he found that during the previous twenty-years five citizens of Cañete and eight of Bujalance had between them illegally sown thirty-two *fanegas* of grain, eight-and-a-half *aranzadas* of new vines (*majuelos*) and nine *aranzadas* of ordinary vines.[54]

The ease with which the judges' verdicts could be defied, either in the courts or on the ground, obviously reduced their effectiveness. However, the severest blow to the whole enterprise was a document issued by Ferdinand on 13 May 1514, in which all penalties for infringements of the pragmatics on land-use which had been exacted by the royal judge, Cuéllar, were annulled. Thus the Crown surrendered in fact all that it had been anxious to demand in theory, the excuse being that the fines would upset the finances of landlords in the area. The document ends with the lame remark that in future, if the pragmatics on enclosures were not observed, 'the penalties contained in them will be carried out'.[55] The collapse of Cuéllar's efforts did not prevent the

Crown from sending Lobón and Galíndez to succeed him, but evidence of penalties' being exacted from offenders or of the effective restitution of lands to Córdoba in this period is non-existent, apart from the ritualistic 'possession' which followed each sentence given by a judge of boundaries. In view of the apparently almost complete failure of the Crown and the local council's attempt to prevent the illegal use of land, it is reasonable to ask why the Córdoba authorities continued to bring cases before the judges. There was clearly the hope, although this was rarely realised, that the costs of the trials would be reclaimed in fines from offenders. Another attraction was that the judges heard cases with amazing speed, in comparison with the normal course of pleas at the *audiencia*. Nearly all verdicts were reached in two or three days and in many cases less than one day was necessary. The sentence, also, was generally carried out at once, even if an appeal removed its effect. It appears, therefore, that the theoretical possibility of punishing offences connected with land-use, and in particular illegal enclosure, was enough to encourage the town to bring a continuous series of actions whenever a royal judge was in residence. However, the total failure to deal with the wealthier landlords and the abject surrender by the Crown in 1514, when added to the other evidence of frequent petty violation of the boundaries fixed by the judges, suggest that the actual achievements in return for years of effort and expense were not great. The town's litigation against private landlords provides a better indication of the general desire to increase grazing-space in the area as rapidly as possible than it does of the restoration of royal lands to the public use for which they were intended.

WOOL TRADE

The destination of the wool produced from the pastures of the Córdoba district is of vital importance in any consideration of the area's economic state and prospects in this period. It is clear that wool was by far the most significant export commodity and, if it could be shown that the surplus was used locally, then Córdoba would have possessed a sound base for an economy dominated by industry rather than commerce. The evidence, however, suggests a very different picture. It is to be found in the notarial archive and consists, in the first place, of over two hundred contracts for the sale of wool for export, between 1471 and 1515. These are supplemented by fifteen transport contracts for wool, which indicate the pattern of the trade.[56]

The city of Córdoba in the late fifteenth century was a centre for the sale of wool, not only from its own district but from a much wider area, including Ubeda and Baeza in the kingdom of Jaén, Baza in Granada, Antequera to the south and Hinojosa, Belalcázar and the Sierra de la Serena to the north. The wool was then transported by bullock-cart along the Guadalquivir to the port of Seville for loading. The carters lived in towns on the river-bank, such as Alcolea, Córdoba itself, Almodóvar del Río, Posadas and Lora del Río. It appears that the wool was taken to Córdoba in April or May and moved to Seville in June. It appears that the two operations were parts of the same trading pattern and in 1513 and 1515 they were included in a single contract.

Unfortunately, there is little surviving material from the period between 1471 and 1484, but it does seem that the pattern of the Córdoba wool trade changed after 1486, when merchants from Burgos appear in the records for the first time. At a council-meeting in May 1499, it was proposed that Alfonso de Castro, a merchant from Burgos, should receive a licence to build a house on royal land, 'below the water-mills of Don Tello, to bring and store the wool which he buys in this city', in return for a ground-rent payable to the council. In the period before the Burgos interests began to dominate the trade, Córdoba merchants seem to have purchased wool from other areas, which was brought to the town, for example from Cuenca and Medinaceli, south-east and east of Madrid. It is impossible to establish whether this wool supplied the local industry or was exported, as no evidence for the movement of wool survives from this period, but there is no doubt of the pattern which developed once Pedro de Arceo, *regidor* of Burgos, appeared as a wool-buyer in Córdoba in 1486, operating jointly with Pedro de Valles of Córdoba. The size of the sample of contracts does not permit sophisticated calculation of the market-shares of Cordoban and Burgos buyers, but in crude figures, the number of sales to local buyers only exceeded the total sales to Burgos merchants in one year between 1486 and 1515. This was 1506, an exceptional year because of political, social and economic dislocation, from which only one contract survives, recording a sale to a local buyer at a low price.[57]

The contracts appear in the notarial registers in a standard form, though not all the particulars of the parties concerned or of the sale were necessarily included every time. The vast majority concern white merino wool, mostly from full-grown sheep but sometimes from younger animals. Black merino wool was also sold on occasions at a lower price. The description 'Castilian' wool appears once in a contract at 130 *mrs* an *arroba*, which was less than half the price of merino wool at its lowest. A typical example of a contract is that made by Lope de los Ríos, *veinticuatro* of Córdoba, on 5 July 1490, with a representative of Pedro de Arceo.

In Córdoba, on this aforesaid day, Lope de los Ríos *veinticuatro* of Córdoba, agreed, in the name of Diego Venegas, his brother-in-law, to sell to Pedro de Raceo [sic], merchant, citizen of Burgos, and to Pedro de Ribas in his name, one hundred and twenty *arrobas* of fine white merino wool of the Puerto del Guijo, at 430 *mrs* an *arroba*, 35 000 *mrs* immediately, and declared himself to be content and paid, and agreed to hand it [the wool] over in a fenced farm, that coming April, on a clear day, after sunrise and in a clean sheep-fold...and that when he handed it over [Ribas or Arceo] should finish paying him the *maravedís* which it amounted to...Each party [pledged] his goods thus.[58]

It is interesting to note the elaborate precautions against fraud and the large advance payment which was made.

From the local evidence, it is not easy to discover the reasons for the growing dominance by Burgos merchants of the Córdoba wool trade. It may be assumed that local producers did not feel particular loyalty to the city's own cloth industry, but obtained the best possible price from whatever source. It cannot be shown that the Burgos merchants consistently offered a better price than their local rivals, but nonetheless, the annual averages of the prices offered by local buyers only exceeded those offered by the Burgos merchants in two years between 1486 and 1515. The limitations of the sample dictate caution in the use of these figures. Both groups of merchants offered advance payments, so that this was not a factor which operated particularly in favour of the Burgos men. What seems to have occurred is that during this period Córdoba became part of an export trade in merino wool on a national scale, which was very largely controlled by mercantile interests in Burgos. Pérez shows that merchants from that city were involved in the export of wool from Cuenca and they seem to have had a similar interest in Córdoba.[59]

Between 1486, when Pedro de Arceo first came to buy wool in Córdoba, and 1515, the annual average price of white merino wool in surviving contracts rose from 346 *mrs* to 449 *mrs* per *arroba*. The Burgos merchants or their representatives tended to make series of annual visits to buy the next year's crop. Sometimes they retained the connection by appointing a local man to represent them. Pedro de Arceo was involved in the trade between 1486 and 1500, Juan de Logroño between 1494 and 1507, Gonzalo López de Polanco between

1492 and 1500 and Alfonso de Lerma between 1495 and 1500. Thirty different Burgos merchants appear at least once during the period as buyers or agents. One factor which may have appealed to sellers was the readiness of some Burgos merchants to make contracts in advance. However, while Arceo began this procedure in 1486, it did not become general until 1515, when thirteen out of the sixteen surviving contracts involved more than one crop, and in one case four were included. It is more probable that the growth of this practice indicates a buyer's market, in which the merchants protected themselves against inflation by committing the producers to a fixed price for several years at a time.

The information included in the contracts reveals the involvement in wool production of virtually all ranks of Cordoban society. As with other rural products, the group of lesser noble and knightly families which controlled the political life of the town was equally conspicuous here. Apart from the widow of the lord of Alcaudete, contracts for the sale of wool were made by fifteen *veinticuatros*, three widows of *veinticuatros*, six *jurados* and an *escribano*, but they were also made by merchants, tradesmen and artisans, and by tenant-farmers, as well as ecclesiastical corporations. Thus it appears that, despite the dominance of the nobility, a wide range of Córdoba's citizens still had access to local pastures, a state of affairs which might conveniently strengthen the council's resistance to interference from the national Mesta, though it could not save the efforts of the judges of boundaries from defeat at the hands of the larger graziers.

TEXTILE INDUSTRY

The export of so large a quantity of wool from the Córdoba area inevitably affected the local textile industry. This had been established in the city since the thirteenth century. Alfonso X gave Córdoba's weavers a privilege in 1258 and in 1280 the Crown gave the local council a privilege for two shops to retail cloth.[60] By the late fifteenth century, the city ranked with the major urban cloth-producers of the southern half of the Iberian Peninsula, such as Cuenca and Toledo.

Although much less is known about the Córdoba industry, its organ-isation seems to have been similar to that described by Iradiel in Cuenca. Apart from preliminary processes, such as the sorting of wool into its different grades, and simple home-based activities such as the spinning of thread, most stages of production took place in the city itself, in contrast to the rural industry of Old Castile. References to cloth-workers, which are confined to carders, weavers, dyers, fullers and shearers, indicate a concentration of these trades in the seven parishes of the Ajarquía, and particularly in St Andrew and St Peter, although they were also found in the Medina, in smaller numbers. Most production seems to have taken place in domestic workshops, though the complex nature of the fulling process and the need for water meant that this activity took place in riverside *batanes* on the Guadalquivir and Guadajoz.[61] The price-lists quoted by Iradiel indicate that Córdoba was capable of producing cloth for the upper end of the market, that is, *veintidosenos*, or cloth with 2200 threads (*hilos*). Cloth of this quality, in addition to *veintenos* (2000 threads), is mentioned in local sources.[62] There is no information about the level of production, though it is known that cloth of lower quality, such as fustians (*fustianes*) and friezes (*frisas*), was manufactured.[63] There is also evidence of cloth production in Bujalance and other places in the *tierra*.[64]

Regrettably, the organisation of labour in the Córdoba cloth industry has to be largely guessed at. The putting-out system seems to have predominated and more will be said shortly about mercantile influence over production. However, the limited evidence available appears to support Iradiel's contention that it is wrong to suppose, as has sometimes been done in the past, that the Castilian Crown was implacably opposed to the development of guilds. The two possible functions of a guild, as a trade association or as a religious brotherhood, were both applied in Córdoba, as in other industrial towns. Attempts have been made to clarify matters by calling trade associations *gremios* and religious brotherhoods *cofradías*, but the Córdoba evidence does not indicate that such a distinction was made. More will be said later about the activities of lay religious organisations, but it is clear that the guilds of cloth-workers, which took an active part in the conduct of their trade, were referred to indifferently as *gremios* and *cofradías*.[65] In late fifteenth-century Córdoba, the cloth-workers were organised into four guilds, representing weavers, dyers, fullers and shearers. Other trades were either subsumed into these guilds or else unorganised.

Regulation of cloth manufacture was shared between the guilds and the town council. Unfortunately, there are no surviving guild records, so that the industry is seen almost entirely from the council's point of view, though some testimony is inadvertently given in private notarial documents. This major limitation should be borne in mind, as it inevitably gives a rather bureaucratic character to the picture of the industry which emerges. It appears that royal intervention, in the form of a letter which reached Córdoba in December 1500, requiring an examination of existing cloth ordinances throughout the kingdom, caused a revision and extension of municipal intervention in the local industry. The municipal ordinances of 1435 referred to a separate, more detailed set of regulations for cloth manufacture, which was confirmed by Ferdinand in 1483, and which survives in the version drawn up in 1458.[66] Up to 1500, the industry was regulated by two supervisors, known as *veedores de los paños* or *veedores de tintas*. The appointment was meant to be annual and was made by the council. However, elections in the 1490s seem to have been irregular and sometimes only one *veedor* (also called a *fiel*) is recorded.[67] After the royal letter had been received, the apparatus for supervising the industry was expanded and the guilds were drawn into greater cooperation with the town council. After 1500, the *veedores de los paños* confined their attention to the dyers, but additional pairs of *veedores* were appointed for the weavers, fullers and shearers. The officials of each trade met each year, more or less, to elect their representatives, whose appointment was then ratified by the council.[68]

Even before royal intervention brought about a greater involvement of the guilds in the control of the industry, the town council was showing the type of concern about the quality of Córdoba's cloths which Iradiel found elsewhere and ascribed to the predominance of mercantile over industrial interests. In 1497, the council appointed a commission to discuss with the dyers possible improvements in the quality of their materials. In 1498, Córdoba council reaffirmed the prohibition, included in its ordinances, of the use of the dye-stuff *orchilla*, also spelt *horchilla*, *urchilla* or *hurchilla* in contemporary documents. This vegetable dye comes from a marine lichen and was imported at considerable cost from the Canaries. It was normally used in conjunction with other dyes in order to produce a red or purple colour. This process was, however, complex and liable to failure, with the result that some textile ordinances, such as those of Córdoba and the draft ordinances of 1500 for the whole of Castile, forbade its use, as a defence against unskilled or shoddy workmanship.[69] Efforts were made at the same time to encourage weavers to produce heavier cloths, and a new town seal, in the form of a crown, was introduced in 1497 for use by the *veedor de los paños*.[70] After 1500, however, the Crown took the initiative, in Córdoba as elsewhere, in the development and control of the textile industry, culminating in the reception of the general ordinances of 1511 by the local council.

In the event, Córdoba protested against the new ordinances at the Cortes of Burgos in 1512, on the grounds that the town's own laws, which had been confirmed by Henry IV, kept the seal for cloths in the hands of a *fiel* (the *veedor de los paños*) who was appointed by the council and might not exercise his office in the trade during his tenure. Under the new laws, which had been foreshadowed in the royal letter of 1500, the town seal was entrusted to practising dyers. Córdoba failed to secure royal confirmation of the 1458 ordinances and had to follow the 1511 rules thereafter.[71]

In view of the economic and political dominance of the ruling families in Córdoba, it is perhaps surprising that the local cloth industry survived the large-scale export trade in merino wool which was so essential a part of the regional economy. Although production figures do not survive, the urban cloth industry retained a fair degree of prosperity until after 1550, despite the council members' personal commitment to mercantile activity. On one notable occasion, the council made a public stand on behalf of local cloth-producers and against the wool merchants. In April 1515, the council discussed some letters which had been obtained by a group of Córdoba manufacturers, Marco Ruiz and his associates, from the *audiencia* at Granada, ordering the enforcement of Henry IV's law of 1462, which reserved a third of Castilian wool production for the home industry. The *regimiento* had apparently joined the protest and now demanded that the *pesquisidor* should enforce the *audiencia*'s ruling. Significantly, the entry in the council *actas* refers to a dispute over whether the third of wool production reserved for local producers meant a third of the total or only a third of what remained after the Burgos merchants had made their purchases. The dominance of commerce over industry was thus clearly indicated.[72]

5

The nobility in regional politics

It should already have become clear that the difference between theory and practice in the life of the region in this period could be considerable. Nowhere is this more true than in its political affairs. It is undeniable that, apart from the Crown itself, the only significant group in Córdoba's politics in the late Middle Ages was the local nobility, so that events in the area cannot be understood without an awareness of the role of aristocrats in regional society.

NOBILITY AND KNIGHTHOOD

In the case of late medieval Castile, the 'pure' concept of rule by the best was of minimal relevance to contemporary qualifications for inclusion in the nobility. By far the most important among these were wealth and breeding. This is not to say, however, that the notion of an aristocracy which earned its privileges had entirely disappeared. It is easy to see that the prolonged crusade for the Reconquest of Spain from the Moors had the effect of raising the military calling in the esteem of society, so that other groups, such as the Christian clergy, burgesses and peasants, were forced to acknowledge their dependence on the soldiers for the ability to live and carry on their own activities. As the Reconquest was still incomplete for most of the fifteenth century, it is natural that the warriors should still have been established at the head of society in this period. Contemporary theorists, such as the chronicler Diego de Valera, complained, as Boethius had done long before, that nobles often obtained their rank on the basis of other people's virtues rather than their own, but the hereditary principle was very far from being threatened under Ferdinand and Isabella. Royal lawyers were indeed dissatisfied with the notion of status being conferred by heredity, but they limited their comments to municipal office-holders, not daring to tackle the nobility as a whole.[1]

If it was accepted without much dispute that nobility might be conferred in perpetuity by the king and that it might properly be granted to those who possessed wealth and breeding and who followed the military calling, it is nonetheless true that many problems of status remained unsolved. It was easy to distinguish the *grandes*, or *títulos*, those who were granted titles and lordships by the Crown as dukes, marquises and counts. More problematical was the relationship between nobles, for whom the usual word was *hidalgos*, and knights, or *caballeros*. That there was a definite distinction between these two ranks had been noted by Valera, who wrote that, '*caballería*, in common law, is not a dignity, nor does it confer nobility, except on the *caballeros* of the Roman curia'.[2] In Valera's view, this state of affairs was justified by the fact that the main motive in his time for seeking the rank of *caballero* was to obtain tax exemptions. However, if the status of *caballeros* was poorly viewed in the late fifteenth century, that of nobility (*hidalguía*) was being steadily enhanced.

The privileges of a *hidalgo* were fairly clearly delineated. *Hidalgos* were less threatened than others by the law and were distinguished from the rest of society. A *hidalgo* had a special relationship with the king and could only be arrested by his express order. Out of respect for his military calling, a *hidalgo*'s horses and weapons were exempt from seizure for debt or any other cause and because of his supposed virtue and purity of blood he might not be judicially tortured. Affairs of honour between nobles were settled by duel and if a noble had for some reason to suffer the death penalty, he was beheaded and not hanged. These privileges naturally applied to the titled nobility as well.

By the fifteenth century, the possession of a fixed family residence (*casa solar*) and membership of a kin-group (*linaje*) were becoming increasingly important. As Valera's work indicates, the concept of blue blood (*sangre azul*), derived from the heraldic significance of the colour blue, which was variously described as the sky, divinity, loyalty and justice, was still firmly established. As a result, far from there being a movement towards individualism, aristocratic notions of lineage were still the inspiration of much political and social activity. Blue blood could only be preserved by avoiding alliances with unworthy persons and it is easy to see the results of this attitude in the marriages of the Córdoba nobility.

In addition to the possession of a *casa solar* and a restriction to marriage within the same social group, the noble had to behave in an appropriate manner in his daily life. Official documents, when describing the characteristics of the 'noble life', often reflected the confusion which existed in contemporary society between the noble, or *hidalgo*, and the knight, or *caballero*. It was clear enough, in principle, that a *caballero*, and the requirement included *hidalgos*, should always keep a horse and weapons, in order to be able to respond to the king's military summons. In practice, this rule was harder to keep, but even more difficulty arose with the other main feature of the noble life, which was that in order to benefit from the privileges of this rank, a man should not live by 'base and vile offices'. A law of John II gave as examples of what was meant by this statement the offices of tailor, leather-dresser, carpenter, stone-cutter, digger, cloth-shearer, barber, spicer, retailer and shoe-maker.[3] Those who failed to fulfil either of these conditions were to lose their privileges and revert to the status of *pechero*, or tax-payer.

THE NOBLE 'LINAJE'

The tension between the military ideal and the practical need to engage in some form of activity for financial gain affected all, from the humble *caballero* to the exalted *grande*, but the first task will be to examine the characteristics of the upper noble *linajes* whose economic and political dominance over the region has already been described. In theory, all nobles were equal before the law, but disparities of wealth were already apparent in the thirteenth century and these gradually created what was in effect a separate class, as the difference of quantity became one of quality. At least until the fourteenth century, the link between wealth and nobility was openly admitted in the title of *rico hombre* ('rich man'), which was the only way in which the leading magnates of Castile were distinguished. In the late Middle Ages, French titles, such as duke, marquis, count and viscount were introduced and the term *rico hombre* became less prominent, disappearing after 1516. In order to understand the political activity of the upper nobility, it is necessary first of all to look at the economic basis of the *linaje*.[4]

Titles of the French type had only begun to appear among the Córdoba aristocracy by 1500. Don Alonso de Aguilar, who dominated the region throughout his political career, was never more than a *señor*, though the head of the rival house of Baena, Don Diego Fernández de Córdoba, was made count of Cabra by Henry IV in 1455, having held the lordship of the town since 1439.[5] Until Don Alonso de Aguilar's son,

Don Pedro, was created marquis of Priego after his father's death in 1501, the only other titled noble in the Córdoba area was the Sotomayor count of Belalcázar. This title was created in 1466. In view of the small number of Castilian *grandes* in this region, the political role of the nobility has to be approached through the families which possessed lordships. The houses of Aguilar and Baena were indeed as pre-eminent as their social rank and economic strength would suggest and the political conflict between them will be considered in due course, but in economic terms, the upper noble *linaje* largely shared the characteristics of the other seignorial families in the area.

The vital importance of royal grants of lands, rents and lordships with judicial, administrative and military powers in the creation of the late medieval Cordoban aristocracy has already been stressed.[6] There were, however, other ways in which the Crown helped to ensure the continued supremacy of the nobility in regional society. Grants of *señoríos* were very rarely revoked and the few contemporary cases did not involve Córdoba. Far more common were additional grants of lordships to existing seignorial families. It was also possible for the king (or the pope) to legitimise the bastard children of the nobility in order to ensure that a suitable heir was available to inherit the family's possessions. However, the most significant contribution which the Crown made to the longevity of aristocratic dynasties was economic.

Often, the Castilian Crown's financial aid to the nobility took the form of transfers of royal revenues to private coffers. These grants, known as *juros*, consisted of a specified sum in cash, which the recipient was thereby entitled to receive from the proceeds of royal tax-collection. Sometimes a specific rent was named in the grant as a source for the cash, while in other cases the money might be obtained from any available rent. The cash was normally handed over annually and grants might be either for life (*de por vida*) or hereditary (*de heredad*). The excessive alienation of royal revenues to private individuals was one of the main weaknesses of medieval monarchs and in Castile the Cortes mounted a campaign against such grants throughout the fifteenth century. These efforts were largely unsuccessful and *juros* developed, as the sixteenth century went on, into a kind of national debt system, in which those below the ranks of the nobility might invest.

As part of their attempt to put the royal administration on a sounder footing, the Catholic Monarchs began in 1480 to reduce the size and number of *juros* and convert hereditary into life grants. According to Matilla Tascón's calculations, over fifty-seven million *maravedís* in hereditary *juros* were granted in 1480 and five million in life *juros*. After the reform, the respective totals were twenty-five million and six million.[7] The spectacular reduction by fifty per cent of royal grants of all kinds, including the governorships of castles (*tenencias*) and feudal retainers in cash (*acostamientos*), did not however prevent certain individuals, and in particular the upper nobility, from continuing to receive a massive income from this source. Two notable local examples are the count of Cabra and the *alcaide de los donceles*, whose *juro* income was halved from 60 000 to 30 000 *mrs* per annum. These were hereditary grants. Such sums were, however, insignificant in comparison with the enormous grant of 1 750 000 *mrs*, 'situated' in the *almojarifazgo* and *alcabala* of Córdoba and its *tierra*, which the duke of Medinaceli received in 1493. The date of this grant indicates how far Ferdinand and Isabella had deviated from their earlier policies by the end of the Granada war. The fact that this huge sum went to a magnate with no interests in the Córdoba area acts as a reminder that the recipients of *juros* did not necessarily collect their cash from local revenues.[8] In her will, Isabella expressed regrets that the financial needs of the Crown during the Granada campaign had caused a reversal of the 1480 reform. *Juros de heredad* were given to individuals in return for loans in aid of the war effort, but the queen stressed that each grant contained a provision that the Crown could buy the *juros* back at any time in the future, at a price equal to the sum originally granted. Her hopes that her successors would revoke these grants were not, however, realised.[9]

In addition to new grants of *juros*, a number of Andalusian nobles received extra lordships in the kingdom of Granada after its conquest. The house of Aguilar gained Almena and El Cerro, the house of Baena Canillas de Aceituna, Archez and Corumbela, and the *alcaides de los donceles* Sedella and Comares, the latter with the title of marquis. The lord of Palma, Don Luis Portocarrero, received Huéjar la Alta and the lord of El Carpio obtained Sorbas and Lubrín.[10] The most important point to notice is that no new family with existing holdings in the Córdoba area joined the ranks of the *señores* in Andalusia as a result of the Granada campaign. Royal largesse was employed to strengthen the position of the existing leaders of local society.

Even more fundamental to the strength and permanence of Castilian *linajes* in this period was the history of the law of inheritance. As in other countries in western Europe, the most important single factor in the creation of huge private estates was the introduction and acceptance of primogeniture as a guiding principle. This was, paradoxically, one of the main results of the reintroduction of law based on the code of Justinian (which in fact assumes partible inheritance) in the thirteenth century. In earlier Castilian law, for example the *Fuero Juzgo*, it was assumed that the parent would divide his goods among his children. Restrictions were placed on attempts by parents and grandparents to favour particular persons or institutions at the expense of others. No one son or grandson could receive more than a third of his father or grandfather's goods in this way (*de mejoría*). The Church could not receive more than a fifth of what remained 'without that third'. Goods received from the king or another lord in return for services were even then excluded from these restrictions, which were known as the *tercia y quinta de mejoría*, and might be disposed of as the testator wished.[11] All this changed with the introduction of Alfonso X's *Partidas*, which established the rights of the eldest son over the rest. The theory of primogeniture was advanced in the context of the succession to the Crown of Castile, but it was rapidly extended to the nobility. In this way, the establishment of private empires in the kingdom was the paradoxical result of a law which was intended to enforce the royal supremacy over all. Whether foreseen or not, one of the results of the permanent adoption of primogeniture in the royal family, a condition which was not achieved until the fifteenth century, was to spread this custom to the leading families of the kingdom, thus accentuating the very evils which the *Partidas* were intended to eliminate.

The arguments used in this code to justify the absolute right of the eldest son to the inheritance of his father were taken from nature, law and custom. The so-called 'natural' argument was in fact based once again on the ownership of property. The main desire of parents was said to be to 'have a lineage to inherit their goods'. As the eldest son arrived first to satisfy this desire, he was naturally the favourite of his parents and thus received the appropriate reward of supremacy over his brothers and sisters. The legal argument was based in the first place on the law of Moses, which stated that the eldest son was set aside as holy for God, taking as an example of the supremacy of the eldest son the power given by Isaac to Jacob, believing the latter to be his eldest son Esau, when he gave him his paternal blessing. 'You will be lord (*señor*) of your brothers and the sons of your mother will bow before you.' The third ground for primogeniture, the appeal to customary law, was more doubtful because, as has already been noted, *fuero* law did not support this principle. The fact was admitted in the

Partidas, which stated that by ancient custom, 'fathers commonly had pity on their other sons [and] did not want the eldest to have everything, but that each of them should have his share'. However, the new code tried to evade this objection by asserting that 'wise men of understanding' realised that, at least in the case of the royal succession, such a partition was not in the interest of the kingdom and had allowed the entire inheritance to pass to the eldest son.[12]

The *Partidas* were on insecure ground, in the context of Castilian law, when they asserted the supremacy of the eldest son and Gregorio López's commentary makes it clear that such statements were the result of Roman law influence. Nonetheless, the principle did become established in Castile in the fifteenth century and it opened the way for the accumulation of huge private fortunes by the families which produced the future *grandes* of Spain. The device which ensured that such fortunes passed intact to the eldest son was the entailed estate or *mayorazgo*. Permission to create such an estate out of the family possessions was granted only by the king, the normal procedure being that the nobleman concerned would obtain a licence to form a *mayorazgo* out of certain, specified goods and properties, in favour of a named individual, generally his eldest son, and a succession of named substitutes in case of the death of one or more of the named beneficiaries. As the example of Córdoba shows, by the end of the fifteenth century there was no important noble family which did not have a *mayorazgo* and the practice was spreading downwards through the echelons of urban society. Indeed, such was the interest which the law of inheritance aroused among the leading citizens of the Castilian towns that the *procuradores* to the Cortes of 1502 demanded new laws on the subject, a request which resulted in the laws of Toro of 1505.[13]

The laws of Toro enforced the *fueros* in all the towns which possessed them, so that inheritance in Córdoba was governed by the *Fuero Juzgo*, with its provisions on the *tercia* and *quinta*. In general, the 1505 laws extended the principles of the *fueros* to the kingdom as a whole, but they added certain definitions in the case of illegitimate children. A 'natural son' was legally a child of parents who were, at the time of conception, in a position to marry without dispensation and whose father recognised him as his son. An illegitimate son could always inherit his mother's goods if she had no legitimate children and if he was born of a union which did not carry the death penalty (*dañado y punible ayuntamiento*). However, a legitimised child did not have precedence if his parents later had a child within wedlock. In such a case, the general rule that an illegitimate child was entitled to a fifth of his father's goods was held to apply.

The most interesting of the laws of Toro, from the noble point of view, were those which referred to the inheritance of *mayorazgos*. The phraseology of these laws reveals the extent to which they had become embedded in Castilian life by about 1500. The need for a royal licence to create a *mayorazgo* was confirmed at Toro but the Crown reserved the right, if it so wished, to ratify one which had already been formed. Licences for *mayorazgos* were held to be valid after the death of the king who had granted them, if they had not by then been used by the beneficiaries. Once a licence had been obtained, the Crown effectively abandoned control of the *mayorazgo* into the hands of its possessors. A nobleman could freely revoke his will to create a *mayorazgo*, without regard to the royal licence which he had obtained for it, provided that he had not already handed over the goods concerned to the beneficiary. After a *mayorazgo* had been created, it passed automatically from one heir to another, according to the terms of the original document and royal licence, without the need for any further intervention by the Crown. A law which was important in certain cases in Andalusia in the reign of Ferdinand and Isabella gave the descendants of the eldest son preference, in the inheritance of a *mayorazgo*, over the younger sons of the founder of the *mayorazgo* and their descendants. The same rule applied if the inheritance was collateral. All descendants of the second son had precedence over the third son and his descendants, and so on. Another law which greatly helped the nobility was that which allowed improvements made to entailed properties, such as fortresses and towns, to be included automatically in the *mayorazgo*, although the Crown was careful to add that entirely new fortifications might not be included without a royal licence, in addition to that required for their construction. The overall effect of these measures is clear. They gave wealthy men the power to preserve and hand on their riches, so that their families obtained a more or less permanent place at the head of society. The weakness of the taxation system also helped to prevent the diminution of wealth, once it had been accumulated. There was no *alcabala* on inherited property and no question of death duties.

As with *juros*, it is impossible to assess in precise numerical terms the extent of the practice of founding and maintaining *mayorazgos* among the Cordoban nobility. Information from later documentation in national archives does however indicate that *mayorazgos* were virtually universal in families whose members held municipal office in the late fifteenth century. Thus in addition to the various branches of the Fernández de Córdoba, families such as the Aguayo, Castillejo, Godoy, Saavedra, Valenzuela and Vargas had *mayorazgos* by 1500.[14] The concentration, so far, on the privileges of the eldest son does not, however, imply that the rest of the children were unimportant. In the first place, all children of noble parents were noble too and not all noble goods were in entail. Secondly, the importance of the nobility in a regional society such as that of Córdoba depended to a large extent on whole families rather than those families' individual heads. In recent years, it has become fashionable in some circles to stress the social and political role of the noble lineage in late medieval west European history. Work has been done on both urban and rural areas, particularly in Italy, but in view of the contemporary use of the terms *linaje* and *bando*, it is clear that such an approach is also relevant to the history of Castile.[15]

Before examining the political role of noble lineages, it is necessary to look at their size and geographical location. For this purpose, a division has been made between families which possessed at least one complete *señorío*, and whose head was thus entitled to call himself *señor*, and those noble houses which, despite having extensive possessions in entail and members who held public office, had not attained the seignorial level. On these criteria, the first group of families contains the eight branches of the Fernández de Córdoba, the Mexía lords of Santa Eufemia, the Portocarrero lords, and later counts of Palma, the Méndez de Sotomayor of El Carpio, the Venegas of Luque, the Sotomayor counts of Belalcázar and two branches of the De los Ríos, lords of Fernán Núñez and Las Ascalonias, respectively. As it is hard, on the basis of the available knowledge of the goods of individual families, to draw an accurate line between the non-seignorial 'upper' nobility and the rest of the *hidalgos*, a fairly arbitrary selection of the former has been made, using as a rough guide the criterion of public office-holding in Córdoba. The second group thus includes the Aguayo, Angulo, Argote, Cabrera, Cárcamo, Cárdenas, Carrillo, Castillejo, Godoy, Góngora, Hoces, De las Infantas and Mesa. About another dozen families might have been included in this category, had sufficient genealogical material been available.[16]

It is particularly hard to provide precise information about the size of noble families. Contemporary genealogies and other documents, such as wills, can rarely be relied on for completeness. Children who died young were often omitted. Illegitimate offspring might well not be recorded and little effort was made, on occasions, to give a precise account of daughters. Thus even if the great age of the falsification of genealogies to prove 'purity of blood' had not yet begun, it is nevertheless unwise to place too much weight on the available figures for noble offspring. In the case of more humble families, the task can scarcely be attempted.

Among the fifteen seignorial families which headed the Cordoban aristocracy, there were few prolific fathers. The largest recorded families are those of Don Alonso de Aguilar, who had five legitimate and four illegitimate children, and the first count of Cabra, Don Diego Fernández de Córdoba, who fathered no fewer than eighteen children, sixteen of them in his two marriages. Most seignorial nuclear families in this period, however, seem to have contained seven or fewer children. The average number for each head of household in this sample was just over four, including illegitimate offspring. Among the thirteen office-holding families included in the second group, there are no recorded families as large as those of the heads of the houses of Aguilar and Baena. The average family size emerges as 3.9, which in view of the dubious nature of the figures used cannot be effectively distinguished from the results for the seignorial houses.

The recorded marriages of Cordoban nobles in the period of the Catholic Monarchs appear to contain few surprises for those who expect little upward or downward mobility and marriage within the existing social group. The heads or heirs of the houses of Aguilar and Baena duly found their spouses in families of national importance. Thus Don Alonso de Aguilar married Doña Catalina Pacheco, daughter of the master of the order of Santiago, while his son, the first marquis of Priego, married Doña Elvira Enríquez, a cousin of the king. In the house of Baena, the second count of Cabra married Doña María, the daughter of Don Diego Hurtado de Mendoza, first duke of the Infantado, while his son, the third count, was married twice, to women from two leading Castilian families, the Enríquez and the Zúñiga. The seventh *alcaide de los donceles*, head of the third most important line of the Fernández de Córdoba, married the sister of Don Alonso de Aguilar's wife, Doña Juana Pacheco. The lesser lords of the Córdoba area generally married members of local families of equivalent rank, though the Fernández de Córdoba lords of Guadalcázar married into other branches of the same original line, the houses of Montemayor and Cabra, respectively. There was some intermarriage between the first and second groups of families, which is not surprising in view of the fact that the division between them is artificial and intended only as an aid to analysis. Thus Fernando Alfonso de Argote married the daughter of the fourth lord of Guadalcázar and Juan Pérez de Godoy, *veinticuatro* of Córdoba, married a daughter of Fernando Alonso de Montemayor. His nephew married the daughter of a *grande*, Don Juan Ponce de León, second count of Arcos. There is no case in this group of office-holding families of marriage with individuals of lesser rank. Unfortunately, the fragmentary nature of the sources makes it impossible to examine the ordinary *hidalgos* in a similar way, but at least it is clear that, while 'good' or 'bad' marriages might be made, in social, economic or political terms, the Cordoban nobles entered the sixteenth century with a determination to seek alliances within their own group.

The distribution of nobles among the parishes of the city is of relevance to an understanding of *linajes* as social and political entities. This question may be looked at from two points of view. First, it is worth asking whether there was any concentration of nobles in certain parishes and, secondly, it is useful to know if each *linaje* lived in a particular quarter, which it might be able to dominate, on the pattern found, for example, in Genoa. If the same criteria for inclusion or exclusion are used as have been applied up to now, the result is an average of about ten upper noble, or office-holding families in each parish. At the two extremes, the ten noble houses in St Nicholas 'de la Villa' included two branches of the Fernández de Córdoba – the house of Aguilar, and the descendants of the former bishop of Córdoba, Don Pedro de Solier – while St Bartholomew and St James each contained only four important office-holding families. It is not possible to distinguish any aristocratic quarter in the city and it is equally clear that individual families had, by the late fifteenth century, become so complex that they might not be said to dominate particular parishes or parts of parishes, as happened elsewhere. The great majority, if not all, of the families above the rank of simple *hidalgo* in Córdoba by about 1500 had come to the region, if not to the city itself, as early as the thirteenth century. They had thus had ample time to intermarry and also to divide into various branches. The result was that, of a sample of forty-nine office-holding families, which excludes all the Fernández de Córdoba, only nineteen were confined to one parish. Fifteen families were divided between two parishes and one between three, while six families resided in four parishes and eight in no fewer than five.

The effect of this distribution on Córdoba's political life will be examined in due course.

It is impossible to establish precisely the number of citizens who were included in the upper noble category as members of families which regularly held public office, for example as *veinticuatros* or *jurados*. However, if the estimates used so far are at all accurate, and the average size of this rank of household was about six, excluding retinues and servants, then Córdoba's leading families may have totalled approximately 350 individuals. In addition, it is possible to make some estimate of the number of citizens with the rank of *hidalgo*. The fullest account from the period is a list which was produced for the city council in May and June of 1514.[17] At the council-meeting on 5 May 1514, a document (*requerimiento*) was read in which the *hidalgos* of the city demanded that the council should investigate the inclusion in the tax-lists (*padrones*) of the parishes of St Marina and St Lawrence of various individuals who, they claimed, were *hidalgos* and therefore exempt from inclusion. The council duly adopted the course suggested in the *requerimiento* and called on all *hidalgos* to prove their title to that rank before the council. This replica of the procedure normally required for proof of *hidalguía* at the royal *chancillería* was implemented during the succeeding month and the results were recorded, parish by parish. This was not the only list of *hidalgos* produced in the period. As a result of a conflict between the *hidalgos* and the *caballeros de premia* over their respective duties in the military service of the Crown, a group of *hidalgos*, eighty-one in number, signed a legal document in Luque on 26 January 1513.[18] Apart from the fact that the 1513 document was not intended as a complete list, the number of names included in it is much smaller than the total of 196 individuals whose titles were accepted by the city council in 1514. Even this larger figure cannot, however, be accepted without modification. Thirty-three names which were included in the 1513 document are not to be found in the 1514 lists. A total of 240 *hidalgos* in 1514 would not seem unreasonable but would clearly be much larger than the figure of 110 which Marie-Claude Gerbet has obtained from Simancas documents.[19] The 1514 lists are incomplete in that there are no names for the parish of St Peter. They also contain the names of twenty-four individuals who were only included after discussion in council and it is matter for speculation whether the doubt was genuine or the result of personal animus. In order to reach some kind of total for the Córdoba nobility in the early sixteenth century it is necessary also to point out that the 1514 lists include many members of the families which have been regarded here as part of the upper or office-holding nobility. It is probable, therefore, that a figure of between 250 and 275 noble heads of household would not be wildly inaccurate.

The only indication of the number of *caballeros de premia* in late medieval Córdoba is a list of those who took part in a parade (*alarde*) on the Campo de la Verdad, to the south of Córdoba, on 5 November 1497. There are 195 names on the list, but it appears to be far from complete, as five parishes are missing altogether and some others are represented by very few names. The occupations of the knights are included in a minority of cases and, as might be expected, they cover a wide range. There were *caballeros de premia* among the cloth-merchants (*traperos*) and general merchants (both *mercaderes* and the apparently lesser *merchantes*). Among industrial workers, the tanners and the dyers seem to have achieved this rank, in some cases, and artisans were represented by silversmiths and furniture-makers, among others. Tenant-farmers (*labradores*), gardeners (*hortelanos*) and woodmen (*silvaneros*) also appear in the lists. The dispute over military service, which surfaced in 1496 and culminated in the *hidalgo* list of 1513, indicates that the distinction between noblemen and *caballeros de premia*, which was in theory precise, was in practice not always obvious. However, the 1497 list does suggest that the practitioners of 'vile and base offices' were still well represented among the *caballeros de premia* of Córdoba around the year 1500 and it will become clear in due course that this particular group had a prominent role to play in the city's politics during the early years of the sixteenth century.[20]

MILITARY FORCES

If the characteristics of noble families are of interest in the study of the aristocratic contribution to local politics, it is equally clear that a knowledge of the distribution of military power in the region is essential for an understanding of the relative strength of different groups within the city and its *tierra*. In a society dominated by a crusade against the infidel, which was rapidly approaching its climax, it was inevitable that political power should correspond closely with the ability to garrison castles and put armies in the field. As far as the larger towns, such as Córdoba, were concerned, the legal basis for the raising of troops was the *fuero* which had been granted in the thirteenth century. The dominant principle was that of the feudal host, whereby the king had the right to summon to his service all men between the ages of twenty-five and fifty who were not excluded for physical reasons or because they were clerics. Those who did not serve had to pay a tribute instead. The militia was paid from council funds and was mustered on the basis of *padrones*, which, like those for taxation purposes, were compiled and used by the *jurados*. The urban forces of Andalusia consisted from the start of *caballeros* and *peones*, two categories which were often more important in social and financial than in military terms. According to Córdoba's *fuero*, the *caballeros* were the most important part of the force. They were only allowed to leave the city outside the campaigning season, that is, between October and May, and if they took their families with them they had to leave a substitute, as a pledge that they would return. The *caballero*, or his deputy, had to maintain a horse for at least eight months of every year. The *peones*, or foot-soldiers, on the other hand, were simply summoned by the *jurados* of their parish, when the order came through from the Crown via the local council, and placed in contingents, each with a certain number of *caballeros*. The whole force was led by the city's *alguacil mayor*.[21]

Even in the *fuero* itself, the *caballeros de premia* were complicating the issue. From the start, these were the members of the trading community which settled in the newly conquered city, who had the wealth to pay for a horse and for the fairly simple knightly accoutrements of the period. They were treated as equals of the *caballeros*. After the laws of Alcalá of 1348, those with goods valued at more than a certain fixed sum were obliged to do knight service. In the fifteenth century, the figure in Córdoba diocese was 4000 *mrs*. Those with goods worth 10 000 *mrs* had to supply two horses and those with 40 000 *mrs* three. By a pragmatic of 20 June 1492, Ferdinand and Isabella raised the minimum figure to 100 000 *mrs*, in Córdoba and the other cities of Andalusia, adjusting the other figures accordingly. According to a Seville ordinance of 1432, *caballeros*, of whatever kind, had to parade in helmet and coat of mail, with sword, shield and lance. The infantry was divided into crossbowmen (*ballesteros*) and lancers (*lanceros*). The latter also had swords, shields and daggers and are not to be confused with the mounted soldiers who were armed with lances. By the time of the Granada campaign, there were also hand-gunners (*espingarderos*), who wore armour.[22]

Ladero's figures for the forces put in the field during the Granada campaign do not, generally speaking, show the types of infantry involved, but they do indicate that Córdoba was in practice capable of raising up to 750 horsemen and 5000 infantry, in case of necessity. The more detailed figures for the period after 1495, which are to be found in local records, reveal that the city was asked to provide up to 400 *espingarderos* and, in one case, 800 *ballesteros*, but that the bulk of its infantry contribution generally consisted of *lanceros*. Another fact which emerges from the *actas capitulares* is that the conquest of Granada was far from being the end of the demands made by the Crown on the city's military resources. Apart from general levies at times of panic, such as the Alpujarras revolt in the kingdom of Granada in 1499, the royal expedition against certain Andalusian magnates in 1513 and the threat of Turkish attacks on the region's coast in 1515, the numbers demanded were lower than they had been during the Granada war, but nonetheless there were few years between 1492 and 1515 in which no troops were required from Córdoba by the Crown.[23]

So far, no mention has been made, in a military context, of the Crown's own 'feudal' vassals, the *vasallos del Rey*, who in theory composed a force of mounted lancers which could form a reliable nucleus for the royal armies. A *vasallo del Rey* agreed to serve the Crown whenever required, on specified terms, and might not become the vassal of any other lord without royal permission. Had this been an effective institution in the period of the Catholic Monarchs, it could have given the Crown a valuable basis of political support among the leading citizens of Córdoba. In fact, however, as Ladero has observed, it was declining steadily in importance during the Granada wars and between 1486 and 1491 the city provided no more than eight *vasallos del Rey* to the royal armies. Marie-Claude Gerbet could find evidence of only eleven in a slightly later period, though her list is admittedly incomplete.[24]

The significance of the Córdoba militia in the region's affairs cannot be assessed only on the basis of numbers. Quality and morale are more important considerations and in these respects the reputation of urban forces in this period was not good. As far as Córdoba is concerned, one guide to the level of military fervour among the citizenry is the effectiveness of the regular parades (*alardes*) of the *caballeros de premia*. While the total of nearly two hundred knights who paraded in Córdoba in 1497 contrasts sharply with the single, pathetic *caballero* who appeared in the only parade summoned in Madrid in that year, Córdoba council seems also to have expected a large-scale failure to meet royal requirements. When ordering an *alarde* for the last Sunday in May 1500, for example, the council added that all *caballeros* who had no horses were to parade nonetheless as *peones*, in accordance with royal instructions. By November 1515, things had deteriorated further. Complaints were made in council that half the *caballeros de premia* failed to turn out, sending their sons or serving-lads instead, while those who did appear were in a state of disarray. The council decided to call another parade for Christmas 1515.[25]

Another sign that military activity was by no means to the taste of many of Córdoba's citizens is the prevalence in the period of substitution in the performance of military service. It was inevitable that many citizens' concern for their own farms or businesses should have outweighed their feeling of loyalty to the Crown and their desire to complete the Granada 'crusade'. This was particularly so once the direct military threat had receded from the Córdoba area, with the result that by the late fifteenth century it was normal for those liable for military service to pay a deputy to march for them. This practice was particularly common among the *caballeros de premia*, but cases involving all ranks are to be found in notarial registers. Thirty-nine examples of substitution are recorded between 31 July and 2 August 1490 and another forty-six between 21 and 24 December 1501. The rush to arrange for deputies was accompanied by a series of disputes over exemptions and status, whenever a demand for troops was received by the council.

The figures provided by Ladero for the troops supplied by leading nobles for the Granada wars give a good indication of the forces at the disposal of the leading members of regional society, as the Andalusian magnates were heavily committed throughout. In contrast with the city militia, seignorial contingents consisted mainly of horsemen, either the lightly armed *jinetes*, who rode in the Moorish style, or the *hombres de armas*, whose equipment and style of fighting corresponded more closely to those customary elsewhere in western Europe. The two categories are not distinguished in the records concerned. Apart from a freak total of 550 horsemen produced by the count of Cabra in 1483, the largest recorded total for the army of a Cordoban magnate is 400, supplied by Don Alonso de Aguilar in 1483, 270 of them being cavalry. Don Alonso never achieved this total again and the count of Cabra and *alcaide de los donceles*, like him, normally produced during these campaigns between 200 and 300 men, most of them cavalry. Lesser lords, such as Gonzalo Mexía and Egas Venegas, provided between twenty and fifty horsemen in most years of the war. Military and economic capabilities seem to have been closely matched among the Andalusian upper nobility and the effect of this state of affairs on the political life of Córdoba is made plain in the whole history of the period.[26]

METHODS OF POLITICAL CONTROL

Any investigation of this question must rest on the assumption that the nobility was involved in the region's politics with the legal sanction of the Crown. The leading families of the Córdoba area were all represented on the city council, except for the Sotomayor of Belalcázar. Don Alonso, the head of the house of Aguilar, was *alcalde mayor* of Córdoba and the count of Cabra, head of the house of Baena, was *alguacil mayor*. These two magnates were among five who held *votos mayores*, or predominant votes, in the council. The others were the *alcaide de los donceles*, Gonzalo Mexía, lord of Santa Eufemia, and Don Luis Portocarrero, lord of Palma.[27] The *voto mayor* seems not to have given an additional vote, but to have been a formal title of honour, beyond the style 'Don', which was restricted to members of the highest rank of the upper nobility and to senior clerics.

It was not, however, by means of honorific titles that the upper nobility exercised its power in Córdoba. The difficulty is that it is not generally possible to discover the mechanism by which this control was effected, although the results were clear enough. In principle, it might be expected that an obvious way in which a magnate could establish a connection with an individual member of Córdoba council would be by means of a simple feudal link between lord and vassal. A lord would pay a retainer (*acostamiento*) to his man, in return for which the latter might live in his lord's house, sharing his table, as a *comensal* or *paniaguado*, although this was not necessarily the case. The recipient of an *acostamiento* was, however, required to serve his lord in battle, when summoned, and in this respect the relationship between a nobleman and a lesser man (who might also be a noble) was similar to that between a magnate and the king. The case of an ordinary citizen who attached himself to the household of a holder of an important municipal office – and in Córdoba all holders of such offices had at least the financial privileges of a noble – might or might not be of great political significance. It is clear, however, that when a *veinticuatro* of Córdoba became the *vasallo* of a local magnate, this was a sign of political alignment. Ladero has noted the growth, after the arrival of the Trastamarans on the Castilian throne in 1369, of the illegal practice of *veinticuatros* and other council officials receiving *acostamientos* from nobles. A law of John II, which forbade office-holders in any royal town to live in the house of any other official of that town, on pain of losing their vote and office, was confirmed by Ferdinand and Isabella. However, the continued existence of this practice was tacitly admitted by the Catholic Monarchs, when they allowed the marquis of Cádiz, and his heir the first duke of Arcos, to pay *acostamientos* to officials in Córdoba, Ecija and Carmona, since they themselves had no offices in these towns. After the admission that nobles might pay *acostamientos* to officials in neighbouring towns, it was difficult in practice for the Crown to stop such payments in towns such as Córdoba where the nobles did in fact hold office.[28] It is, unfortunately, as hard to work out in detail the political significance of noble use of *acostamiento* payments as it is to establish the effect of marriage alliances and the action of noble *linajes* as political entities. The only way in which the attempt may be made is through an examination of the main episodes in the political history of Córdoba and its region from the late 1460s until 1516.

POLITICAL DEVELOPMENTS

The reign of Henry IV

Political alignments in the whole of western Andalusia in the reign of the Catholic Monarchs were largely determined by the conflicts of Henry IV's period. The significant years came after 1464, when national and local rivalries combined to cause turmoil in the region. When prince Alfonso became the centre of noble resistance to his half-brother, the king, in 1465, the Andalusian upper nobility split into two opposing camps. In Córdoba, Don Alonso de Aguilar became the leader of a party supporting Alfonso, while the count of Cabra led those who remained loyal to Henry. These two *bandos* were to be the main feature of Córdoba's politics at least until the early years of the sixteenth century. From the start of hostilities, Don Alonso de Aguilar, accompanied by the *alcaide de los donceles* and Luis Méndez de Sotomayor, lord of El Carpio, was dominant in the city. He held the *alcázar* of Córdoba and the tower known as the Calahorra, which controlled the southern end of Córdoba's bridge across the Guadalquivir. He also held the castles in the *tierra* at Santaella, Bujalance, La Rambla, Adamuz, Peñaflor and Puente de Alcolea. The Cabra party, in contrast, normally functioned in the *tierra.* It was supported by Martín Alonso de Montemayor, lord of Alcaudete, Egas Venegas, lord of Luque, and Luis Portocarrero, lord of Palma. The Cabra side held the castles of Castro del Río, Castro Viejo, Pedro Abad, Aldea (now Villa) del Río and Montoro.

Many skirmishes and raids took place during the next four years, but the most important was the capture of Ecija, in July 1466, by the count of Cabra and his son-in-law, Luis Portocarrero. The Aguilar party continued to control Córdoba, however, and after Don Alonso had granted a truce to his rivals, in November 1467, the next major event on the national stage was the death of prince Alfonso at the end of June in the following year. His demise filled king Henry's supporters with new enthusiasm, and the count of Cabra unsuccessfully attacked Bujalance and Córdoba itself. Initially, the backers of prince Alfonso transferred their allegiance to the king's sister, princess Isabella, but after the agreement between the two sides had been made at Guisando, in September 1468, whereby Henry recognised Isabella as heiress to the throne, the king attempted to restore his authority in the rebel areas. As a part of this campaign, he came to Andalusia in May 1469, entering Córdoba at the end of that month. The count of Cabra and his supporters came back to the city with the king, but the settlement treated both sides equally. All the royal castles which had been seized in the fighting were to be restored to the control of the council, but the king also decreed that the two leaders, Don Alonso and the count, were to be compensated by the citizens of Córdoba, through a *repartimiento*, for the cost of garrisoning the usurped castles and for works carried out within them. Henry seems previously to have promised to the count of Cabra the sum of 1 400 000 *mrs* in return for his efforts to restore the city to the king's obedience. Numerous members of the two parties signed an agreement in Córdoba on 5 June 1469, to the effect that they would restore the integrity of the city's possessions and never allow any of them to be alienated again. The following day, three *veinticuatros* of Córdoba were appointed to find out the magnates' expenses and five members of the council offered to mortgage various of their farms if public funds proved insufficient to pay the compensation.[29]

Not surprisingly, the king's visit to Córdoba failed to end the conflict between the two *bandos*. Henry installed his ally, the count of Cabra, as *teniente* of the *alcázar* and the Calahorra tower, but in October 1469, Don Alonso de Aguilar made a surprise attack on the count's son, the *mariscal* Don Diego and his brother Don Sancho, the former being imprisoned in the castle of Cañete. Don Alonso then besieged the

Córdoba *alcázar* and the Calahorra and succeeded in recapturing them, while his ally, the *alcaide de los donceles*, was despatched to secure the defences of the castle at Castro del Río, which in theory belonged to Córdoba council. The *alcaide* had estates nearby, in his town of Espejo. Once Don Alonso had regained control of Córdoba, he graciously agreed to obey the king and release the *mariscal* Don Diego, but only into the hands of two nobles with whom he had connections and in return for a promise that the king would grant him, by June 1470, the governorship of the important frontier fortress of Alcalá la Real, which was one of the Crown's defences against the Moors of Granada. Once he had regained his freedom, the *mariscal* challenged Don Alonso to single combat and, although the fight never took place, the chivalric correspondence which survives concerning the affair illustrates one aspect of the aristocratic mentality of the period.

The king's failure to restore order in the Córdoba area was largely the result of political pressures on a national scale. Don Alonso de Aguilar's virtual immunity from attack owed much to the support which he received from the marquis of Villena, Don Juan Pacheco, to whose daughters both he and the *alcaide de los donceles* were later married. The aim of the marquis of Villena seems to have been to dominate Castilian politics purely on his own behalf, but he was happy to help his future son-in-law govern Córdoba virtually as a seignorial town. King Henry in effect had no supporters in the area, as his superficial ally, the count of Cabra, now supported princess Isabella, and after she had been disinherited once more by her brother, signed, on 22 December 1470, an alliance with the duke of Medina Sidonia, who largely controlled the city and region of Seville. In 1471, Don Alonso expelled from Córdoba its bishop, Don Pedro de Solier, who was a member of the Fernández de Córdoba family but a supporter of the count. With the help of the marquis of Villena and the marquis of Cádiz, the latter the arch-rival of the duke of Medina Sidonia, Don Alonso held on to Córdoba until the early years of the following reign.

In May 1472, king Henry was in Córdoba once more, attempting vainly to make peace between the *bandos*, and in the following year the political tensions in the city became entangled with the problems of Christians newly converted from Judaism, with the result that riots erupted, both there and elsewhere in the region. The implications of these events will be discussed later, but the next major development was the capture and imprisonment by the *mariscal* Don Diego of Don

Alonso's brother, Gonzalo Fernández de Córdoba, who was later known as the 'Great Captain' for his military exploits in Italy. This less glorious episode, early in his career, took place in September 1474 and resulted in Gonzalo's incarceration in Santaella castle, where he remained until February 1476, together with his wife and some supporters. This was despite the fact that, after the death of Don Alonso's mentor, the marquis of Villena, the two sides signed a peace-treaty, in November 1474, in which they agreed that the garrison in Santaella would be reduced, that Gonzalo Fernández would be released and that Don Alonso de Aguilar would marry Doña Francisca, the daughter of the count of Cabra, as had been arranged some years before. None of the terms of this treaty was carried out and it was at this stage that Don Alonso married Doña Catalina Pacheco, hoping that her brother would secure him the king's favour.[30]

The reign of Ferdinand and Isabella

In the event, Henry died in the following month and was succeeded by his sister Isabella. However, her claim was strongly disputed by his daughter Joanna and her Portuguese allies, and while the outcome remained obscure the politics of the Córdoba area, with the *bandos* in stalemate, remained virtually frozen. This meant that when Isabella and her husband Ferdinand, having secured their position, eventually arrived in Andalusia in 1477, the balance of power in Córdoba was as it had been in 1474. The Cabra party was exiled to its lordships in the *tierra*, while Don Alonso occupied Córdoba itself and the castles of Hornachuelos, La Rambla, Santaella, Bujalance, Montoro, Villa Pedroche and Castro del Río. The Catholic Monarchs obtained the restoration to the Crown of all these castles, but like Henry IV they found it necessary to compensate the magnates for their losses. It was by no means a foregone conclusion that the new rulers would be obeyed, especially as one of the queen's tasks when she reached Córdoba was, it is said, to sue for the release of her *corregidor*, Diego de Merlo, who had been arrested in 1476 by Don Alonso, in his capacity as *alcalde mayor* of Córdoba. In order that Isabella might save face, Merlo was reinstated, although he was soon replaced. The main achievement of the royal visit, however, was the recovery, apparently by the sovereigns' will-power, of the royal castles and the expulsion from the city of the leaders of the two *bandos*. Don Alonso remained as *alcalde mayor* and the count as *alguacil mayor*, but they were both suspended and their powers were vested in the *corregidor*, who was henceforth the Crown's chief representative in the area.[31]

Before assessing the effectiveness of the settlement brought about by Ferdinand and Isabella in 1477–8, it is worth looking more closely at the composition of the *bandos* which had virtually destroyed the authority of the Crown for a number of years. The available information on the residence, marriage policy and political activity of the Cordoban nobility suggests that the unit of political conflict was not the family 'clan', or *linaje*, but the far more amorphous and complex *bando*. There were only two such groupings, the Aguilar *bando* and that which supported the house of Baena. Each was led by a magnate who was also the head of one of these two rival branches of the Fernández de Córdoba family, and the citizens of Córdoba, in the reign of Henry IV, had little choice but to join one of these groups or else keep out of politics. In practice, the latter option probably did not exist, except for the most insignificant members of Cordoban society.

The limited amount of evidence available for the composition of the two *bandos* indicates that each must have been supported by far more people than could have had feudal or marriage ties with the houses of Aguilar and Baena. It is known that the Cabra party was present in Córdoba for Henry IV's visit in 1469, during which a document of reconciliation was signed. It is also known that the *cabristas* were expelled three months later, in October, by Don Alonso de Aguilar. Lists of members of Córdoba council during the period of the expulsion survive in the Córdoba Cathedral archive. One is to be found in the excommunication of Don Alonso, together with various members of the council, by the bishop of Córdoba, Don Pedro de Solier, after the latter had been expelled from the city for supporting his cousin, the count of Cabra. This document is dated 1 July 1472. A document lifting the excommunication, issued by the bishop on 24 September 1475, contains council-lists for 21 June 1473, 6 November 1473 and 18 August 1475. If these later lists are compared with that of the signatories of the 1469 agreement, those who disappear after 1469 include members of the Aguayo, Angulo, Argote, Aranda, Bermúdez, Cabrera, Castro, Figueroa, Godoy, Heredia, Mayorga, Molina, Noguera, Ramírez, De los Ríos, Méndez de Sotomayor, Vargas, Velasco and Venegas families. Those who remained in Córdoba with Don Alonso included members of the Aguayo, Angulo, Argote, Baeza, Berrio, Cabrera, Cárcamo, Cárdenas, Castillejo, Castillo, Cea, Figueroa, Gahete, Godoy, Herrera, Hinestrosa, Hoces, Infantas, Luna, Mesa, Molina, Parias, De los Ríos,

Sosa, Méndez de Sotomayor, Tafur, Torreblanca and De la Torre families. It is obvious from these lists that a number of families were apparently involved in the conflict on both sides.[32]

It must be clear from the events between 1464 and 1474 that royal control over Córdoba and its region was no more than theoretical and that the local council and its financial and political structure had been swept aside by the rival factions of the upper nobility and their supporters. In contrast, the period between the restoration of royal authority, in 1478, and the death of Don Alonso de Aguilar, fighting Moorish rebels in the Sierra Bermeja in 1501, reveals a virtually complete absence of activity by the *bandos*. The leaders of the two sides seem to have accepted, albeit with reluctance, the suspension of their offices in Córdoba and, at least in the years for which records exist, to have taken no part in council affairs. Indeed, the surviving documents suggest that political life, in the sense in which that term had been understood in the previous reign, had ceased. Even if it is necessary to chronicle and try to explain the resurgence of seignorial power after 1500, the subsequent setbacks of royal policy should not detract from Ferdinand and Isabella's earlier achievement. Between 1478 and 1500, Córdoba and its *tierra* were governed in a manner which was probably more in accordance with royal intentions than had been the case in any previous period under Castilian rule. While it is by no means obvious that the interest of the Crown coincided with that of Córdoba's citizens, it nonetheless appears that the regular succession of *corregidores* who were sent to the city to represent the Crown after 1478 gave individuals a better chance of escaping, if they so wished, from the tyranny of the *bandos* than they had had before or were to enjoy again for many years. It was in this period that the governmental structure which was described earlier corresponded most closely to reality. It remains to be seen what tensions survived in the political society of the region and to what extent they undermined or even destroyed the work of the Catholic Monarchs.

The early sixteenth century

The return to prominence of the old leaders of the *bandos* began with the apparently irrelevant episode of the annexation by the count of Cabra of the lordship of Valenzuela. The Valenzuela family had come to Córdoba at the time of the Reconquest. The exact date of the grant of the *señorío* to the family is not known, but in the fourth generation after this the line reached an heiress. She married Martín Sánchez de

Castro and their descendants bore the name of Valenzuela. The family become closely involved with the house of Baena and in the later fifteenth century Juan Pérez de Valenzuela was household steward (*maestresala*) to the count of Cabra. However, the rival house of Aguilar was also interested in the lordship and, between them, the two great houses extinguished its independence.[33]

On 5 May 1501, Alfonso Fernández de Valenzuela, lord of Valenzuela, made an agreement with Doña Francisca de Zúñiga, countess of Cabra, to sell her the little town (*lugar*) of Valenzuela. The price was to be 30 000 *mrs* per *yugada* of land, 5000 *mrs* per citizen (*vecino*) and 150 000 *mrs* for every 1000 *mrs* of rent produced by the town.[34] However, he seems to have repented of this transaction, as on 15 June 1501, he made another agreement with Don Pedro Fernández de Córdoba, marquis of Priego and lord of Aguilar, whereby he put all his property, including the castle and town of Valenzuela, under the protection of the marquis and became his vassal, agreeing to serve the marquis with a small band of horsemen, in return for an *acostamiento* of 40 000 *mrs* per annum. Alfonso stated in this document that he had made this agreement because he was 'fatigued by the annoyance given him by the count of Cabra over the said *lugar* of Valenzuela'. As a result of the count's pressure, he had agreed to sell Valenzuela to the house of Cabra, but he now formally withdrew his approval of this agreement, replacing it by his arrangement with the marquis of Priego.[35]

This confused state of affairs was resolved as part of a much more significant event for the history of Córdoba, that is to say, a permanent peace between the two *bandos* which had fought over the area for so many years and which had been restrained only with great difficulty by Ferdinand and Isabella. Negotiations between the houses of Aguilar and Baena were conducted, on the side of Don Alonso's son the marquis of Priego, by Don Enrique Enríquez, the marquis's father-in-law and uncle of the king, who acted not merely in the interest of family peace but also with the full support of the Crown, which was anxious to secure permanent stability in the Córdoba area. Don Enrique first of all attempted to obtain the implementation of an agreement which had been made at Granada between the young count and the dowager countess of Cabra, on the one hand, and the marquis of Priego on the other. This had included the handing over of Valenzuela to the house of Baena, in return for the demolition of its castle. However, Alfonso Fernández de Valenzuela had proved unwilling to sacrifice his patrimony in the interest of peace between the two great noble houses and although, as has been mentioned, he had duly agreed to sell Valenzuela to the count of Cabra, he had since attempted to extricate himself by concluding the agreement which made him a vassal of the marquis of Priego, no doubt hoping to profit from the marquis's misgivings about the general peace. Don Enrique Enríquez, however, was determined to see the sale and demolition go through and was ordered by Ferdinand and Isabella to hold Valenzuela castle until the agreement between its lord and the countess of Cabra had been implemented. Don Enrique extracted a promise from the young count of Cabra that he would demolish the castle as soon as he had taken possession of the town and told the marquis of this promise by means of a letter from Seville, dated 22 February 1502, in which he stated baldly that the agreement would go through regardless of Alfonso Fernández de Valenzuela's views on the matter. Don Enrique also told the marquis in this letter that he had summoned Alfonso to Seville to resolve the issue, telling him this was a royal command. In addition, he wrote to Fernán Páez de Castillejo, a *veinticuatro* of Córdoba, asking him to use his good offices to persuade Alfonso to come to Seville and effect the sale of Valenzuela.[36]

Alfonso duly succumbed to the combined pressure of the Monarchs, the king's uncle and the houses of Aguilar and Baena and gave up his *señorío*. With this obstacle removed, a general peace was made between the marquis of Priego and the count of Cabra, at Seville on 3 March 1502. This fulfilled the second count of Cabra's wish that the rivalry between the two great houses of Córdoba should cease, a wish which he expressed in his will, made at Baena on 4 April 1487.[37] It was perhaps natural that the desire for peace should have been strong on the side which had generally done less well in the struggle, but in any case, at Seville in 1502, the new heads of the two houses publicly buried their predecessors' rivalries. It was agreed that a messenger should be sent to obtain from the Crown a licence for the agreement for the sale of Valenzuela to the house of Cabra to be implemented. On the same day, the marquis and the count agreed a series of articles between themselves. First, in accordance with a general royal directive to the Cordoban nobility, the two lords agreed not to acquire any property within each other's lordships, or less than a league (about 5.5 km) from the territory of the other. They also agreed not to harbour malefactors escaping from each other's lands, not to receive each other's vassals except by mutual consent, and to settle all future disputes by diplomacy and not by force.

The agreement hardly reveals a high degree of trust between the old rivals, but it was to have a drastic effect on the strength of royal authority within the area. The Valenzuela affair itself illustrates the continued influence of the upper nobility, which Ferdinand and Isabella could in reality do little to reduce.[38]

Before the reconciliation took place, the marquis of Priego had been offered by the Crown a basis on which he might in the future exercise power in the region. On 7 October 1501, as soon as his father had been killed in the Sierra Bermeja, Don Pedro Fernández was granted Don Alonso's office of *alcalde mayor* of Córdoba, as well as the title of marquis, an honour which Don Alonso himself had never gained. The new marquis was received as *alcalde mayor* by a full session of Córdoba council on 27 October 1501. After receiving the staff (*vara*) of office, Don Pedro went to his lodgings in the bishop's palace, accompanied by the *corregidor* and council.[39] This implies that at this stage the marquis continued his father's practice of not attending council-meetings and indeed his presence was not recorded at any session until 1504. In the meantime, however, the marquis and other local nobles had placed the city in their debt, both morally and financially, by supplying it with grain and then cash, during the emergency of the years after 1502. The efforts of the local nobility in this connection were to reach a peak in 1506.[40] On 18 November 1504, the marquis of Priego attended a meeting of the council, although there was a *corregidor* in the city, and this meant that he was suspended from office as his father had been since 1478. It might be thought that Don Pedro was profiting from the demise of the queen, but her death did not occur until 26 November and Córdoba council only received news of the event from Ferdinand on 4 December, when Diego López Dávalos' term as *corregidor* was extended. The city formally raised Joanna's standard as queen on 8 December, in the presence of the *corregidor*, the marquis of Priego, the count of Cabra and the *alcaide de los donceles*, all holders of *votos mayores*, thirty-three *veinticuatros* and twenty-nine *jurados*.[41]

It is impossible to tell, from the available evidence, whether the marquis acted in this way because he had heard of Isabella's ill-health and being aware, as all those concerned with national politics must have been, of the doubts about the future, hoped for a relaxation of royal control. However, leaving aside the possible prophetic powers of the marquis, there is no doubt that he began at this point to attend some council-meetings, but by no means all. He was absent for the rest of

1504, but in 1505 he appeared on 3 February, 20 February, four times in late July, twice in late August and once at the beginning of September. By early 1506, the grain shortage had caused a serious situation in Córdoba and on 18 March, the *corregidor* told the council that 600 'Swiss' soldiers (*çoyços*) were available to quell food-riots in the *tierra*. At this time, a number of *veinticuatros* left the city, presumably to protect their own property from attack, and on 10 June 1506 they were followed by the *corregidor* himself.

Thus it was that on 15 June 1506 the royal provision of *corregidores* or *pesquisidores* broke down, for the first time since Francisco de Valdés' appointment in 1478. The marquis of Priego, as *alcalde mayor*, and the count of Cabra, as *alguacil mayor*, took the *varas* of office from the *corregidor*'s officials, although the previous *alcalde mayor*, Lic. Andrés de Palacio, declared that they should not have them without a specific royal command. There was some discussion in the council about the propriety of the nobles' action, a fact which itself indicates the success of the intervening period of stable royal government in erasing the former system of seignorial control. The deputy town clerk (*escribano del concejo*), Diego Rodríguez, recorded in the *actas* that Martín Alonso de Montemayor declared himself to be in favour of the new arrangement, unless he saw a royal document which forbade it, and this view prevailed at the meeting. The former officials withdrew, leaving the marquis and count in charge. It is worth remembering that without the reconciliation between the houses of Aguilar and Baena, which had been at least partly engineered by the Crown, a united noble government of Córdoba at this stage would scarcely have been imaginable.

The period of control by the marquis and the count, the latter having appeared in council for the first time to accompany the marquis on this occasion, lasted only until Don Diego Osorio was received as *corregidor* on 19 August, but its importance lies in the fact that it in some sense broke the spell which had kept the upper nobility from direct involvement in urban politics. The arguments used to justify the takeover were set down in a memorandum which was presented to Córdoba council by Gonzalo de Hoces, the city's *procurador mayor*. They were twofold. First, the *corregidor* Dávalos had absented himself from the city secretly, without informing the council as he was required to do, and secondly, in view of his absence, the intervention of the magnates was essential to the preservation of order in the current difficult situation. Such views bear a marked resemblance to those generally held in aristocratic circles in the later years of Henry IV's reign.[42]

The argument about the danger of disorder seems to have been advanced with at least some degree of sincerity, as in March 1507, when plague threatened, a formal *requerimiento* was issued by the council to *corregidor* Osorio, that he should remain in the city and not escape like his predecessor. This suggests that, in such an emergency, strong government would be welcomed by the council, from whichever quarter it came. However, the marquis and the count were given occasion to intervene once more when, on 25 August 1507, the *corregidor*, who had left the area in April after the worst of the plague was past, failed to present himself when a document extending his term of office was read in council. The marquis seems to have intended at this stage to make a political challenge to the authority of Ferdinand as administrator of the Crown of Castile, because, in expelling Osorio's officials from the council-chamber, he stated for the record that he would only accept the *corregidor*'s extension if it was commanded by queen Joanna, 'by her letter patent, signed with her royal name, as is customary with the provision of offices of *corregimiento*'.[43] This, he must surely have known, was impossible because of her insanity, and the gesture may not have been unconnected with the news of Ferdinand's return to Valencia from Italy, which had been received by the council on 19 August. Whatever the truth of the matter, the marquis ruled the city, with Don Antonio de Córdoba as deputy for his brother the count of Cabra, until, in December 1507, Diego López Dávalos returned to the post which he had deserted in 1506, armed, ironically, with a royal provision given in Joanna's name but signed by Ferdinand. This was accepted without demur by the marquis and Don Antonio.[44]

The third episode in the progressive alienation of the marquis from the authority of the Crown is not recorded in the city's *actas capitulares*, which, perhaps significantly, do not survive for the years 1508–9. However, the events of the summer of 1508 can be fairly well established from other sources. The chronicles of Bernáldez, Santa Cruz and Alcocer give accounts of varying length, but do not differ in their statement of the basic facts. Bernáldez's account is used here, as it is contemporary, whereas Santa Cruz's chronicle was not completed until 1551–3. Alcocer's version contains nothing which is not to be found in Bernáldez, except for one small incident, mentioned below, which may well be fictitious. Bernáldez is, however, supplemented by the *Libro de los escribanos*, which is an account of contemporary events by two successive town clerks of Jerez de la Frontera, Juan and Gonzalo Román.[45]

Bernáldez states that trouble arose in Córdoba in 1508 between the supporters of the *corregidor*, Diego López Dávalos, and members of the household of the bishop, Don Juan Daza. Violent incidents occurred and were investigated by Nuño de Argote, who held the *vara* of an *alcalde mayor* for the *alcaide de los donceles*. However, the marquis of Priego, 'who followed, in friendship and favour, the party (*parcialidad*) of the bishop', broke Nuño's staff, because he had not received it in the council-chamber.[46] Ferdinand heard of this affront to the dignity of the magistracy and decided, in view of the disorder prevailing in the city, to send an *alcalde* of the royal household as *pesquisidor*, to investigate the marquis's behaviour. He formally ordered the marquis to leave Córdoba, but Don Pedro's reply was to arrest the *alcalde* and imprison him with the *alcalde* of the Hermandad, Juan Estrada. The marquis then took the royal official to Montilla castle, announcing to the public that he was obeying the king's orders by leaving Córdoba and that the *alcalde* was accompanying him voluntarily. Despite this, the marquis released the magistrate in Montilla and returned to Córdoba.

Ferdinand decided that this defiance could not be tolerated and informed Córdoba and other Andalusian towns, from Dueñas on 25 July 1508, that he was coming to the area to restore order. The royal towns were told to place their forces in readiness to assist. The king took the royal garrison of Burgos to Andalusia, this consisting of 600 *hombres de armas*, 400 *jinetes*, and 2500–3000 infantry – hand-gunmen, crossbowmen and lancers. The marquis's brother, the 'Great Captain', Gonzalo Fernández de Córdoba, attempted a reconciliation, even persuading the marquis to come to Court and ask for Ferdinand's pardon, but the king refused to see him and kept him in captivity two leagues from the Court.

The military expedition was therefore punitive in character and not aimed at restoring order. A contemporary document gives the sentences which were meted out to the marquis's supporters in this venture. He himself was condemned to perpetual banishment from Córdoba and the rest of Andalusia and was deprived of all his royal offices – the *alcaldía mayor* and *veinticuatría* of Córdoba and the governorship of Antequera – and 300 000 *mrs* of *juros* in the rents of Córdoba. His castles were all confiscated by the king and that at Montilla, in which the royal *alcalde* had been imprisoned, was demolished, despite the pleas of the Great Captain, who was born there. Thirteen men, including Alonso de Cárcamo, Bernaldino de Bocanegra, Juan de Saavedra, two lawyers called Herrera and Mexía, Juan de Luna and two members of the Valenzuela family, were sentenced to death, with the confiscation of their goods and the demolition of their houses. Others, such as the governor of Montilla, who had received the prisoner, the *jurado* of St James, Alonso Ruiz de Aguayo, who had led him out of town in chains, on a mule, and the *alcalde* of the Hermandad, who lent the marquis a horse for the occasion, were sentenced to lose limbs. The *alférez* of Córdoba, Don Diego de Córdoba, four *veinticuatros* and two *jurados* and several other members of leading Cordoban families, were sentenced to terms of imprisonment. The marquis was also condemned to pay the entire cost of the military expedition and the subsequent trials, which was estimated at twenty million *mrs.*[47]

The reasons for the revolt and for the king's savage reaction are complex. Bernáldez's view was that the marquis bore a particular grudge against Ferdinand because he had not adequately punished the Moors who killed his father, Don Alonso de Aguilar. Ferdinand had attempted to secure his loyalty by marrying him to his cousin, Doña Elvira Enríquez, whose father had been responsible for bringing the houses of Aguilar and Baena together. Nonetheless, Bernáldez argued that a concern for the family honour had led to rashness on the part of the young marquis. The earlier acts of defiance, which seemed to prepare for the 1508 revolt, could fit in with this theory, but the issues involved were probably more complex. Alcocer recounts the story that, when resting at the Venta del Puerto del Mulador, on the way to Andalusia, Ferdinand began to feel misgivings about the expedition, fearing that the marquis might humiliate him. However, a courtier, Hernando de Vega, heard what was in the king's mind and said to him, 'My lord, to Córdoba, or to Aragon!' Whether this episode actually took place or not, there is no doubt that many Andalusian magnates, including the marquis of Priego and the count of Cabra, were anxious that Ferdinand should not govern Castile. After Philip I's death in 1506, many of them had signed a document of confederation which on the surface was intended to keep order in the region, but which was in fact directed against Ferdinand. It was not only in Córdoba that the king faced seignorial defiance in 1508.[48]

Recently, Bartolomé Yun has forcefully asserted that the *bando* politics of Córdoba in these years cannot be properly understood without an awareness of the role of the *alcaide de los donceles*. He suggests that Ferdinand had endeavoured, since 1502 or earlier, to build up the power of the *alcaide* in order to balance that of the marquis and count. However, in reality it is hard to see the *alcaide de los donceles* as the focus of opposition to the newly combined *bandos* of Aguilar and Baena, because he played so little part in the events of 1506–8. At a vital stage, in 1506, the *alcaide* left Córdoba altogether, in order to command the expedition to Mazalquivir, in North Africa, and in view of this fact and of the earlier strenuous efforts of the Catholic Monarchs to bring about the reconciliation of the houses of Aguilar and Baena, it is difficult to accept Yun's analysis. It may well be that archbishop Deza of Seville was right when he referred, in a letter, to the *alcaide de los donceles* as a faithful servant of Ferdinand, but the boundaries disputes between towns belonging to the *alcaide* and the marquis of Priego, which Yun notes in support of his view and which are more fully examined by Quintanilla, were typical of relations between the different agricultural communities of the region. It is possible that Ferdinand did realise early on that the new alliance between the Aguilar and Cabra *bandos* threatened to weaken royal control of the area, and it is also possible that the *alcaide de los donceles* for some reason resented the rapprochement between his relatives, but until the family papers of that branch of the Fernández de Córdoba, which are in the archive of the dukes of Medinaceli, have been fully investigated, it is unwise to be dogmatic on the subject.[49]

Despite the apparent strength and speed of Ferdinand's expedition in 1508, the Crown did not press home its advantage, as it had done in 1478. It is not known if the sentences summarily passed on the rebels were actually carried out. According to Alcocer, the marquis spent his banishment in Toledo, even appearing at Court at the request of Ferdinand's new queen, Germaine of Foix. This hardly suggests that he was out of favour and so it is perhaps less surprising that, on 21 August 1510, Pedro de Valles arrived in Córdoba with a royal letter restoring the marquis to his offices of *alcalde mayor* and *veinticuatro*. On 26 November 1511, the marquis made his first personal appearance at a meeting since 1508, a fact which may have been connected with the demolition of Montilla castle, which according to Alcocer was carried out at this time. The king seems to have been satisfied with symbolic retribution and a limited period of banishment as, in August 1510, ten *veinticuatros*, including the marquis's son, Don Francisco Pacheco, were restored to their offices by royal command. Six *jurados* reappeared at the same meeting.[50]

As these events suggest, the Cordoban nobility and its supporters on the city council were not seriously affected in the long run. Indeed, in some ways the nobles were allowed to improve on the position which they had attained by 1500. A growing tendency was the return of royal castles in the area to noble governors, but this time in complete legality and not by usurpation, as under Henry IV. Almodóvar castle had been in the hands of minor members of the Fernández de Córdoba family since 1478, but in 1511 Ferdinand granted it to the count of Palma. The city council's protest was overruled and the count continued to expand his influence in the area by obtaining the governorship (*tenencia*) of the royal castle of Hornachuelos. This castle was transferred in 1512, first to the 'Great Captain' and then, later in the same year, to the marquis of Priego's son, Don Francisco Pacheco. Bujalance castle was granted by the Crown to another of the Fernández de Córdoba.[51] Tension over boundaries and land-use between the citizens of Palma and those of the neighbouring royal possessions of Hornachuelos and Peñaflor, both under Córdoba's control, erupted in 1513 into an open challenge by the count of Palma to the Crown's authority. On 15 July, the council in Córdoba received a *requerimiento* from Palma, demanding action in the case of the arrest of a servant of the count of Palma by citizens of Hornachuelos. It transpired that the count's men had illegally occupied some royal land, known as the Haza del Cerro de la Cabeza. After Córdoba council had appointed a commission to defend the royal patrimony, two of its agents reported that, on 26 July, the count's men had marched into the lands of Peñaflor and put up gallows as symbols of seignorial jurisdiction. In a letter sent to Córdoba later on 27 July, the council's men reported that the count of Palma's forces for this operation consisted of a hundred cavalry and four hundred infantry. Eventually, the dispute was settled by the *audiencia* at Granada through the time-honoured procedure of sending a *pesquisidor*. The success of the Crown's legal agencies in ending the violence was to be at least as significant for the future as the continued readiness of local magnates, even after 1508, to pursue their interests by military means. In this case, the count was punished for his invasion of royal territory by the loss of the governorship of Almodóvar castle.[52]

That the balance of power in the region still strongly favoured the upper nobility was soon to be confirmed from another source. The *actas capitulares* for 1515 contain copies of three petitions to the Crown from Antón de la Mesta, on behalf of the *caballeros de premia* of Córdoba.[53] They amount to a damning indictment of the leaders of local society and suggest that whatever the *caballeros de premia* had lost in military vigour, they had in effect taken over from the *jurados* as the guardians of communal tradition. The behaviour of the *jurados*, 'who will be lords of the people', was the main burden of the second petition, but it was the first which made the most wide-ranging accusations. The *veinticuatros* and *jurados* were said to be residing in the houses of the principal *caballeros* and to be representing their interests. Because council members were *avasallados*, the citizens dared not complain, and the *caballeros de premia* were offered the rank of *hidalgo notorio*, with exemption from direct taxes, if they remained silent. The *corregidor* and his officials condoned this behaviour. The result was bad government in the city, with the council conniving at crime provided it was in its members' interest. The solution proposed by the petitioners was radical and provides an interesting parallel to the later Comunero movement. Along with other Castilian cities of the period, the people of Córdoba, on this evidence, referred to themselves as the *comunidad*. Córdoba took no part in the uprisings of 1520–2, but here the *caballeros de premia* asked the Crown to allow the *comunidad* to enter the *cabildos* of the council and also to hold separate assemblies. The *comunidad* was to join with the magistrates to provide for the government of the city. Some of the present council members might take part in these meetings, apparently as individuals. The third petition urged that the Crown should give more support to the activities of its judges of boundaries in the area.

The fact that the council kept a copy of these petitions may suggest the sublime self-confidence of Córdoba's rulers in 1515. In any case, nothing came of the protests and the nobility continued to dominate the area. The *bandos* had ended, but this only strengthened seignorial power.

6

Religion and society

Religious life is in some ways the most complex and the most delicate area which the historian ever has to tackle. Nevertheless, such an effort must be made, if it is ever to be possible to establish whether the term 'Christian Córdoba' was any more than a means of chronological definition. This, however, is not the full extent of the problem. Córdoba and its region were obviously included in the society of three religions which existed in Spain in the Middle Ages, so that apart from institutional and personal Christianity, the question arises of the character and role of Judaism and Islam in local life. While much of the evidence is fragmentary and much work remains to be done, it is nonetheless possible to say a great deal about some of the main features of the city's religious life and even about the attitudes and beliefs of its citizens.

CHRISTIANITY

There can be no doubt that institutional religion loomed large in Córdoba's life. The Church, understood theologically as Christ's physical presence on earth, naturally included all baptised Christians. Nonetheless, it had long been established, largely as a result of the contempt for the 'world' in its material manifestations which had become a part of Christianity almost from the start, that a life devoted to God would ideally consist of worship and prayer rather than work in the home or outside it. Thus arose the distinction between 'full-' and 'part-time' Christians, later to be described as 'clergy' and 'laity'. The value of the clergy to the rest of society was recognised in the theory of the three estates or orders, so that, just as the nobles provided military protection for their fellow-Christians, the full-time priests, monks and nuns formed the front line against the spiritual enemies of Man. That these ideas were more than abstract notions or clichés was indicated in the clearest possible way by the Church's position as a landowner and appropriator of much of the produce of lay society.

There is no possibility of establishing how many of Córdoba's citizens were in holy orders in this period. The incidental testimony of the 1502 list of grain-holdings suggests the size of the Cathedral staff, but does not detail the bishop's household. Other religious institutions are known, but many of them in little more than name. In 1502, the clergy of the Cathedral, leaving aside any who may have served the surrounding parish of St Mary, consisted of the dean, the *maestrescuela*, or chancellor, the prior, the archdeacon of Pedroche, the precentor (*chantre*), the treasurer, the apostolic protonotary, the steward (*mayordomo*) and thirty-eight major or minor canons. One was absent and four benefices were vacant. In addition, thirteen chaplains served the various chantries in the Cathedral, six in the chapel founded by the former precentor, Fernán Ruiz de Aguayo, three in the chapel of the precentor Hoces, three in the chapel of the archdeacon of Badajoz and one in the chapel of St Peter.[1] Although sizable by modern standards, this establishment would not have seemed large at the time. Seville Cathedral had eighty canons in the early sixteenth century.[2] Four chantries, in the case of Córdoba, seem few, when this type of devotion was apparently so popular in much of western Europe. The size of the staffs of secular clergy which served the fourteen parish churches of Córdoba, together with the parish of St Mary, is not known.

When Córdoba was reconquered, Ferdinand III founded four religious houses for men and his choice of orders reflected contemporary developments in the Church. The result is that there were no monastic houses on the Benedictine model in the Córdoba area and the Cluniac and Cistercian orders, which had been so active in earlier stages of the Reconquest, never established themselves to any significant extent in Andalusia. Instead, the newly settled city became a field of operation for the Augustinian canons and the more recently formed orders of friars. Ferdinand established the Dominicans in the house of St Paul, the Franciscans in St Peter 'el Real', the Trinitarians in La Trinidad and the Mercedarians in La Merced. The Augustinians were set up, later in the thirteenth century, in the house of St Augustine. The Cistercian house of the Holy Martyrs Acisclus and Victoria was founded by Father Alfonso Ruiz in 1332, while, for women, a house of Clares, dedicated to St Clare, had been established in 1264 and the convents of St Cross and St Inés were added in the fifteenth century. St Martha, a house of Jeronymite nuns, was founded in 1464 and there were other convents bearing the names of the Incarnation and 'Las Dueñas'. The late medieval movement for reform of the religious life led, in the Córdoba area, to the foundation of three Franciscan houses, St Francis 'del Monte' within the boundaries of Adamuz, in 1394, St Francis 'de la Arruzafa', in the Sierra of Córdoba, in 1414, and, in 1452, Mother of God, outside the walls of Córdoba itself, adjoining the parish of St Marina. The austere Dominican house of St Dominic 'de Scala Coeli' was founded in or around 1423, while the more splendid Jeronymite foundation of St Jerome 'de Valparaíso' began in 1408. In addition to these friaries, the Sierra of Córdoba also contained a number of sanctuaries and hermitages, especially around La Arruzafa and La Albaida.[3]

With research in its present state, it is difficult to say a great deal about the economic presence of the institutional Church in the Córdoba area. However, it is clear that in terms of jurisdictional lordships, the Church received very little after the Reconquest and by the fifteenth century had lost even this. In western Andalusia as a whole, ecclesiastical lordships had included 5.7 per cent of the land at the end of the thirteenth century, but by the early sixteenth century this had been reduced to 3.8 per cent. Córdoba Cathedral held the lordship of Lucena for a time, apparently without jurisdiction, but under the Catholic Monarchs its only possession was the castle of Toledillo, which was attached to the bishop's household. In 1497, the Crown tried to reverse the sale of the castle to the count of Palma, but apparently without success.[4] In terms of taxes and rents, on the other hand, the Church's presence was very much felt throughout the region.

It is not possible to compose anything approaching a complete list of properties held by the churches and religious houses of Córdoba, but there are strong indications of the Church's role as a landlord. The Cathedral chapter and the bishop's household, which were separate entities for this purpose, were important landlords in city and country-side. The 1502 survey refers to five arable farms (*cortijos*) and a half-share of some grain-mills in Castro del Río and one farm each in Adamuz and Bujalance, which were held by the Cathedral chapter. More comprehensive information about the possessions of the bishop's household is to be found in a document which was drawn up after the death of bishop Juan Daza in 1510. Apart from details of the tithes collected for the bishop, which have already been used for the study of agricultural production, the document also gives an account of the rents payable from the properties attached to the *mesa obispal*. In 1510, the sum of 227 702 *mrs* was paid in cash as rent, equivalent to 12.33 per cent of the household's rents for that year. The bulk of the bishop's properties were either in Córdoba itself or else in the valley of the Guadalquivir, at Adamuz, Montoro, Trassierra (in the mountains behind Córdoba), Posadas, Hornachuelos and Palma del Río. Outside the valley, the bishop held property at Fuente Obejuna, in the Sierra, and Santaella and Castro del Río in the Campiña. The bishop owned many houses, the majority of them in Córdoba itself, where the highest rents were obtained. His most valuable land was enclosed in *dehesas*, many of them on the left bank of the river opposite Córdoba. While the urban properties were generally let for the tenants' lifetime, the rural lands appear to have been rented out on one-year contracts, providing ample opportunity for rents to rise with inflation. A single document cannot, of course, indicate whether such adjustments were in fact made. Nonetheless, the available evidence is sufficient to show that the bishop was able to live as a wealthy, absentee landlord, exactly like his secular equivalents. The only property directly exploited by his officials was the fruit- and vegetable-garden alongside the bishop's palace.[5]

At least as interesting as the collection of rents by the officials of the bishop's household was the effect of the produce accumulated in kind on the provisions markets of the city. Either in the form of tithes or as rent for property, the bishop received far more grain than he or his household could possibly consume. Some of the surplus was distributed in the form of salaries for his officials, such as his personal chaplains and sacristans and the gardener who looked after his fruit and vegetables. The chaplains and sacristans seem to have received up to a third of their salary in the form of grain. Most of the bishop's grain, however, was sold, either in Córdoba itself or in the places in the *tierra* where it was collected. Surviving evidence for such sales is to be found in a book covering the period from early January to the end of May 1510.[6]

It is impossible to find similar information about the possessions of the religious houses of Córdoba, though the available fragments indicate, not surprisingly, that they, like the bishop and the Cathedral chapter, followed the secular pattern of land-holding. A study of the religious life of Córdoba's Christians in this period is, however, greatly assisted by an examination of the relationship between laymen and monastic houses, in terms of new foundations, donations and burial customs.

The growth of seignorial power in the secular world in the later Middle Ages was matched in the formation of new religious houses. Although the first friaries set up in reconquered Córdoba were the result of royal initiative, those founded afterwards were all examples of noble patronage. The hermitage of St Joseph, which later became a hospital, was founded by Doña Mayor Martínez, a member of the family of the Fernández de Córdoba, lords of Belmonte, in 1385. The convent of Las Dueñas had been set up by the Venegas of Luque in 1370. Among fifteenth-century foundations, the convent of Clares dedicated to St Cross was set up as a daughter house of St Clare itself in 1464 by Pedro de los Ríos, lord of El Morillo and *veinticuatro* of Córdoba. The nunnery of the Incarnation, whose first abbess came from Las Dueñas, was founded by the will of a precentor of the Cathedral, Antón Ruiz de Morales, who was also a member of a local noble family. The Jeronymite convent of St Martha received a bull from Paul II in 1464, having been founded by Doña Catalina López de Morales, widow of Juan Pérez de Cárdenas. Some of its first nuns were associates of the bishop, Fernando González Deza, and the *alcaide de los donceles.* The Franciscan house known as Mother of God was founded by Ruy Martínez de Pineda, a tertiary of the order. Outside Córdoba, St Francis 'del Monte' was set up by Martín Fernández de Andújar, and St Francis 'de la Arruzafa' by Fernando de Rueda. The family of the *alcaide de los donceles* was associated with Brother Vasco's foundation of St Jerome 'de Valparaíso', so that only St Dominic 'de Scala Coeli' seems to have been established by an initiative which came entirely from within the order concerned.[7]

It is significant that not only did Córdoba's nobility show continued enthusiasm for the friars and their equivalent orders of nuns in the late fifteenth century, but it also channelled quite considerable resources into charitable foundations. As elsewhere in medieval Europe, care for the sick and for the poor were often supplied by the same institutions. There were eighteen hospitals in late medieval Córdoba for which records of some kind survive and this figure is very probably not complete. Of the foundations for which the date of origin is known, the earliest is the Hospital of St Lazarus, which was set up under a privilege of Sancho IV in 1290, to help the poor and sick. Otherwise, most of the surviving information concerns fifteenth-century foundations. The Hospital of the Blood of Christ, for example, was founded in 1430 in the parish of St Andrew to care for the insane, by Luis de Luna, *veinticuatro* of Córdoba, while in 1441, Lope Gutiérrez de los Ríos, *maestrescuela* of the Cathedral, set up the Hospital of St Mary of the Orphans. In addition to caring for those mentioned in the title, it also provided a home for some of the less fortunate members of the De los Ríos family.[8]

Several hospitals were begun in Córdoba during the reign of the

Catholic Monarchs. The Hospital of St Andrew, for instance, had its statutes approved by bishop Iñigo Manrique in 1483, while the tiny, four-bed Hospital of the Holy Cross, which cared for abandoned children, came into the hands of the *cofradía* of St Nuflo in 1496. It is rare to find details of the size of these hospitals, though it is probable that they were all fairly small.[9] Two foundations of this period may, however, be described in greater detail. The first is the hospital for thirty-three poor women, which was founded by a document of 29 October 1496, in the former dwelling, in the parish of St Mary, of Doña María de Sotomayor, the daughter of Luis Méndez de Sotomayor, lord of El Carpio and Morente. The hospital was set up by her executors, her sister Doña Beatriz, who was married to Don Diego López de Haro, the current lord of El Carpio, and Fray Francisco de Sotomayor, formerly guardian of the friary of St Francis, though which house of that name is not specified. Under the terms of Doña María's will, dated 24 August 1496, the new hospital was to be administered jointly by her executors, the Cathedral chapter and the successive heirs of her *mayorazgo*. The foundation was initially endowed with three sets of houses in the parish of St Mary, adjoining the hospital itself, two olive- and wine-producing properties, one of them at Trassierra, and various tracts of arable land in the Campiña, some near Córdoba itself and some in the family's lordships of El Carpio and Morente or the adjoining territories of Córdoba council at Bujalance and the military order of Calatrava at Villafranca.[10]

Consideration of the other hospital founded in this period about which more is known inevitably raises the question of religious brotherhoods and their role in the life of the city. On 14 February 1493, Alonso de Fuentes, *provisor* and vicar-general for the bishop of Córdoba, Don Iñigo Manrique, granted a licence to the chief brother (*hermano mayor*) and members (*cofrades*) of the Brotherhood of Charity (Cofradía de la Caridad) to establish a hospital in the houses which the *cofradía* had rebuilt, in the parish of St Nicholas 'del Ajarquía', adjoining the Plaza del Potro, where mass might be celebrated and a bell-tower built, under the jurisdiction of the bishop.[11] The brotherhood in question was the most influential of the large number which existed in Córdoba at the time. Teodomiro Ramírez, though unfortunately not stating his sources, mentions about a dozen *cofradías* of medieval origin, all of them religious rather than occupational in character. It is important to note, though, that the religious and economic functions were often combined in these organisations and that, even if the guild structure was fairly weak, this is not to say that lay brotherhoods were not a vital aspect of the Christianity of the period. In view of the impossibility of producing a full study of the composition and activities of Córdoba's *cofradías* to match that which exists for Cáceres, the example of the Caridad must stand for the rest.[12]

The brotherhood appears to have undertaken a wide range of duties concerned with the marginal groups in Córdoba's society. There is little evidence concerning its own social composition, but a document of 1481 suggests that the *hermano mayor* might come from the ranks of the *caballeros de premia* or *peones*, although he was exempt, *ex officio*, from military service. An indication of the *cofradía*'s work may be found in a royal provision of 1483, in which the king instructed the local magistrates not to tamper with the alms which the brothers received for the purposes of providing burials for convicts without financial means and for outsiders who died in Córdoba, and of finding husbands for orphan girls of an honest life. In 1503, Juan Pérez, *hermano mayor de la Caridad*, who is described in the document as a merchant (*mercader*), presented to Córdoba council a royal document which instructed its treasurer, Alonso de Morales, to hand over to the steward of the brotherhood a sum of money which the Crown had granted from its income from the sale of confiscated goods, for the relief of the prisoners in the city gaol. The sum in question, which was 50 000 *mrs*, was to be paid by the brotherhood for the maintenance of the prisoners at the rate of one *real* (thirty-five *maravedís*) per day. It is not known if other *cofradías* engaged in similar activities, in addition to supporting the cult of saints and running hospitals, but this testimony suggests that the Caridad enjoyed considerable prestige both within and outside Córdoba.[13]

Much has been made, in other parts of Europe, of individual donations to Christian activity as an indication of the existence, or the lack, of religious fervour among the laity. In the case of Córdoba, it is not possible to make a complete survey of such donations, but certain examples, taken from the surviving notarial documents, may serve to illustrate the religious predilections of at least a few of the leading members of local society. The preference for the work of the friars and their female equivalents, which has already been noted in the case of new foundations, also applies to donations made in wills. Some donors supported the older churches, for example Egas Venegas gave 2000 *mrs* in his will, in 1472, to the parish church of St Peter, while Pedro de Aguayo gave some houses in St Nicholas 'del Ajarquía' to the

Cathedral in 1483. Pedro de Hoces, *jurado* of St Michael, gave a vineyard to a local convent and a few directly charitable donations were made. In 1483, Inés González de Mesa, widow of the *veinticuatro* Rodrigo de Aguayo, left money to provide shirt and shoes for four poor inhabitants of the parish of St Mary, 'for the love of God', while Egas Venegas left 2000 *mrs* to the convent of St Mary 'de las Dueñas' to pay for clothing for the poor.[14] The religious benefactions of the leaders of Cordoban society are indicated by the wills of Doña Catalina Pacheco, widow of Don Alonso de Aguilar, and Martín Alonso de Montemayor, *veinticuatro* of Córdoba.

In her codicil of 21 September 1503, which was further added to on 3 November 1503, Doña Catalina increased the donations which she had made in her will to religious and charitable activities. The main project for which Doña Catalina wished to provide funds was the hospital which was being set up in the house of the *veinticuatro* Antón Cabrera, in the parish of St Nicholas 'de la Villa'. In the codicil, a gift of 20 000 *mrs* per annum from the rents of Córdoba was increased to 60 000. Doña Catalina also asked her sons, the marquis of Priego and Don Francisco Pacheco, to buy linen from her estate for the twenty beds which she had supplied to this hospital. She asked her executors to pay for a chapel in the hospital, to supplement the 250 000 *mrs* which Antón Cabrera himself had given to the project. The 1503 codicil refers to a wide range of other religious benefactions. Doña Catalina used 50 000 *mrs* of perpetual *juros* which she held in the rents of Córdoba to endow three chaplaincies. The pope was to be petitioned to ensure that the three chaplains were Jeronymites and they were intended to serve local convents. Other gifts mentioned in the codicil include 10 000 *mrs* to the abbess of St Clare, for a female slave to serve the convent, two chalices for churches in Córdoba and Ubeda, devotional objects such as jewels and an alabaster image of Our Lady to her daughter, Doña Elvira de Herrera, a Clare in the convent of St Inés, Ecija, and other devotional objects to her other daughter, María, who was also a nun. The two daughters were also to have the pick of her library, but the titles are not given. Doña Catalina gave 15 000 *mrs* and 100 *fanegas* of wheat, together with some cloth, to the religious women (*beatas*) of El Canuelo, in Córdoba, and 15 000 *mrs* and clothing to the nuns of St Catherine of Siena, Córdoba. She also gave cash or religious objects to three other local convents.[15]

Martín Alonso de Montemayor's will is an example of a wealthy layman's attitude to Christian giving in the face of death. As usual, it concentrates initially on measures to secure the salvation of Martín's own soul and those of his relatives. He endowed a chaplaincy in the family chapel of St Peter, in the Cathedral, where he was to be buried. The money was to come from *juros* in the butcheries of Córdoba and houses in the city. Martín also paid for the saying of masses for the soul of his brother, Fernán Pérez de Montemayor. He agreed to pay 15 000 *mrs*, from his late wife's goods, to the convent of St Clare in Alcaudete, which their daughter Ana had joined before she was twelve. Martín's will does not contain the profusion of religious gifts, many of them indicating the personal interest of the donor in the establishments concerned, which is to be found in Doña Catalina's codicil. Nonetheless, some generalisations may be risked on the basis of these wills.[16]

As might be expected, all the wills contain some kind of provision for burial and the saying of masses for the souls of the testator and, generally, his close relatives. The choice of church for burial seems, on the basis of a sample of wills of leading citizens, to have fallen more or less equally between local parish churches, including the Cathedral, where the important noble families normally had vaults or private chapels, and the friaries and convents which other evidence shows to have been so fashionable.[17] Another striking feature of religious donations, on this evidence, is their small size, even in the comparatively grandiose cases of founders of hospitals. The Córdoba nobility does not seem to have wished to divert many of its financial resources to securing personal salvation. Noble wealth might be measured in hundreds of thousands, or even millions, of *maravedís*, but gifts to religious institutions normally amounted only to hundreds or, at best, a thousand or two. The only exceptions were sums given to support friaries or convents where relatives of the donor were members. Here, such gifts might be construed as parallel to the normal provision made for the children of the nobility in the secular world.

While it may be argued that the allocation of goods in wills to religious causes is a strong indication of the giver's feelings about Christianity, such material can only provide part of the answer to a question of this kind. What has been revealed so far about Christian institutions and the support which they received from Córdoba's citizens seems to be in line with what is known about other areas of Castile and of the rest of western Europe in the period. As Sánchez Herrero found, for example, in the kingdom of León, the Church provided a complex and expensive framework in which the individual Christian might express his religious faith.[18] This visible structure is obvious in the Cathedral and its staff, the bishop and his household, the fourteen parish churches, the many and various friaries, convents, shrines and hermitages, the religious confraternities and their charitable enterprises. The place of Catholic conformity in the public life of the city was shown equally clearly in the boom in fish sales in Lent and the official attendance of the city council at such functions as the Corpus Christi procession and the Lenten sermons. Such rites are certainly not to be dismissed and the social effects of religious conformity will be further considered shortly. Nonetheless no study of Christianity in Córdoba in the late Middle Ages can avoid the delicate subject of personal belief.

Often, historians have in practice accepted the medieval Church's assumption that the ideal Christian is a 'professional', or in other words a clerk in holy orders. Thus the quality of the Church tends to be judged by its clergy. In the case of Córdoba, however, it is not possible to say a great deal about the character of the clergy. Clearly, institutions such as the Cathedral would defend their rights, or believed rights, in the same way as the city council or any other secular body. The municipal *actas* would suggest that one of the most contentious issues in Córdoba was not the conquest of Granada, or even the antics of the houses of Aguilar and Baena, but whether the Cathedral clergy should pay customs duties on the wine which they imported, in theory for their own consumption, but in practice, according to the council, for resale. The problem is that it is extremely difficult to tell whether this rather uninspiring behaviour was the sum total of the capabilities of Córdoba's clergy or whether a Christian life based on less mercenary values flourished among them.

That the conduct of individual Christians fell far short of the standards set by Jesus' teaching is a proposition which would surely have been accepted by virtually everyone in the late medieval Church. The desire for reform was expressed in both institutional and individual terms, though the result was often the exclusion of persons and movements from the Church as heretical. In the case of Castile, much work has been done in recent years on the attempts which were made in the fourteenth and fifteenth centuries to raise the standards of the clergy and to encourage, or force, a return by religious communities to the primitive standards of their orders. In this tendency, the Catholic Monarchs had an important role and their efforts were channelled particularly into improving the quality of the bishops and increasing the zeal of the regular clergy.[19]

Very little is known about the nature of life in the religious communities of Córdoba in this period. The earliest evidence for the existence of the reform movement in the area is the adherence of St Francis 'del Monte' to the Franciscan Observance in 1415. In or around 1423, the friary of St Dominic 'de Scala Coeli' was founded by Blessed Alvaro of Córdoba, a local Dominican holy man who wanted the new house to return to the early simplicity of the order. Although it did not formally join the Dominican Observant Congregation until 1489, St Dominic 'de Scala Coeli' functioned as a study-house from 1434 at the latest, and its members exercised an urban apostolate from a building near the Mercedarian friary in Córdoba itself, which had been given by one of Alvaro's followers, Fray Juan de Valenzuela. Otherwise, the only evidence is negative, consisting of the efforts of the Poor Clares to resist a similar 'observance' of the Franciscan rule in their convent.[20] The role of religious communities as landlords obviously posed a threat to their vocation, but it is not generally known if this worldly interest was balanced by fervent worship and prayer.

Some of the problems of tackling reform through the standard of the clergy are illustrated by the succession of bishops who presided over the diocese of Córdoba in the late Middle Ages. When Isabella came to the throne in 1474, Don Pedro de Solier was bishop. He founded an illegitimate line of the Fernández de Córdoba family and his part in local politics, including expulsion from the city for supporting the Baena faction, has already been described. Don Pedro's death, in 1476, no doubt helped to reduce seignorial influence in local politics, but it is not clear that it did much to provide better spiritual leadership for the Córdoba Church. The succeeding appointments to the see, which for historical reasons was in the province of Toledo rather than that of Seville, were illustrative of the Crown's approach to the choice of bishops, thanks to the share which Ferdinand and Isabella obtained in papal investitures of such offices. The next seven bishops of Córdoba, who together spanned the years from 1476 to 1510, were all outsiders and all royal servants. Fray Alonso de Burgos (1476–82) was a Dominican friar, at one time the queen's confessor. Significantly, both he and the next bishop, Don Tello de Buendía (1483–4), were members of the princess Isabella's council during the last, stormy years of her brother's reign. Don Tello showed his devotion to the Crown by acting as a royal witness in the legal case concerning the Crown's repossession of the marquisate of Villena.

The next bishop, Don Iñigo Manrique, was a lawyer, like his predecessor, and it is improbable that he saw much of Córdoba during his ten years' occupation of the see (1486–96), because he presided over the *audiencia* of Valladolid and later of Ciudad Real. Don Iñigo was succeeded by two more courtiers, Don Francisco Sánchez de la Fuente (1496–8), who was a diplomat, and Don Juan Rodríguez Fonseca (1499–1505), who served the Crown with distinction, particularly in connection with the Indies. Don Juan Daza, who held the see from 1505 to 1510, had the misfortune of presiding over some very difficult years, including the revolt of the marquis of Priego in 1508, which is said to have been precipitated by some of his retainers. He was succeeded by the first locally born bishop since Solier, Martín Fernández de Angulo, whose period of office lasted six years. The careers of these prelates do not suggest that Catholic reform under Ferdinand and Isabella increased the level of pastoral care exercised by diocesans. The merits which led to the appointment of these individuals as bishop of Córdoba seem to have been more concerned with the government service than with Christian leadership. The two local men who obtained the job were members of noble families, and while there is no reason to suppose that bishop Angulo's character was as fiery and non-ecclesiastical as that of Don Pedro de Solier, a commitment by both prelates to the aspirations of the local aristocracy was more or less inevitable. In some cases, late medieval Castilian bishops brought their administrative skills to bear on pastoral problems, in the context of provincial councils and diocesan synods, but although bishop Manrique was one of those despatched by the Crown in 1487 to reform the Benedictines elsewhere in Castile, there are no surviving records of diocesan synods in Córdoba before the 1520s.[21]

If the bishops were frequently preoccupied with non-pastoral matters, what of the Cathedral clergy? The Córdoba chapter, in common with others in the Peninsula in this period, contained a number of local aristocrats, from families such as the Ponce de León, Sotomayor and Valenzuela. It also included men of humbler origin, some of whom became entangled with the Inquisition.[22] Canons, whether in the Cathedral chapter or in collegiate churches such as St Hippolytus in Córdoba, were not normally expected to undertake pastoral duties. It is, however, worth enquiring into their level of culture and in the case of the Cathedral this may be done through an investigation into the chapter library.

There is some evidence that bishops and canons used the library and also owned books themselves. In January 1508, the chapter received a legacy of books from the late canon Juan Alfonso de Astorga, including two manuscript commentaries on the Decretals, three others in print and a 1485 printed edition of sermons preached at the council of Basle by Lodovico Pontano di Roma. The most important benefaction to the Cathedral library in this period was in 1516, when bishop Angulo died, leaving his books and manuscripts to be sold in order to help pay for a monstrance made by Enrique de Arfe to display the Blessed Sacrament in procession. In the event, the papal nuncio, who had been entrusted by Angulo with carrying out the terms of his will, ordered the chapter to keep the books and find the money for the monstrance from some other source. Among the items thus added to the library was a manuscript containing thirteen of the bishop's judgements in civil and canon law cases. His printed books were also legal texts and commentaries. There is some evidence that chapter members borrowed books and manuscripts and even the notorious bishop Solier returned some in 1476. Not surprisingly, the library was strongly biased towards theological works and, even more, towards the law, but there were also a few Classical texts of authors frequently found in fifteenth-century libraries, such as Cicero, Ovid and Seneca. There was also a supply of liturgical texts for use in the Cathedral services. Between 1502 and 1505, bishop Fonseca paid for thirty-one illuminated choir-books and another thirty were added in bishop Daza's time. This production, at least, took place despite the disturbances of the years 1506–8.[23]

To what extent erudition radiated from the Cathedral is not entirely clear. The theoretical position regarding the education of the Cathedral clergy is set out in a *Statute made in favour of students*, dated 23 August 1466. The document refers to two categories of scholar, those who studied grammar, logic or philosophy in Córdoba itself and those who went away to university. The Córdoba students were required to attend the choir at the hour of Nones, before beginning their studies, and to be present at the High Mass on Sundays and major festivals. All their fees were paid by the chapter, as were the fees and expenses of those who went away to study theology or laws at Salamanca or Valladolid universities. Sigüenza and Alcalá de Henares were later added to this list. The 1466 statute required students to produce a residence certificate, called a *mora tracta*, each year. They were allowed eight years to complete their courses and their fee allowance from Córdoba was cut by half if they acquired benefices or prebends in their university town. Natives of Salamanca or Valladolid were sent to study in each other's towns, so that they would not be distracted from their work.

The grammar and logic courses in Córdoba, which had to be completed before a student went away to university, lasted four years. According to the *actas* of the Cathedral chapter, the grammar master had a bachelor's degree. According to the terms of appointment of Bach. Alfonso Rodríguez in 1498, the master received a salary from the chapter in grain and cash and in addition he might claim a florin per annum for each student he taught. He was also required to report his students' expenses to the chapter, so that they might be reimbursed. It appears that there were facilities for the study of music in the Cathedral, though there are no surviving details of a formal choir school apart from what is implied in the documents already quoted. The success or otherwise of these measures cannot be accurately assessed, but a statement in the chapter *actas* for 3 January 1464 that, 'all holders of benefices in this church, present or future, who cannot read or sing, should work in order to learn', hardly inspires confidence. In fact, the next day's chapter recorded a long list of offenders and such provisions were regularly repeated in later years. It was not uncommon for canons to be excused from choir services in order to prepare for such ordeals as preaching a sermon.[24]

If ignorance of the basic priestly skills was so prevalent even among those who had the most opportunity to study, it seems improbable that the lay Christians of Córdoba suffered from a surfeit of instruction in the faith. As the historian cannot have a window into another man's soul, it is inevitable that Christianity in the city must be judged by the public conduct of the majority of citizens who adhered to that religion. There is good reason, based on the Scriptures, for arguing that a revealed religion cannot be said to affect the world, or indeed exist, unless it shows itself in the conduct of human society. Such is the explanation for the stress which has been laid up to now on the institutional manifestations of Christianity. However, historically, Christianity was neither the first nor the last revealed monotheistic religion and it is arguable that one of the most effective criteria for judging the practice of Córdoba's Christians is their behaviour towards the adherents of the other 'religions of the Book', Islam and Judaism, who lived for so long in their midst.

ISLAM

In view of Córdoba's past as the capital of the caliphs, it may be best to consider first of all the surviving influence of Islam in the late medieval city. Although the population of Muslim Córdoba was cleared out soon

177

after the Reconquest, a certain number of Muslim artisans were soon reimported and thereafter a small community survived many vicissitudes until its final expulsion in 1502. To judge from its contribution to the special tax (*pecho*) which the Moors paid in addition to normal levies, the Córdoba community in 1293 was about half the size of that in Seville. The real number is not known, but a Cathedral document states that after the treaty concluded between Ferdinand IV of Castile and Muhammad III of Granada in 1304, some of Córdoba's Muslims emigrated to Granada, leaving behind a shortage of skilled stonemasons. Nieto speculates that the loss was more significant in quality than in quantity, but in any case the problem of depopulation in the Muslim community (*aljama*) is referred to once again in a privilege of John I, dated 2 January 1386. This time the cause is said to be excessive tax-demands, though the Crown appears to be more interested in the difficulties thus created for the municipal finances than in the plight of the Moors.[25]

Such insensitivity was to recur all too often in the succeeding century or so and it is perhaps significant that the tone for dealings between Christians and Muslims should have been set in the gloomy and defensive atmosphere of Castile in the 1380s. The royal protection which was used to justify the additional tax-demands made on the Moors did not save them from social restrictions. *Mudéjares*, as Muslims under Christian rule were known, had reduced rights at law and were, at least in theory, debarred from public office. There is little doubt, however, that as a result of the policy towards religious minorities which was defined by the Catholic Monarchs at the Cortes of Toledo in 1480, the Moorish *aljamas* of Castile began their decline into oblivion. Tax-demands were raised once more, on a series of occasions, after 1482, but even more grave a threat was the policy of separate development, interestingly known as *apartamiento*, which was revived in 1480. The Córdoba *aljama* seems to have been affected even before that date, as in a document dated 29 January 1480, which reveals a great deal about the city's Muslim community, the Crown refers to Moorish protests at their removal to another part of town. Until the *corregidor* Francisco de Valdés had tried, recently, to move them to a street in the old castle (Alcázar Viejo), in the parish of St Bartholomew, they had lived in streets near the central square, the Plaza de las Tendillas de Calatrava, in houses which they either owned or rented, where they had carried on trades such as boot- and shoe-making and ironwork, and useful occupations such as veterinary surgery, 'ever since the aforesaid city has been Christian', 'serving with them well and famously the welfare of the aforesaid city and the pleasure and honour of its citizens'.

The Córdoba Muslims' reward for this loyal service was to be evicted from their traditional quarter and the move seems to have been disastrous. In the Alcázar Viejo, their health deteriorated and thirty out of the thirty-five married Moors died as a result. Apparently cut off from their former means of economic support, the rest were soon suffering from malnutrition. They also lost their Mosque. Strenuous complaints by the Muslim community to its official protector, the Crown, produced an instruction to the *pesquisidor* in Córdoba, Diego de Proaño, to investigate the situation and if possible find a remedy. In response to Proaño's report, the Monarchs ordered that a new Moorish quarter (*morería*) should be found, but insisted that the Muslims should continue to be separated from the rest of the community.[26] In this unhappy state they seem to have continued until their forced conversion or expulsion in 1502. The Crown asked its *corregidor* to report on the Moors' goods and the *apartamiento* question in 1488 and 1490, while in 1495, Córdoba council sent *jurado* Pedro de Pedrosa to Court to discuss the taxation of the Muslim community. The last reference to this group in local records is a petition from converted Muslims to the council in which they successfully asked that they should not have to pay their last, thrice-yearly instalment of the special *pecho* on the Moors, because they had become Christians.[27]

This evidence from 1502, that some at least of Córdoba's Muslims preferred conversion to expulsion, raises wider questions about the contemporary relationship between Christianity and Islam. Ladero has observed that although Castilian legislation traditionally offered incentives to Muslims to change their religion, there is little sign of this offer being taken up until 1501.[28] Up to then, Muslim communities, such as that of Córdoba, had kept their identity, often against heavy odds. Once the pressure to convert or leave became overwhelming, these small groups of humble artisans in Castile quietly vanished from the scene without ever causing problems of the kind which disturbed the Crown of Aragon.

The weakness of Córdoba's Muslim community in the late Middle Ages and the ease with which it was eventually suppressed contrast with the strongly Islamic character of the city's physical appearance and artistic life. Reference has already been made to the survival of the complex street plan and market-sites of Muslim Córdoba, but even more interesting than the urban environment is the attitude of Christian citizens towards it. Recent work has suggested that the relationship between the two sides in the Reconquest was far more complex than had previously been thought. The society of the frontier thus became unique in Europe. Moors and Christians adopted the same military technique and they also evolved elaborate structures for dealing efficiently with problems such as the exchange of prisoners, theft and kidnapping. It was normally the responsibility of the local authorities to deal with such matters. As an important military base and frequent home of the Court during the Granada campaign, Córdoba was inevitably affected by the results of violent contact with the Moors, although it was no longer close to the frontier. It might be thought that the war effort and the exploits in the field of the local aristocracy would have raised tensions between the Christian majority and the Muslim minority within the city. In fact, though, the available evidence suggests that the state of war against the Moors coexisted with a continued admiration for Islamic culture. Angus MacKay has studied this phenomenon in the context of ballad poetry, but there is further evidence in the earliest known description of the city of Córdoba. This anonymous Latin piece, attributed to one 'Jerónimo' and found in Salamanca Cathedral library, diverges from the conventional form of medieval descriptions of cities in one particular and significant respect, that is, in its eulogy of the Cathedral of St Mary.[29] The former Mosque is said to surpass the seven wonders of the Ancient World and its twelve doors, its arcades and its minaret are admired apparently without regard for the fact that they were products of Islamic art and religion. The former minaret, no longer extant, is illustrated in a Cathedral choir-book of 1502.[30]

It would be wrong to assume from the survival of the Mosque that Córdoba under Christian rule lived in continued subordination to Islamic cultural values. Nieto has argued forcefully that the artistic achievement of late fifteenth-century Córdoba was fully integrated with the Hispano-Flemish cultural idiom which was typical of most of Spain at the time. Jerónimo's text was apparently written in the first half of the century and by that time there were many books illuminated in the Gothic style in the Cathedral library. International Gothic was affecting some detailed additions to the Mosque itself by the time of bishop Fernando González Deza (1398–1424). The first major modification to the building, however, was the construction of a new choir in the Gothic style, begun under bishop Manrique (1486–96). While insignificant in comparison with the drastic alterations carried out in the sixteenth century, this project is indicative of the artistic tastes of Christian Cordobans in the time of Ferdinand and Isabella. The illuminations in the early sixteenth-century Cathedral choir-books and the works of contemporary painters such as Bartolomé Bermejo, Pedro de Córdoba and Alfonso de Aguilar (not the magnate!), were typical products of the Hispano-Flemish style.[31] The Hospital of Saint Sebastian, opposite the Cathedral, remains a fine example of the Isabelline architectural school, more splendid than the almost contemporary Hospital of Charity, at the end of the Plaza del Potro.

Tolerance, or even admiration, of Islamic art had, therefore, its limitations. Whether or not it is true that Córdoba's attachment to its Islamic past diminished in the latter part of the fifteenth century, in favour of the Hispano-Flemish Gothic, it appears in any case that the city's Christian majority managed to separate completely in its mind the culture which produced the Great Mosque and the worthy Muslim artisans who, in the Catholic Monarchs' reign, still made and repaired its boots and shoes and healed its sick animals. Nonetheless, however much the physical survival of a Muslim community in the city may have strained the powers of assimilation of the Christians, the problems caused by the Muslims were as nothing in comparison with those posed by the past or current adherents of the oldest 'religion of the Book'.

JEWS AND CHRISTIANS

There had probably been no time, at least since the eighth-century Muslim conquest, when Córdoba did not boast an important Jewish community. The golden age of coexistence (*convivencia*), which had so much benefited believers in all three religions, seems not to have ended, as far as the Jews were concerned, with the conquest of the city by Ferdinand III. In the mid-thirteenth century, the Cathedral chapter protested at the construction by Córdoba's Jews of a synagogue which it regarded as excessively ostentatious and a danger to the Christian faithful. Pope Innocent IV, in a bull dated 13 April 1250, ordered the bishop to investigate. No doubt there were other medieval synagogues in Córdoba, but the one which survives, in the traditional Jewish quarter to the north-west of the Mosque and the bishop's palace, probably dates from the beginning of the fourteenth century.[32] The size of the Jewish community in this period is not known, but there is no doubt that it suffered a crippling blow in 1391, when riots, which had been fomented in Seville, in part by the preaching of the archdeacon of Ecija, Ferrand Martínez, spread to Córdoba. Here, the main motive seems to have been robbery, but the result was many forced conversions to Christianity, as well as some killings.[33] The Crown was much displeased by the attacks and Henry III immediately forbade any further violence against the Jews. As a result of his visit to Córdoba in 1395, the king ordered the royal lodging-master (*aposentador*), Pedro Rodríguez de Fonseca, to compile a full report of events, but no resulting documents survive. Nonetheless, it is clear that the Jewish community never recovered from the 1391 attack and many recent converts to Christianity are recorded in the Cathedral archive.[34]

As with the Muslims, the final destruction of Córdoba's Jewish *aljama* resulted from the policies of the Catholic Monarchs. On 16 March 1479, Ferdinand instructed the *corregidor* not to allow the Jews to leave the quarter in which the Monarchs had ordered them to be placed during their visit to the city in 1478. The *apartamiento* policy did not last long, however, as in 1483, in response to pressure from the newly established Inquisition, the Crown ordered the expulsion of all unconverted Jews from the archdiocese of Seville and the diocese of Córdoba. The order was not immediately effective, as the Córdoba Jewish community was still referred to in the allocation of tax contributions for the Granada war in 1485, but thenceforth there was no further mention of Jews in the city.[35]

Although Jewry ended its connection with Córdoba before the expulsion from Castile as a whole in 1492, the Jews had long since been replaced as the main social preoccupation of Christian Castilians by Jewish converts to Christianity, the *conversos*. After 1391, Jewish communities faithful to the old religion were to be found mainly in small towns or in the countryside, while those in cities such as Córdoba either moved or converted.[36] By the mid-fifteenth century, these converts had begun to be as much disliked as their Jewish ancestors by the rest of the community. In 1449, during a rebellion in Toledo against John II, led by Pedro Sarmiento, the council of that city passed a *Sentence-Statute*, which debarred all New Christians and their descendants from holding public office in the city for evermore, on the grounds that *conversos* 'of Jewish descent', were 'suspicious in the faith of Our Lord and Saviour Jesus Christ'.[37] Although this first 'purity of blood' statute was strongly opposed by the papacy and by Castilian *converso* writers, the notion of *limpieza de sangre* slowly seeped into contemporary society. In Córdoba, the precentor Fernán Ruiz de Aguayo excluded *conversos* from serving the altar in the chantry which he founded in the Cathedral in 1466.[38]

The most significant outbreak of anti-*converso* feeling in Córdoba in this period was, however, the riot of 1473. A number of chronicles may be used to establish the main events. In March of that year, the *cofradía* of Charity was holding a street procession. As it passed through the market-square known as the Rastro, a girl spilt what has been described as water (though other interpretations have been suggested) from a balcony on to a statue of Our Lady. The house concerned belonged to a *converso*. Fighting broke out in the street and a blacksmith called Alonso Rodríguez quickly took the lead. Other *converso* houses were attacked as well and the authorities were forced to act. Don Alonso de Aguilar, who effectively controlled Córdoba at the time, attempted to intervene, but he found it impossible to restrain the rioters and withdrew to his headquarters in the Alcázar for three days, emerging when it was all over to decree that no New Christian should ever again hold public office in the city. Many *conversos* fled during the attacks, some to Seville and later, when similar trouble broke out there, to Gibraltar. Others went to North Africa.[39]

On the face of it, the riots were religious in origin, the pretext being the insult offered to the Mother of God and hence to the Christian faith by the dropping of water on the statue. The procession took place in Lent, when Christian religious fervour was at a particularly high level, and was organised by the most influential of Córdoba's confraternities. Contemporary writers, however, suggested other interpretations. The *converso* chronicler Valera described the Brotherhood of Charity as a 'conspiracy in the city, under the colour of devotion'. He refers to a split among the lesser nobility which formed the municipal government, some of the nobles supporting the *conversos* and others, notably Pedro de Aguayo, joining in enthusiastically with the rioters. Modern work has tended to support Valera's view that robbery was a major motive for the 1473 riots. Documents in the Cathedral archive show that the *conversos'* houses burnt down in the attack were mainly in commercial districts, such as the fish-market, the meat-market, the fair-quarter (Calle de la Feria and surrounding streets) and the Plaza de las Tendillas. The Cathedral chapter afterwards referred to the riots as 'the robbery of the *conversos* which was carried out in the city'. It is, however, clear that the riots were also connected with the *bando* conflicts of the years 1464–74. All contemporary writers agree that the *conversos* had attached themselves to Don Alonso de Aguilar, and the chronicler Palencia claims that they financed 300 knights for him. Some *converso*s had, through upper noble support, obtained various council posts, though lack of evidence makes it impossible to provide names. Palencia states that *converso*s illegally purchased offices in Córdoba, but this was probably not in fact necessary, as it was not difficult for a magnate such as Don Alonso to secure their appointment by the Crown, in the normal course of events.[40] What is clear is the connection between *converso*s and the upper nobility and hence the links between anti-*converso* feeling in Córdoba and, on the one hand, seignorial faction-fighting and, on the other, lower-class resentment of wealthy *converso* financiers and traders and their upper-class protectors.

The issues raised by the 1473 riots were further highlighted after the introduction of the Inquisition to Córdoba in 1482. This measure followed Ferdinand and Isabella's visit to Andalusia in 1477–8 and appears to have been part of their policy of restoring order in the region. There was a widespread conviction that many of those who benefited from noble protection were not really converted to Christianity at all, but were continuing their Jewish practices without suffering the social disabilities which went with public loyalty to the Jewish faith. The Inquisition was thus intended not only to enforce religious purity but also to curb seignorial influence. On 4 September 1482, Córdoba Cathedral chapter gave permission to Pedro Martínez de Barrio, Bach. Alvar García de Capillas and Bach. Antón Ruiz de Morales, canons, who had been appointed to the city as inquisitors by the Crown and the pope, to be absent from choir services while carrying out their duties. Antón de Córdoba was instructed to accept the post of notary to the Inquisition, provided that he appointed a deputy to record the acts of the chapter.[41]

The impact of the Holy Office was quickly felt in Córdoba in various ways, the most obvious of which were the reconciliation and the burning of heretics. 'Reconciliation' involved the heretic's confession of guilt and readmission to the Church. Burnings normally involved those who relapsed, or returned to their heretical ways, but even reconciliation could mean death, as the inquisitors believed that they were saving their victims' souls from an eternity in hell. Only a selection of the Inquisition's convictions are recorded, as the Córdoba trial documents for this period are not extant. At least two *jurados* and two *escribanos* lost their offices for judaising between 1484 and 1486. From 1484 until 1492, ten individuals reconciled to the Church after admitting their guilt had their obligation to pay their debts postponed by the Crown because their goods had been confiscated by the Inquisition. Debts incurred before conviction were to be paid when they had acquired some more wealth. Apart from office-holders, the Holy Office's victims in this period included a tanner, a dyer, a spicer, a shoe-maker and a farmer (*labrador*).[42]

Another effect of the inquisitors' activity in the early years was the traffic in confiscated goods. From 1481, the receiver of goods for Andalusia was Lic. Fernán Yáñez de Lobón, an *alcalde* of the royal household and Court. By 1487, he had been replaced by Diego de Medina, and in 1502, Don Luis de Sotomayor, the Franciscan son of the third count of Belalcázar, was appointed by the Crown to this office.[43] The Crown often used goods confiscated in this way to reward its servants, for example the secretary Francisco de Madrid, the chief accountant Dr Juan Díaz de Alcocer and the royal chaplain Lorenzo de Valverde. Local beneficiaries from this particular kind of royal largesse included the Cathedral chapter and Don Alonso de Aguilar.[44] However, despite the fact that, to begin with at least, the upper classes in Córdoba had this reason to support the Inquisition, the long-term threat which that institution posed to the *conversos* was bound eventually to change that state of affairs.

The conflict between the noble and *converso* interests was highlighted by the career of Diego Rodríguez Lucero, a canon of Seville who became inquisitor of Córdoba in 1495. Once he took over, the rate of convictions increased and in 1503 five *escribanos* were arrested. As early as 1487, the Crown had found it necessary to order the magistrates of the seignorial town of Chillón not to obstruct the work of the inquisitors. By 1501, such tension had spread to Córdoba itself, with the result that the *alguacil mayor*, no less, attacked the Inquisition's notary, who recorded confiscated goods, while he was about his lawful business. The constable was duly dismissed and banished by the Crown, but the incident turned out to be only the beginning of the trouble between the city and the inquisitors.[45]

A leading role in the successful campaign against Lucero was played by the Cathedral chapter. The canons had been suspicious of the inquisitors from the start and when prominent Cathedral officials such as the chancellor (*maestrescuela*) began to be arrested and even burnt, it may be imagined that relations deteriorated fairly rapidly. The city council and the Cathedral chapter sank their differences and mounted a propaganda campaign, directed both at the archbishop of Seville, as Inquisitor-General, and at the Crown, which culminated in the condemnation and forced retirement of Lucero at a Catholic Congregation in Burgos in July 1508. The campaign coincided with the economic, social and political dislocation of the years 1506–8. It is important to note, however, that not all the citizens of Córdoba supported the secular and ecclesiastical authorities in their opposition to Lucero. Although in early 1507 the council and chapter seem to have organised the breaking open by a mob of the Inquisition prison in the Alcázar, after which Lucero had to escape by the back gate on a mule, there are clear statements by contemporaries that some of the lower classes were keen to see the inquisitors' work continue, because it involved the arrest of wealthy *conversos*.[46] As a servant of the marquis of Priego wrote to his master at the time, 'Your lordship knows the condition of the common people in this case, that they would like there to be many heretics, to see them arrested and burnt.'[47]

Apart from its obvious drastic effect on the *converso* community, Lucero's period as inquisitor left its mark on the city as a whole, both physically and mentally. At a council-meeting on 1 February 1514, it was agreed that Francisco de Aguayo should be told to speak to the current inquisitors about 'the account of the synagogues' (*la relación de las synogas*). The phrase is explained more fully in one of a list of petitions to the Crown, drawn up to be taken to Court by Gonzalo Cabrera. During his time in Córdoba, Lucero had ordered the demolition of two houses, one of them belonging to Juan de Córdoba, 'who was known as the mad *jurado*' (*rabio*), on the grounds that they were used as synagogues by judaising *conversos*. The Congregation of Burgos had, on royal orders, declared the accusation to be untrue and Córdoba council now petitioned the Crown to grant the sites for rebuilding as public property. If the Crown had already given them to private individuals, the new owners should similarly be required to rebuild as soon as possible, 'in order that such a memory may disappear'.[48]

Were it not for the Holocaust of the twentieth century, it might be hard to understand the fury which the presence of Jews, and in particular those who had converted to Christianity but retained some of their old habits, aroused among the Old Christian citizenry of Córdoba. In the aftermath of the 1391 attack on the city's Jewish community, so many of the remaining Jews converted that those still faithful to the old religion, like the Muslims, seem not to have attracted the odium of the Christians. The role of the Inquisition in Spanish society between its refoundation in 1478 and its final abolition in 1836 was so extensive that it is tempting to think of its introduction as inevitable. Such was far from being the case. The establishment of the

Holy Office in Andalusia was preceded by a fierce theoretical debate which appeared to have been won by those who argued that, in the words of Nicholas V's bull *Humani generis inimicus*, dated 24 September 1449,

Between those newly converted to the faith, particularly from the Israelite people, and Old Christians there should be no distinction in honours, dignities and offices, whether ecclesiastical or secular.[49]

The bull and the other texts in the debate arose out of the Toledo rebellion of 1449 and the *Sentence-Statute*. The adoption in practice of the policy of *apartamiento* for Muslims and Jews and inquisitorial investigations to establish the degree of sincerity of new converts to Christianity seems to have arisen in the first instance out of political and social pressures. It may certainly be argued that the instability of Andalusia in the latter part of Henry IV's reign was a contributory factor towards the rioting in Córdoba and other cities of the region in 1473, and Wolff, MacKay and Nieto have all attempted to explain the outbreak of anti-Jewish and later anti-*converso* feeling in this way. The argument goes that the deterioration in the circumstances of the Castilian Jews, which led up to the attacks of 1391, was caused in large measure by a social crisis of long standing. This in turn resulted from the weakness of the Christian settlement in Andalusia after the thirteenth-century Reconquest, to which were added the general European problems of the fourteenth century. Social tensions within Castile were accentuated by the Black Death, the civil war which brought the Trastamarans to the throne with French help, and other difficulties. Each group, nobles, merchants, townsmen, peasants and so on, attempted to adjust to the new circumstances and the Jews became scapegoats.

After 1391, attention shifted to the *conversos*. Just as in the fourteenth century the Jews had become the focus of general discontent, partly because some of them were successful government financiers and tax-collectors, so in the fifteenth jealousy among Old Christians was caused by the ease and rapidity with which former Jews achieved success in ecclesiastical and secular society, once a change of religion had removed the bar to their holding office. This general dislike of Old Christians for New was focused in each of the violent incidents which preceded the introduction of the Inquisition.[50]

It is nonetheless striking that, although the Jewish and Muslim minorities ultimately suffered the same fate, it was the Jews and Jewish converts to Christianity who attracted the real hatred of the Old

Christian majority. The higher social status of some Jews and *conversos* undoubtedly explains this in part, but it seems hard to avoid the conclusion that another vital factor was the theological place of Judaism in a predominantly Christian society. In the minds of medieval Christians, the Jews were not only corporately guilty of the crucifixion of Christ but, by refusing to accept Him as the Messiah, forfeited their previous role as God's chosen people. The new Israel was the Church and the surviving Jews were a guilty and blind minority which existed on the margin of Christian society, alternately the recipients of royal protection, which simply served to isolate them from their fellow-citizens, and the victims of a theology which in its practice vacillated between acceptance that Jews would remain as wanderers and exiles on Earth until Jesus' second coming and efforts to convert them to Christianity by blandishments or by force. Thus although attacks on Jews and *conversos* may largely be explained by political, social and economic circumstances, there was always the theological role of Judaism to add fury to the intolerance of the majority. In late medieval Córdoba, the Christian failure to come to terms with the origins of that faith added a special ingredient to the political and economic tensions of the region. In addition, the obsession with Judaism, in its religious and racial aspects, had a significant effect on the character of Christianity in Córdoba. The city followed the fashion of other parts of western Europe in the parallel tendencies towards charitable works and mysticism, the former represented predominantly by the brotherhoods and the latter by groups of religious women, living in small communities which were often not part of any specific order. However, there is no sign of theological radicalism either in the official reform movement, which is hardly surprising, or in more spontaneous religious manifestations. There is a little evidence of Béguines in late fourteenth-century Seville, but none, as yet, in Córdoba. Foreigners, including the sceptical Guicciardini, were not impressed by the level of devotion among Spanish Christians. The concentration on the defence of the faith against real or imaginary attack by Jews or Muslims seems to have consumed energies which might otherwise have been employed in criticism of traditional Catholic theology and hierarchy. Thus the contemporary identification of religious belief with social conformity was particularly accentuated and a gulf developed between the preoccupations of Christians in Spain and those elsewhere in Europe which was to have a dramatic effect on hopes for unity in the Reformation period.[51]

Conclusion

Both mentally and physically, the society of Córdoba and its region was becoming narrower and more restricted when Ferdinand died in 1516. In the political sphere, the apparently harsh repression of the marquis of Priego's revolt had not loosened the ever-tightening grip of the nobility on local government. Symptoms of this process were continued noble dominance of council offices, the rehabilitation in 1510 of the rebels of 1508, the continued allocation of governorships of royal castles to members of the upper nobility, despite local laws and protests, and the violence of Córdoba's disputes with the count of Palma. The *caballeros de premia*'s petitions of 1514 reflect lesser men's frustration at the Crown's active participation in the strengthening of the political power of the local aristocracy. At the highest social level, immobility was the main feature. No new families joined the ranks of the seignorial nobility as a result of gains made in the Granada war. Instead, royal grants of newly conquered lands were used to confirm the dominance of an aristocracy which had largely been created as a result either of the thirteenth-century Reconquest or of the Trastamaran accession to power in 1369. The achievement, in 1502, of permanent peace in the long-standing conflict between the houses of Aguilar and Baena brought stability to the area, but at the cost of a reversion of power from the Crown and its *corregidores* to the leading noble families.

The economy, too, showed signs of stagnation which predated the better-known difficulties of the mid-sixteenth century. Córdoba had always lived primarily from agriculture and this state of affairs continued, despite the problems of grain and meat supply in the period between 1502 and 1508. It has been argued in the case of grain, and the same may apply to meat, that the shortages were due to a refusal by producers, mainly nobles, to bring their goods to market, rather than a failure of production. There is no doubt, in any case, that the nobility gained considerable political advantage from the population's dependence upon it for the means of subsistence. The history of Córdoba's grain supply in the first decade of the sixteenth century is, however, only a symptom of more deep-seated problems. Not only did secular lords hold more than a third of the land of the kingdom of Córdoba, together with about half of the population, but they also had enormous political and economic influence in the city and its possessions. There can have been virtually no citizen of Córdoba who did not in some way feel the influence of the aristocracy in his or her personal life. The nobles had town-houses and retinues, they or their supporters filled the council and represented the city in the Cortes. The surplus production of their estates, along with the rent and tithe income of the Church, dominated the markets. Thus even if the level of seignorial violence in Córdoba was significantly reduced by Ferdinand and Isabella's policies, the economic dominance of the nobility was undiminished.

The consequences of this fact are particularly obvious in the case of Córdoba's main industry, the manufacture of cloth. It is clear that cloth-producers in the city were gradually being defeated in the early sixteenth century by the commercial exploitation of the area's wool production. The aristocracy, in its role as a producer of raw material, had no particular interest in the development of local cloth manufacture and was content to use its political and economic power to cooperate with mercantile interests in the export of wool from the region. The nobility certainly had no inhibitions about engaging in trade, but its wealth and power removed any incentive to take risks of an entrepreneurial nature.

It is less clear what effect the burden of taxation had on economic activity. Possibly, the sales-tax, or *alcabala*, acted as a brake on trade and industry, but so little is known about the relationship between tax-yield and the productivity of the economy that a statistical approach to the problem is impractical. In theory, a small agricultural producer who lived in Córdoba might be liable for rent on his house and land, the tithe of his grain, wine or oil production and an *alcabala* of up to ten per cent on any market purchases. He would be included in the tax-list by the *jurados* of his parish and would thus have to contribute a sum in cash to Cortes levies and the city's share of the expenses of the Hermandad. The prices he paid for goods would also include customs-dues, notably the *almojarifazgo*, and often extra municipal taxes, the *sisas*. It is known that there were many anomalies in the working of the tax system but their effect on the individual tax-payer cannot be accurately assessed. Nonetheless, certain facts stand out. The seignorial sector of the economy made a totally inadequate contribution to public revenues in comparison with its wealth. The burden of taxation very largely fell on those least able to bear it, in other words agricultural and urban workers who did not produce their own food and were thus dependent on the market. Major landholders not only escaped direct taxation because of social privilege, but also evaded indirect taxes through their economic self-sufficiency. There is no sign in the period of a wider distribution of land among the population. Indeed, if anything, the tendency was in the opposite direction, towards greater concentration of land-holding and the development of commercial crops, particularly wool, at the expense of those needed for subsistence.

The role of the Crown in this process was probably less conscious than has sometimes been thought. Ferdinand and Isabella tried to regulate all sectors of the economy, but their efforts were generally unsuccessful in restraining or diverting market forces. It is true that royal intervention did not encourage Castilian agriculture and cloth manufacture, but it is improbable that this was the intention. It seems more likely that the main obstacle to economic progress was the disproportionate amount of wealth and power which was concentrated in the hands of the seignorial nobility. The Crown was responsible in so far as it acquiesced in this state of affairs. As far as the cloth industry was concerned, a surfeit of control rather than a lack of official interest was probably the main factor in stifling innovation.

In contrast, royal policy appeared to be devastatingly effective in the area of relations between the Christian majority and the Jewish and Muslim minorities. It has been argued that the period saw the replacement of the former myth of coexistence in Castile by one of national unity, both political and religious. There is no doubt that relations between the three religions were particularly bad in Ferdinand and Isabella's reign and that some Christian contemporaries harked back to the last united Spanish state, the Visigothic monarchy, as an inspiration. While it does indeed appear that such notions were popular in royal circles, they do not seem to have had much effect on the ground. Christian reactions to Jews and Muslims varied from time to time, from place to place and from person to person. In general terms, though, it may be suggested that Christianity in Castile took on a particularly militant and formalistic character as a result of its long and by no means unconstructive confrontation with Islam and Judaism. It is tempting to see the growth of Christian bigotry in Ferdinand and

Isabella's reign as part of a more general narrowing of political, economic and social horizons.

The experience of Córdoba thus serves to illustrate the achievements and the limitations of the Catholic Monarchs. Political order was restored as a result of their visit to the city in 1478 and the gains thus made were consolidated by their almost annual return during the Granada war, between 1482 and 1492. It may well not be accidental that the local nobility began its return to power after 1500, when Córdoba remained unvisited by its rulers until Ferdinand arrived, breathing fire and slaughter, in 1508. It is equally clear, however, that the undoubted vigour of the Catholic Monarchs' rule was far from being exercised in the cause of a wider distribution of power and wealth. If their reign was revolutionary, it was a conservative revolution, confirming those distinctive features of Spanish society which were soon to cause such pain and misunderstanding in the country's relations with its European neighbours and with its new colonial subjects.

Glossary

All Spanish words in the text are explained when first used. The list below includes contemporary measurements, with both metric and Imperial equivalents, although only metric conversions are given in the text. The rest of the list consists of a selection of the more commonly used words.

acostamiento	feudal retaining fee, normally cash
actas	minutes of council or chapter
aduana	customs
alcabala	sales-tax
alcalde	senior magistrate
alcalde de la Real Casa y Corte	magistrate of the royal household
alférez	standard-bearer
alfoz	territory governed by a city
alguacil (*mayor*)	(chief) constable
alhóndiga	grain market
almojarifazgo	customs duty
almotacén	official in charge of weights and measures
aranzada	land-measure, primarily for non-arable land; in Córdoba, 36.7 ares (0.9 acres)
arrendador	tenant- or tax-farmer
arroba	measure of weight: 11.5 kg or 25 lbs; or capacity: 18.25 lit. or 32 pints
azumbre	liquid measure: 2 lit. or 3.5 pints
Bachiller (Bach.)	University bachelor's degree
barbechos	fallow land
caballero	knight
cabildo	chapter or council
cahiz	grain measure: 6.66 Hl or 19 bushels
cántara	liquid measure: 16 lit. or 3.5 gals.
ciudad	city or large town
concejo	council
converso	convert, generally from Judaism to Christianity
corregidor	chief royal magistrate in a town
cortijo	farmstead
dehesa	enclosed land
Doctor (Dr)	University doctor's degree
encabezamiento	method of collecting *alcabala* (see ch. 3)
escribano	notary or scribe

fanega	dry measure: 55.5 lit. or 1.6 bushels; or a measure of of land-area: in Córdoba, 61.2 ares or 1.5 acres
fiador	guarantor
fiel	subordinate municipal official
Hermandad (Santa)	Brotherhood (Holy)
hidalgo	nobleman
huerta	irrigated land
jurado	parish representative on council
labrador	tenant-farmer
Licenciado (Lic.)	University licentiate's (M.A.) degree
lugar	small centre of population
mayordomo	steward
montazgo	tax on use of pasture
monte	high ground
oficio acrecentado	office above the legal number
padrón	tax-list
partidor	allocator of lands for the Crown
pecho	direct tax
peón	foot-soldier
pesquisa	investigation
portazgo	tax on internal trade
pragmatic	royal legal provision in written form on a specific issue
regidor	member of town council
regimiento	office of *regidor*, or the *regidores* as a body
repartimiento	allocation or distribution
renunciación	resignation
ruedo	cultivated land surrounding a centre of population
señorío	lordship
servicio	direct tax
tercias reales	two-ninths of Church tithe, granted to Crown
término	boundary or territory
tierra	land or territory
tributo	royal tax
vasallo	vassal
vecino	citizen
veedor	overseer
veinticuatro	member of city council
velas	patrols
villa	town
yugada	yoke, as a land-measure; variable in area, but in the order of 32 hectares or 80 acres

Appendix 1

Tables of magistrates and public finances

Table 1. *Chief magistrates in Córdoba, 1476–1516*

1476	Diego de Merlo, member of royal council and royal *guarda mayor*	*Corregidor*
1477 (June–Sep.)	Diego de Osorio, royal *maestresala* (lit. head waiter, a courtier)	*Pesquisidor*
1477 (Sep.)	Diego de Merlo	*Corregidor*
1477 (Nov.) –1479	Francisco de Valdés, member of royal household	*Corregidor*
1480 (Jan.)	Diego de Proaño, *alcalde* of the royal household and Court	*Pesquisidor*
1480 (May)	Francisco de Valdés	*Corregidor*
1484 (Sep.) –1487	García Fernández Manrique	*Corregidor*
1488 (by July)	Francisco de Bobadilla, *maestresala*, captain of the royal guard	*Corregidor*
1490 (Feb.)	Bach. Gonzalo Sánchez de Castro, *alcalde* of the royal household and Court	*Juez de Residencia*
1494–5	Lic. Juan Fernández de Mora	*Pesquisidor*
1495 (Jan.)	Francisco de Bobadilla	*Corregidor*
1497 (Feb.)	Alfonso Enríquez	*Corregidor*
1499 (June)	Lic. Alvaro de San Esteban	*Pesquisidor*
1499 (Sep.)	Alfonso Enríquez	*Corregidor*
1500 (May)	Lic. Alvaro de Porras	*Pesquisidor*
1500 (Aug.)	Diego López Dávalos	*Corregidor*
1506 (June)	Don Pedro Fernández de Córdoba, marquis of Priego	*Alcalde Mayor*
1506 (Aug.)	Don Diego Osorio	*Corregidor*
1507 (Aug.)	Marquis of Priego	*Alcalde Mayor*
1507 (Dec.)	Diego López Dávalos	*Corregidor*
1508 (Oct.)	Alfonso Enríquez	*Corregidor*
1511 (June)	Fernando Duque de Estrada	*Corregidor*
1514 (June)	Lic. Diego Ruiz de Briviesca	*Pesquisidor*
1515 (May)	Don Antonio de la Cueva	*Corregidor*

Note: Unless otherwise specified, each magistrate's term of office lasted until the next date mentioned in the table.

Sources: RGS 27.6.1477, 3.9.1477, 7.11.1477, 13.1.1480, 2.5.1480, 6.9.1484, 15.7.1488, 12.2.1490, 10.2.1494.
AMC Actas 2.3.1479, 19.1.1495, 11.2.1497, 19.6.1499, 30.9.1499, 30.5.1500, 22.8.1500, 15.6.1506, 19.8.1506, 25.8.1507, 17.12.1507, 13.6.1511, 12.6.1514, 9.5.1515.

Table 2. *The municipal accounts of Córdoba, 1452–3*

These accounts were produced, at the order of Juan de la Sarte, *receptor* (receiver) of evidence at the *audiencia* of Granada, for a hearing of Córdoba's case for the restoration to public control, by the count of Belalcázar, of the *dehesa* of Madroñiz. The document containing these details was read to Córdoba council on 22 December 1506 (AMC Sec. 12 Ser. 4 No. 14 fols. 342–6v and 352–7).

Accounts for Midsummer 1452 to Midsummer 1453

Income	*maravedís*
Almojarifazgo of Almodóvar, with Guadarromán and Santadís (?)	800
„ „ Posadas	3652
„ „ Peñaflor	100
Derechos of Moratilla, including both rivers but not the *dehesa*	1347
Almojarifazgo of Hornachuelos	3125
„ „ Villar	not known
„ „ Belmez, Espiel, Nava de Obejo and El Allozán, occupied by master of Alcántara	not collected
Almojarifazgo of Fuente Obejuna	3225
Bread-oven in Fuente Obejuna, annual rent (another occupied by master of Alcántara)	400
Almojarifazgo of Villa Pedroche	5011
„ „ Obejo	50
„ „ Puente de Alcolea	50
„ „ Adamuz and Algallarín	3547
„ „ Pedro Abad	200
„ „ Montoro	10 824
„ „ Aldea del Río	1612
„ „ Bujalance	13 060
Bread-oven in Bujalance	60
Former bread-oven in Bujalance	5
Almojarifazgo of Castro del Río and Castro Viejo	14 500
Charcoal rent, farmed by Gómez Fernández de Santa Eufemia	10 605
Almojarifazgo of Santaella	4000
„ „ La Rambla	17 500
Bread-oven in La Rambla	800
Bread-oven in Santaella	20
Grazing in Santaella	373
Grazing of *dehesa* of La Parrilla, let to Gonzalo Carrillo, *veinticuatro*	6000
Roda of Alnatar, with both its roads	21 746
Dehesa of Los Engeneros	3648
Income from vacated lands alongside the Guadalquivir, either side of Córdoba, excluding Hornachuelos	1895
Grazing on the river below Córdoba	250
Half of the *dehesa* of Villalobillos	5333
Velas of the countryside around Córdoba	9800
„ up-river from Córdoba	2042
„ down-river from Córdoba	1600
„ of Fuente Obejuna	700
„ „ Pedroche	300

Income	maravedís
Dehesa of Moratilla	750
,, ,, Algallarín, let to *jurado* Gonzalo Ramírez	1500
Dehesas of Madroñiz, El Hinojoso and Torrecatalina. These were occupied by the master of Alcántara, but Córdoba seized them back, put in Juan Rodríguez de Baeza as *fiel*, and obtained as rent from the master's tenants	38 830
Fines paid by brokers (*corredores*) who charged more than six *maravedís* per thousand as commission	16 906
Penalties under the municipal ordinances	46 000
Rent of the water-carriers (*aguadores*)	1700
Media, or tax on linen and coarse woollen cloths (*sayales*)	100
Duty on meat for the Moorish community	1000
Poll-tax on the Moors	6000
Dye-houses of the Aduana, let to Gonzalo Díaz de Jerez and Jaime Martín, dyer	900
Houses in the Corredera, let to Juan Rodríguez, wine-skin maker (two sets of houses)	1350
Houses 'de la Red'	600
Properties let in return for *censos*:	
Haza de los Barreros, to Luis Mexía	20
Mill at Gahete, to Martín Alonso, citizen of Gahete. Said to be occupied by the master of Alcántara	10
La casilla (small house) at St Paul's fountain, to Alonso Méndez	10
Land and fishery at the Arroyo de la Cabrilla	10
Public land enclosed by Torremilano council	10
TOTAL INCOME	267 466

Expenditure	maravedís
Alfonso del Castillo, *veinticuatro*, for journey to Court	5000
Alvar Sánchez, *veinticuatro*, for taking a letter	2376
Salary of the collector (*recaudador*) Juan Rodríguez	3000
'Care of the Body of God'	1066
Salary of 3000 mrs and *castellanías* of 1000 mrs for 21 *veinticuatros*	84 000
Salaries (*quitaciones*) for Juan Martínez de Argote and Luis Méndez de Sotomayor, lord of El Carpio	6000
Quitación for Fernando Alonso, *veinticuatro*	3000
Gonzalo Sánchez, *fiel* in charge of the council-house	1000
Past *quitaciones* for Pedro de Montemayor, *veinticuatro*	11 000
Alguacil mayor in charge of the gates	3250
Two council *fieles*	5000
Luis Sánchez, lawyer	2000
Grant from the council fines to a broker	100
Torches to light the council-chamber at night	180
Alcaide Juan de Berrio of Adamuz	1000
Payment by Bartolomé de Briones, farmer of the fines under the ordinances, towards a bill of 120 000 mrs for damage to a bishop's house	35 000
Gonzalo de Córdoba, for governorship of Almodóvar	2000

Expenditure	*maravedís*
Don Pedro, lord of the house of Aguilar, for holding the castle of Hornachuelos, since returned to Córdoba council	50 000
For the men whom Don Pedro led to restore property to Córdoba in February 1453. The money thus used was that collected in rent from the *dehesas* of Madroñiz, El Hinojoso and Torrecatalina	30 000
To the council property fund	27 465
Jurado Bach. Pedro Fernández de Mesa, for taking a message to Baena	200
To the two municipal accountants (*contadores*), salary of 1000 *mrs* each	2000
Salary of their *escribano*	300
Pedro Méndez the younger, salary and *quitación* as *procurador* of the council	3000
Quitación of the *escribano del concejo*, Gonzalo Rodríguez de Baeza	2300
Juan González, municipal accountant and auditor	2000
Marshal Diego Fernández, as *alguacil mayor* and *alférez*	8000
Gómez Fernández de Santa Eufemia, from the charcoal rent	10 705

TOTAL EXPENDITURE 300 942

DEFICIT ON ACCOUNT FOR 1452–3   33 476 *mrs*

Table 3. *Taxation revenue in the diocese of Córdoba, 1429–1504*

(a) *Alcabalas*

	Income per annum	
Years of tax-farm	Value in *maravedís*	Value in florins
1429	1 952 950	44 385
1430	1 652 952	31 787
1431	1 994 046	38 347
1432–4	1 843 316	35 448
1439	2 634 208	50 657
1440–3	2 876 700	55 321
1444–5	3 326 708	63 975
1446–7	3 140 467	60 393
1448–50	2 384 000	45 846
1451–2	3 383 371	33 833
1453–4	2 908 150	29 081
1455–8	3 100 000	31 000
1459–62	3 362 579*	33 625
1463–5	4 078 500*	40 785
1468–9	4 480 000	29 866
1480	9 303 785	35 108
1481	9 298 543	35 088
1482	9 298 500	35 088
1483	7 508 000	28 332
1484	7 308 000	27 579
1485	7 308 000	27 579
1486	7 737 750	29 199
1487	7 801 500	29 439
1488	7 801 500	29 439
1489	7 803 000	29 445
1490	7 803 000	29 445
1491	8 386 546	31 647
1493	8 593 377	32 427
1494	8 611 225	32 495
1495	9 786 000	36 928
1496	10 106 590	38 138
1499	9 509 500	35 884
1501	10 286 493	38 816
1502	10 841 000	40 909

* Excluding income from *señoríos*.

Note The annual totals set out above, dated according to the different farms which were granted by the Crown, include the four *partidos*, entitled *alhóndiga, rentas mayores, rentas menores* and *término realengo*. In the years 1480–7, the rents of Fuente Obejuna were accounted separately. They have been included above in the totals for those years.

Sources Ladero, *Hacienda real*, Tables 1–3. AMC Actas 1.4.1502, 26.3.1505. AMC Sec. 18 Ser. 3 No. 9.

(b) *Tercias reales*, collected in cash

	Income per annum	
Years of tax-farm	Value in *maravedís*	Value in florins
1429	100 962	2294
1430	100 962	1941
1431	111 211	2138
1432–4	106 988	2057
1439	126 300	2428
1440–3	131 621	2531
1446–7	275 743	5302
1448–50	275 000	5288
1451–2	425 000	4250
1453–4	450 000	4500
1455–8	543 500	5435
1459–62	677 500	6775
1463–5	937 500	9375
1488	470 500	1775
1489	470 500	1775
1490	470 500	1775
1491	470 500	1775
1493	520 000	1962
1494	520 750	1965
1496	575 645	2172
1504	2 117 733	7991

Source Ladero, *Hacienda real*, Tables 1–3.

(c) *Almojarifazgo castellano*

	Income per annum	
Years of tax-farm	Value in *maravedís*	Value in florins
1428–33	271 906	6179
1440–3	441 283	8486
1444–5	882 566	16 972
1448–50	752 669	14 474
1455–8	1 266 666	12 666
1459–62	1 274 583	12 745
1463–7	1 553 466	15 534
1480–2	1 625 000	6132
1483	1 275 000	4811
1484–7	1 111 111	4192
1488–91	1 205 500	4549
1493–4	1 185 000	4471
1495–7	1 200 000	4528
1498–9	1 100 000	4150
1501–2	1 258 000	4747

Note These figures are for the city only.

Source Ladero, *Hacienda real*, pp. 129–30.

(d) *Servicio* and *montazgo* for the Crown of Castile

	Income per annum	
Years of tax-farm	Value in *maravedís*	Value in florins
1429–31	834 000	18 954
1432–3	912 237	17 543
1438–41	1 518 750	29 206
1441–4	1 616 975	31 095
1445–8	2 129 888	40 959
1449–52	2 031 250	39 062
1453–4	2 440 683	24 406
1456–61	1 300 000	13 000
1462	1 440 000	14 400
1463–7	2 062 000	20 620
1468–9	2 400 000	16 000
1480–3	4 560 000	17 207
1484–7	5 570 000	21 018
1488–91	5 400 000	20 377
1493–4	5 780 000	21 811
1495–7	6 351 000	23 966
1498	5 453 000	20 577
1499–1501	5 583 000	21 067
1502–3	5 859 000	22 109
1504	5 920 590	22 341

Note: These figures for the whole Crown of Castile illustrate the declining relative importance of this source of revenue.

Source: Ladero, *Hacienda real*, p. 164.

Appendix 2

Money and its value

The coinage of the Crown of Castile, unlike that of most of western Europe in the Middle Ages, was not based on the Carolingian currency but on that of the western Muslims. Thus the earliest known gold coins in Castile, minted in Toledo for Alfonso VIII in the late twelfth century, had the same value as the dinars which had been minted by the earlier, Almoravid dynasty. They were called *morabetinos* (from Ar. *murabiti*, 'relative to the Almoravids'), which developed into *maravedís*. Alfonso's son, Henry I, continued to mint gold *maravedís* during his short reign, but his sister Berenguela and his nephew Ferdinand III made a coin which was equivalent to the Muslim half-dinar, or *masmudina*. This was also called a *maravedí*, although its value was only three-fifths of that of the *maravedí* of Alfonso VIII. After this new, lower-value coin appeared, the Muslim dinar became known among the Castilians as the 'double' *maravedí*, or *dobla*. The Christians' version of the *dobla* survived in Castile until it was replaced by a copy of the Venetian ducat, the *ducado*, in 1497. The Muslim rulers in North Africa and Granada meanwhile continued to mint *masmudinas* up to the reign of Ferdinand and Isabella.

The ancient measure of Mecca, ordained by Muhammad for the use of the faithful and known in Castilian as the *mitcal de la ley*, continued to be the basis for measuring the metal content of the Castilian coinage in the late Middle Ages. The Castilian mark was thus smaller than that used in the rest of western Europe, so as to correspond with the *mitcal*. The *dobla* survived in this form until the reign of the Catholic Monarchs, but there were many vicissitudes in the history of Castilian coins in the intervening years, not least in the reigns of John II and Henry IV. One complication was the minting by John II of some *doblas* which were made out of the metal of coins from Muslim Málaga. These were called *doblas de la banda* and were current for many years, although they were not of such fine metal as the *doblas* of the traditional type, which in that reign were called *doblas cruzadas*, after the cross which was included in their design.

At the Cortes of Segovia in 1471, Henry IV attempted to put an end to the monetary anarchy then prevailing in his realm. He revalued the gold currency by restoring the old *dobla* to replace the *dobla de la banda*, calling it the *enrique*, *castellano* or *dobla castellana*. He also confirmed the *real* as the standard silver coin and the *blanca* and *media* (half-) *blanca* as low-value, silver alloy currency (*vellón*). The hundred or more legal mints and many illegal ones were reduced to six, in Burgos, La Coruña, Cuenca, Segovia, Seville and Toledo. The problem with so many of Henry IV's laws was that he lacked the means to enforce them, and Ferdinand and Isabella soon found it necessary to confirm the 1471 monetary ordinances. In their pragmatic, issued at Segovia on 20 February 1475, they took over Henry's coinage and fixed the values of the *doblas* and *reales* in terms of the *maravedí*, which by the fifteenth century had degenerated into a *vellón* currency. Under the 1471 ordinances, only half-*maravedís*, or *blancas*, were minted. The 1475 pragmatic fixed the *real* at thirty *maravedís*. The standard gold coin, the *dobla castellana*, was entitled the *excelente* and valued at 870 *mrs*, while the *enrique* and *castellano* continued at 435 *mrs*. The *dobla de la banda*, which was still in circulation although no longer minted, was valued at 335 *mrs*.

The ordinary people of Castile were more concerned with the low-value, *vellón* coins than with gold and silver, and petitions in the Cortes tended to concentrate on the elimination of false *blancas* and the valuation of true coins. At Toledo in 1480, the *procuradores* to the Cortes complained of a shortage of *vellón*, which was making life difficult for the poor. In one of the ordinances of Toledo, in January 1480, the *real* had been valued at thirty-one *maravedís* of three *blancas* each. As a result, the quarter-*real* was worth $24\frac{1}{4}$ *blancas*, a fact which shows the need for smaller coins. In practice, the gap was filled by the use of foreign coins, such as *tarjas* (*écus*) from Béarn, France and Brittany and *placas* from Flanders. These supplemented Henry IV's *blancas*, which were gradually being used up, as the 1475 pragmatic had not ordered the minting of any more.

The most important document of Ferdinand and Isabella's reign concerning monetary matters was the pragmatic of Medina del Campo, dated 13 June 1497. Its main feature was a change from the *excelente* to the *ducado* as the main gold coin, 'because it was found that ducat coins are more common in all Christian kingdoms and provinces'. The Venetian ducat had been imitated earlier in the century by John II of Aragon, but its general adoption in Spain dates from 1497. The minting of ducats, double-ducats and half-ducats was ordered, but in fact most of the coins produced were double-ducats. The silver coinage was unchanged, apart from its design, but on this occasion *blancas* were ordered and a new valuation of coins was established. The value of a *real* was increased to thirty-four *maravedís* and henceforth there were two *blancas* in a *maravedí* instead of three. The new gold ducat (*ducado de oro*), which was also known as the *excelente de Granada*, was valued at 375 *mrs*.

Although the 1497 coinage quickly became established and lasted until 1566 without significant alteration, the attempt in the Medina del Campo pragmatic to end the use of illegal or foreign *vellón* was unsuccessful. The intention was to call in all Castilian and foreign *blancas* then in circulation and melt them down to make the new *vellón*, but the shortage of Castilian *blancas* continued and *tarjas* and *placas* are referred to in Spain as late as 1566. During Ferdinand and Isabella's reign, the *maravedí* remained the standard money of account, although a coin of this value was no longer minted, and the *dobla de la banda* was still current, although it had in theory been replaced by Henry IV's *dobla* and the Catholic Monarchs' *ducado*. In the early sixteenth century, there was a growing tendency to reckon in *reales* or *ducados*, rather than *maravedís*, but an equivalent in terms of the latter can always be found by using the values in the 1497 pragmatic.

Where different tax-yields are compared in this work, they are given both in *maravedís* and in a gold equivalent. The coin selected for this purpose is the Aragonese florin, which was minted in the Crown of Aragon in imitation of the Florentine original. This Aragonese coin had no part in the Castilian monetary reforms of 1497, but it has the advantage over the Castilian candidates for this purpose, the *dobla de la banda* and the *ducado*, that it was in circulation throughout the period. Ladero has supplied figures for the value of the Aragonese florin in *maravedís* as follows:

| 1400 | 44, | 1430 | 52, | 1450 | 100, |
| 1465 | 150, | 1474 | 240, | 1480 onwards | 265 |

In the conversion of totals from *maravedís* to florins, the nearest recorded value for the florin has been used. As each new ordinance probably acknowledged a revaluation of the florin which had already taken place, such a practice inevitably involves some inaccuracy, but it is not possible to speculate on the value of coins in a given year, so that this risk must be run.

It is certainly arguable that precious metals are not an ideal indicator of the real value of money, because they are, in the medieval economy, poor guides to purchasing power. Most people made most of their purchases by means of Castilian or foreign, legal or illegal, *vellón* coins. This means that the prices of food and other basic commodities would give a better indication of the real value of the ordinary Castilian's money than the ever-increasing equivalent in *maravedís* of *doblas, ducados* and florins, which resulted from the bullion shortage which preceded the massive influx of precious metals from the New World.

Unfortunately there are serious difficulties in the use of commodity prices in fifteenth-century Castile. The main problem is that the available figures are irregular and unreliable. The adequate supply of grain was fundamental to the living standards of the population, but its price varied from day to day and, in times of scarcity, from hour to hour. It is possible to gain a fair impression of the prices of meat, olive oil and soap in Córdoba over the period 1493–1514, thanks to the *actas capitulares*, but this information unfortunately covers the least interesting period for prices, which followed Ferdindand and Isabella's efforts to stabilise the coinage. While the prices of these three commodities in Córdoba rose in that period by an average of forty-six per cent, such figures are no substitute for coin values, as they cover such a short period. In general, it appears that over a longer period the trend in prices was steadily upwards, but with marked reversals from time to time. It may well be that if fuller information on prices were available, the picture of the value of the *maravedí* which would emerge would not greatly differ from that obtained by the use of gold coins. This choice is not now open, however, though in the context of public and seignorial finance it is in any case more appropriate to quote values in terms of the gold currency.

Notes

1 CÓRDOBA AFTER THE RECONQUEST

1 *Primera crónica general de España que mandó componer Alfonso el Sabio*, ed. R. Menéndez Pidal (Madrid, 1955), ii, 772, as translated by Angus MacKay.

2 Emilio Cabrera Muñoz, 'Tierras realengas y tierras de señorío a fines de la Edad Media. Distribución geográfica y niveles de población', *Actas del Primer Congreco de Historia de Andalucía (1976)* (Córdoba, 1978), *Andalucía Medieval*, i, 296–7.

3 Juan Ocaña Torrejón, *Historia de la villa de Pedroche y su comarca* (Córdoba, 1962), pp. 12–16, 33–4, 36. Edrisi, *Description de l'Afrique et de l'Espagne*, ed. R. Dozy and M. J. de Goeje (repr. Leiden, 1968), pp. 263–5.

4 Manuel González Jiménez, 'Ordenanzas del concejo de Córdoba (1435)', *HID*, ii (1975), 67–97. Torremilano ordinances in AMC Sec. 13 Ser. 10 No. 5, especially fols. 7–8. Córdoba's 1478 ordinances in AMC Sec. 13 Ser. 10 No. 2 (eighteenth-century authenticated copy).

5 Pascual Madoz, *Diccionario geográfico–estadístico–histórico de España y sus posesiones de ultramar* (16 vols., Madrid, 1848–50), from which much of the information in this section is taken.

6 The original manuscript of Colón's *Itinerario* is in the Biblioteca Colombina in Seville (MS BB 148–27). It was edited by Antonio Blázquez, appearing in parts in the *Boletín de la Real Sociedad Geográfica* between 1904 and 1908, and in a three-volume edition published in Madrid in 1915. A map of land-use in Andalusia, based on Colón's findings, was published by Michel Drain and Pierre Ponsot in their article, 'Les paysages agraires de l'Andalousie occidentale au début du XVIᵉ siècle', *MCV*, ii (1966), 73–85.

7 Jerónimo, *Descriptio Cordubae*, ed. with Castilian translation by Manuel Nieto Cumplido (Córdoba, 1973), pp. 63–4.

8 Angus MacKay, *Spain in the Middle Ages; from frontier to empire* (London, 1977), p. 5.

9 Emilio Cabrera Muñoz, *El condado de Belalcázar (1444–1516). Aportación al estudio del régimen señorial en la baja Edad Media* (Córdoba, 1977), pp. 52–4.

10 Julio González, *Repartimiento de Sevilla* (2 vols., Madrid, 1951).

11 *Ibid.*, i, 42–6, 53.

12 *Ibid.*, i, 20–1, 47–51. The *Libro de las Tablas* is in ACC, MS 125, fols. 4v–7v and its contents are summarised in A. García y García, F. Cantelar Rodríguez and M. Nieto Cumplido, *Catálogo de los manuscritos e incunables de la catedral de Córdoba* (Salamanca, 1976), pp. 220–1. Part of it was published by M. Muñoz Vázquez in 'Notas sobre el repartimiento de tierras que hizo el rey don Fernando III en Córdoba y su término', *Boletín de la Real Academia de Córdoba*, no. 71 (1954), pp. 251–70.

13 Ramón Carande, *Sevilla, fortaleza y mercado. Las tierras, las gentes y la administración de la ciudad en el siglo XIV* (Seville, 1975), p. 24.

14 Manuel González Jiménez, *La repoblación de la zona de Sevilla en el siglo XIV. Estudio y documentos* (Seville, 1975), pp. 10–12, 22–5.

15 J. A. García de Cortázar, *Historia de España Alfaguara*, vol. ii: *La época medieval* (Madrid, 1973), 382.

16 Antonio Ubieto Arteta, 'Cronología del desarrollo de la Peste Negra en la península ibérica', *Cuadernos de Historia anexos a Hispania*, v (Madrid, 1975), 63. González Jiménez, *Repoblación*, pp. 31–40. N. Cabrillana, 'Villages désertés en Espagne', in *Villages désértés et histoire économique, XIᵉ–XVIIIᵉ siècle* (Paris, 1965), p. 480.

17 González Jiménez, *Repoblación*, pp. 41–2. Antonio Collantes de Terán, 'Nuevas poblaciones del siglo XV en el reino de Sevilla', *Cuadernos de Historia anexos a Hispania*, vii (Madrid, 1977), 288.

18 González Jiménez, 'Aspectos de la economía rural andaluza del siglo XV', in *Huelva en la Andalucía del siglo XV* (Huelva, 1976), p. 18. Sobrequés in J. Vicens Vives (ed.), *Historia social y económica de España y América*, ii (Barcelona, 1957), 52. Antonio Collantes de Terán, *Sevilla en la baja Edad Media. La ciudad y los hombres* (Seville, 1977), pp. 156, 163.

19 Cabrera, 'Tierras realengas', pp. 295–308.

20 Miguel Angel Ladero Quesada, 'La población de Andalucía en el siglo XV. Notas provisionales', *Anuario de Historia Económica y Social*, ii (1969), 483.

21 Cabrera, 'Tierras realengas', pp. 298–9.

22 González, *Repartimiento de Sevilla*, i, 236–93.

23 González Jiménez, 'Aspectos', p. 26, and *Repoblación*, p. 78.

24 Collantes, 'Le latifundium sévillan aux XIVᵉ et XVᵉ siècles. Ebauche d'une problématique', *MCV*, xii (1976), 101–25.

25 González Jiménez, 'Aspectos', pp. 26–31.

26 Collantes, 'Le latifundium sévillan', pp. 115–23.

27 González Jiménez, *El concejo de Carmona a fines de la Edad Media (1464–1523)* (Seville, 1973), pp. 96–7, 99–102, 123–5. A *fanega* here equals 55.5 litres.

28 *Fuero Juzgo*, bk 4 title 5 law 1, in *Los códigos españoles concordados y anotados* (12 vols., Madrid, 1847–51), i.

29 *Partidas*, 4-17 and 4-18. In accordance with convention, the edition cited here is that of the Real Academia de la Historia (3 vols., Madrid, 1807). The *Códigos españoles* reproduce in preference (vols. ii–v) the text and glosses of Gregorio López de Tovar, which were declared by Charles V in 1555 to be the sole version with legal force.

30 The best description of the different types of nobility and vassalage in late medieval Castile is that provided by Marie-Claude Gerbet in *La noblesse dans le royaume de Castille. Etude sur ses structures sociales en Estrémadure de 1454 à 1516* (Paris, 1970), pp. 105–42.

31 Montalvo 5-9-2, 3. *Partidas* 5-4-9. *Ordenamiento* of Alcalá 27-2.

32 *Partidas* 2-1, preamble and law 8.

33 Montalvo 3-16-5, 2-4-7, 2-1-3.

34 Montalvo 3-2-4. *Partidas* 3-3-5, repeated in Montalvo 3-2-14. Montalvo 3-1-1.

35 Alfonso María Guilarte, *El régimen señorial en el siglo XVI* (Madrid, 1962), pp. 117, 121, 233–7. *Partidas* 4-25-2. See also Gregorio López's gloss of *Partidas* 5-4-9 in *Códigos españoles*, iii, on Montalvo 8–17–1 and 4.

36 *Partidas* 3-4-2. Guilarte, *El régimen señorial*, p. 281.

37 Montalvo 5-9-2. Guilarte, *El régimen señorial*, p. 155.

38 Montalvo 2-11-7.

39 Guilarte, *El régimen señorial*, pp. 185–6. *Partidas* 3-29-16.

40 Miguel Angel Ortí Belmonte, 'El fuero de Córdoba y las clases sociales en la ciudad. Mudéjares y judiós en la Edad Media', *Boletín de la Real Academia de Córdoba*, yr 25 (1954), 7–94.

41 AMC Sec. 1 Ser. 2 Nos. 5 and 14.

42 AMC Sec. 1 Ser. 2 No. 3.

43 ACC Caj. S. No. 27.

44 Rafael Ramírez de Arellano, *Historia de Córdoba desde su fundación hasta la muerte de Isabel la Católica* (4 vols., Ciudad Real, 1915–17), iv, 135.

45 *Cortes de los antiguos reinos de León y Castilla* [hereafter *Cortes*] (Madrid, 1861–1903), iii. 393–401. For an account of the Sotomayor *señorío* see Cabrera, *El condado de Belalcázar*.

46 The documentation of the legal cases involving Fuente Obejuna is to be found in AMC Sec. 2 Ser. 30 and ACC Caj. O. The 1513 compromise is in AMC Sec. 2 Ser. 30 No. 15 and the 1557 sale agreement is reproduced in Guilarte, *El régimen señorial*, App. 28. Rafael Ramírez de Arellano's interpretation of the role of Córdoba council in the 1476 revolt, in 'Rebelión de Fuente Obejuna contra el comendador mayor de Calatrava', *Boletín de la Real Academia de la Historia*, xxxix (1901), 446–512, is being revised, with fuller documentation, by Emilio Cabrera and others. A preliminary report is to be found in *Actas del Primer Congreso de Historia de Andalucía (1976)*, *Andalucía Medieval*, ii, 113–22, under the title, 'La sublevación de Fuente-ovejuna contemplada en su V centenario'.

47 Ladero, 'Algunos datos para la historia económica de las órdenes militares de Santiago y Calatrava en el siglo XV', *Hispania*, xxx (1970), 655, and *Andalucía en el siglo XV. Estudios de historia política* (Madrid, 1973), pp. 37, 64–6.

48 Ladero, *Andalucía*, pp. 37, 47. RGS 1497 fols. 307 (21 Feb.) and 41 (10 Aug.).

49 The remainder of this chapter owes much to Ladero, *Andalucía*, pp. 1–56. For comparative purposes it is best to consult Gerbet, *La noblesse*, which refers mainly to the neighbouring region of Extremadura. For the Sotomayor, a fuller account may be found in Cabrera, *El condado de Belalcázar*. For the house of Aguilar, see Concepción Quintanilla Raso, *Nobleza y señoríos en el reino de Córdoba. La casa de Aguilar (siglos XIV y XV)* (Córdoba, 1979).

2 STRUCTURE OF URBAN GOVERNMENT

1 *Fuero de Usagre*, ed. Rafael de Ureña and Adolfo Bonilla (Madrid, 1907), art. 392.

2 Hipólito Sancho de Sopranis, *Historia de Jerez de la Frontera desde su incorporación a los dominios cristianos* (2 vols., Jerez, 1964–5), i, 75. Quintanilla, *Nobleza*, p. 31.

3 Rafael Ramírez de Arellano, *Historia de Córdoba*, iv, 30.

4 AMC Sec. 19 Ser. 4, libros varios, i, fol. 7v and Sec. 19 Ser. 4 Nos. 2 and 3. Cited by Fernando Mazo Romero in 'Tensiones sociales en el municipio cordobés en la primera mitad del siglo XV', *Actas del Primer Congreso de Historia de Andalucía, Andalucía Medieval*, ii, 87.

5 AMC Sec. 13 Ser. 10 No. 4, ordinances of Ferdinand, 2 September 1483, fol. 3. See also González Jiménez, 'Ordenanzas del concejo de Córdoba (1435)', *HID*, ii (1975), 204. On *alguaciles de espada*, see the pragmatic of Catholic Monarchs, Seville, 24.2.1491, in AMC Libro de ordenanzas, iv, fols. 7–12.

6 *Partidas* 3-19.

7 *Partidas* 3-27-6. AMC Sec. 13 Ser. 10 No. 4 fol. 3.

8 AMC Actas 10.5.1497, 9.2.1498, 23.5.1498.

9 AMC Actas 7.5.1498.

10 AMC Actas 13.7.1479, 22.6.1479, 27.6.1496, 13.11.1493, 2.10.1510, 13.2.1493, 12.6.1499, 13.11.1495.
11 Montalvo 2-16-3.
12 The available information is to be found in Emilio Mitre Fernández, *La extensión del régimen de corregidores en el reinado de Enrique III* (Valladolid, 1969), and Benjamín Gonzalez Alonso, *El corregidor castellano, 1348–1808* (Madrid, 1970).
13 Ladero, *Andalucía*, pp. 89–90.
14 Mitre, *La extensión*, p. 28.
15 *Cortes*, iii, 92.
16 For a list of Córdoba magistrates, see Table 1, p. 195.
17 Ladero, *Andalucía*, pp. 139–46.
18 Alfonso de Palencia, *Crónica de Enrique IV*, trans. A. Paz y Melia (5 vols., Madrid, 1904–9), iv, 401–4. RGS 27.6.1477, 15.9.1477, 7.11.1477.
19 AMC Actas 20.10.1496, 30.1.1497.
20 AMC Actas 15.6.1506, 19.8.1506, 25.8.1507, 17.12.1507. The 1508 revolt is discussed below, on pp. 158–61.
21 *Cortes*, iii, 127 (Montalvo 2-16-2).
22 See Table 1.
23 *Cortes*, iii, 272.
24 AMC Actas 13.2.1497, 28.8.1499, 19.8.1506, 26.10.1513. Montalvo 2-16-6.
25 AMC Actas 28.8.1500, 13.7.1500, 2.8.1514, 16.8.1514, 22.9.1514, 11.12.1514,
26 Hernando del Pulgar, *Crónica de los Reyes Católicos*, ed. Juan de Mata Carriazo (2 vols., Madrid, 1943), i, 141–4. *Capítulos de corregidores* (Seville, 1500) (BN R31.811), and in Diego Pérez, *Pragmáticas de los Reyes Católicos* (Medina del Campo, 1549) (BL 504.g.3), law 57, fols. 47v–52.
27 D. Pérez, *Pragmáticas*, law 61.
28 Montalvo 7-2-1.
29 Montalvo 7-2-7.
30 Ladero, *Andalucía*, pp. 86–7.
31 Sancho, *Historia de Jerez*, i, 155.
32 Montalvo 7-2-18, 7-2-2, 7-2-6, 7-2-8.
33 Montalvo 7-2-2.
34 Montalvo 7-2-13.
35 Montalvo 7-2-22.
36 For example, RGS 14.2.1477.
37 RGS 4.12.1478. See Chapter 6.
38 AMC Actas, 26.3.1479.
39 Ladero, *Andalucía*, pp. 86–7.
40 Montalvo 7-1-23.
41 AMC Sec. 19 Ser. 4 No. 64.
42 APC Of. 18 vol. 8 fols. 437–40. AMC Sec. 19 Ser. 4 Actas, i, fols. 11v–13v.
43 AMC Actas 8.2.1484, 20.2.1484, 27.2.1484.
44 RGS 19.3.1479.
45 AMC Actas 19.11.1498, 10.3.1501. AMC Sec. 2 Ser. 21 No. 4.
46 RGS 8.3.1484, 20.2.1485, 6.3.1490, (10).1492, 20.7.1494, 10.12.1494. AMC Actas 19.6.1500, 10.2.1505, 6.3.1505.
47 AMC Actas 10.6.1496.
48 RGS 3.2.1478, 21.2.1478, 10.11.1475, 9.11.1475. AMC Actas 24.5.1504, 22.8.1505, 15.3.1506, 27.7.1496.
49 AMC Sec. 2 Ser. 17 No. 2, Sec. 2 Ser. 20 No 8.

50 AMC Actas 8.6.1498.
51 AMC Actas 13.7.1479.
52 For the national organisation of the Hermandad, see Celestino López Martínez, *La Santa Hermandad de los Reyes Católicos* (Seville, 1921), and Luis Suárez Fernández, 'Evolución histórica de las hermandades castellanas', *Cuadernos de Historia de España* (Buenos Aires), xvi (1951), 5–78. See also M. Lunenfeld, *The council of the Santa Hermandad, a study of the pacification forces of Ferdinand and Isabella* (Coral Gables, Fla., 1970).
53 AMC Actas 30.3.1479, 5.1.1502, 16.5.1496, 26.4.1499.
54 See *Don Quijote*, part 1, chs. 22–3.
55 See Chapters 5 and 6.
56 Montalvo 7-1-1.
57 Rafael Fernández González, 'El castillo de Almenara', *Boletín de la Asociación Española de Amigos de Castillos*, no. 54 (1966), pp. 361–8 and AMC Libro de ordenanzas, i, fol. 258v. AMC Actas 13.8.1479, 30.3.1493.
58 AMC Actas 1479, fols. 60–1.
59 AMC Actas 15.3.1493.
60 Montalvo 7-1-2, 3, 4. AMC Actas 6.10.1503, 11.10.1503.
61 Montalvo 7-1-5.
62 AMC Actas 4.11.1496, 3.9.1512.
63 AMC Actas 1.8.1493.
64 AMC Sec. 19 Ser. 4 No. 107. AMC Actas 14.5.1498.
65 AMC Actas 17.2.1497, 2.12.1500.
66 AMC Sec. 19 Ser. 4 Actas, i, 28.9.1510, 19.7.1511, 26.7.1511. Although there is no record of fines for absence from council-meetings in Córdoba, the practice did exist in Carmona in the early sixteenth century, where *regidores* were fined one *real* for each inadequately explained absence (González Jiménez, *Ordenanzas del concejo de Carmona* (Seville, 1972), p. 7).
67 AMC Sec. 13 Ser. 10 No. 1. AMC Actas 2.9.1493, 23.12.1495, 15.1.1498, 2.6.1501.
68 Montalvo 7-2-9. RGS 9.1.1478, 10.11.1480, 10.7.1485. AMC Actas 27.7.1479, 10.11.1501, 5.11.1507, 3.4.1510, 21.10.1506, 31.8.1513.
69 AMC Sec. 13 Ser. 10 No. 6, Sec. 13 Ser. 10 No. 5 fol. 1. AMC Actas 2.1.1496, 15.1.1496, 28.4.1497, 18.2.1512. AMC Sec. 13 Ser. 10 No. 4 fol. 4.
70 AMC Actas 6.10.1497, 3.12.1498, 3.6.1495, 26.6.1495, 12.12.1505.
71 AMC Sec. 19 Ser. 4 Actas, i, 9.6.1513, 19.11.1510, 30.8.1511, 20.9.1510, 28.2.1512.
72 AMC Sec. 16 Ser. 4 No. 8.
73 AMC Actas 15.1.1498, 18.9.1500, 26.10.1513, 3.7.1500. AMC Sec. 17 Ser. 7 No. 1.
74 *Cortes*, ii, 189. Francisco Mendizábal, 'La real chancillería de Valladolid', *Revista de Archivos, Bibliotecas y Museos*, 3rd ser., xxx (1914), 62–4.
75 Mendizábal, 'La real chancillería', xxxi, 96–9 and 'En torno a la real chancillería de Valladolid', *Hidalguía*, vi (1958), 357–64. Montalvo 3-1-1, 3-2-14.
76 RGS, v, pp. xxi–xxii. RGS 30.10.1494, 25.11.1494.
77 AMC Actas 22.1.1496, 4.4.1498, 3.7.1499, 20.3.1500, 10.5.1501, 23.7.1501, 26.7.1501, 30.10.1495, 2.11.1495, 18.11.1506, 10.9.1511, 15.5.1506, 2.11.1506, 18.11.1506.
78 AMC Actas 8.7.1495, 22.1.1496, 20.6.1496, 9.9.1496, 17.9.1501.
79 AMC Actas 20.8.1499. AMC Sec. 6 Ser. 1 No. 1, Sec. 12 Ser. 4 No. 1, Sec. 12

Ser. 4 No. 3 fol. 1, Sec. 6 Ser. 1 No. 16, Sec. 12 Ser. 4 No. 14,

80 AMC Actas 3.1.1498, 10.1.1498, 28.2.1498, 28.9.1498, 28.6.1499. AMC Sec. 6 Ser. 1 No. 7.

81 AMC Actas 3.3.1497, 14.3.1502.

82 AMC Actas 27.7.1504, 16.9.1504, 20.6.1502, 23.9.1504, 17.8.1495, 6.2.1493, 15.2.1493, 9.8.1497, 13.12.1497.

3 ROYAL TAXATION AND MUNICIPAL FINANCE

1 Miguel Angel Ladero Quesada, *La hacienda real de Castilla en el siglo XV* (La Laguna, 1973).

2 Ladero, *La hacienda real*, pp. 220–1, 89.

3 *Ibid.*, pp. 199, 201.

4 *Ibid.*, pp. 152–3.

5 María del Carmen Carlé, 'Mercaderes en Castilla, 1252–1512', *Cuadernos de Historia de España* (Buenos Aires), xxi–xxii (1954), 214.

6 Ladero, *La hacienda real*, pp. 21–32.

7 *Cortes*, iii, 441–3.

8 *Cortes*, iii, 629–30.

9 Ladero, *La hacienda real*, pp. 199–211.

10 RGS 20.8.1478.

11 AMC Actas 17.7.1497, 13.9.1497, 11.8.1505. APC Of. 1 vol. 1 fols. 460–3.

12 Ladero, *La hacienda real*, p. 214. AMC Actas 18.1.1496, 13.11.1495. AMC Sec. 19 Ser. 4 Actas i, fol. 76v. AMC Actas 23.2.1502, 30.10.1495, 3.7.1500.

13 Montalvo 4-2-6.

14 AMC Actas 13.11.1495, RGS 7.11.1477.

15 AMC Actas 22.5.1479, 21.3.1496, 19.1.1501. D. Pérez, *Pragmáticas*, fol. 146. Juan Ramírez, *Pragmáticas de los Reyes Católicos* (Alcalá de Henares, 1503), no. 199(5). AMC Actas 17.9.1501, 24.5.1501, 4.9.1500, 29.5.1500, 6.2.1497, 16.7.1505.

16 Ladero, *La hacienda real*, pp. 214–17. Archivo Municipal de Jerez, Vitrina 5 fols. 1–13. AMC Actas 7.9.1495, 5.2.1496.

17 AMC Actas 9.3.1496, 12.9.1496, 18.9.1495, 21.3.1496, 15.6.1496, 16.3.1496, 29.7.1496, 5.8.1496.

18 AMC Actas 24.4.1500, 22.5.1500, 19.6.1500, 14.8.1500, 15.2.1496, 19.2.1496, 22.2.1496, 16.3.1496, 2.5.1496, 13.5.1496, 8.7.1496, 18.7.1496, 14.9.1496, 7.12.1496, 27.10.1497, 3.1.1498.

19 Values of *servicios* in Córdoba.

Córdoba	maravedís	Aragonese florins
1500	2 600 000	9811
1502	6 106 652	23 043
1504	5 988 952	22 599
1506	5 000 000	18 867

(AMC Actas 30.3.1500. RAH Colección Salazar y Castro M-98 fols. 69–71v. AMC Sec. 18 Ser. 7 No. 2)

Total *servicios* for the Crown of Castile:

	maravedís	Aragonese florins
1476	162 000 000	675 000
1502	100 000 000	377 358
1504	102 656 000	387 381

(Ladero, *La hacienda real*, p. 214. RAH Salazar M-98 fols. 69–71v.)

20 AMC Actas 16.3.1479, 29.8.1495, 1.7.1496. Ladero, *La hacienda real*, p. 216.
21 For the 1452–3 municipal revenues see Table 2. Ladero, *La hacienda real*, p. 219. AMC Actas 8.4.1496, 14.8.1500.

Totals for the *moneda forera* in the diocese of Córdoba

	maravedís	florins
1440	239 536	4606
1446	239 526	4606
1458	215 066	2150
1464	240 000	2400
1482	240 000	905
1488	255 000	962
1494	421 346	1589

(Ladero, *La hacienda real*, p. 221.)

22 Ladero, *La hacienda real*, p. 61.
23 Salvador de Moxó, *La alcabala: sobre sus orígines, concepto y naturaleza* (Madrid, 1963), pp. 15–30, 46–7.
24 Modesto Ulloa, *La hacienda real de Castilla en el reinado de Felipe II* (Rome, 1963), pp. 114–15.
25 Ladero, *La hacienda real*, pp. 65–7. Moxó, *La alcabala*, p. 39. The term *hombre bueno* could mean a townsman, or a lesser noble or ecclesiastic at Court, but already, in certain *fueros*, it applied to men who assisted the *alcaldes* in justice or administration, a meaning which appears to cover the present case. See Evelyn S. Procter, *Curia and Cortes in León and Castile, 1072–1295* (Cambridge, 1980), pp. 144–5, 161–2.
26 Ladero, *La hacienda real*, pp. 67–9.
27 APC Of. 18 vol. 6 sec. 7 fol. 6.
28 AMC Actas 4.1.1497.
29 AMC Actas 14.11.1496, 28.11.1496, 2.12.1496, 17.9.1493, 16.12.1496, 7.4.1497.
30 AMC Actas 6.5.1495, 30.12.1495, 4.1.1497, 30.5.1498, 27.11.1499.
31 Ladero, *La hacienda real*, pp. 70–1. AMC Actas 4.1.1497, 11.9.1495.
32 Ladero, *La hacienda real*, p. 71. AMC Actas 7.9.1502, 8.5.1504.
33 Ladero, *La hacienda real*, p. 70. AMC Sec. 18 Ser. 3 No. 7 (copy).
34 Agreements for the *alcabala* on hides (1491, 1498, 1500): APC Of. 14 vol. 24

sec. 3 fols. 18v–29, Of. 14 vol. 24 sec. 6 fol. 11v, Of. 14 vol. 5 sec. 19 fol. 42, Of. 18 vol. 7 fols. 81–2, 83–4, 96–102; iron *alcabala* (1486, 1491, 1500): APC Of. 18 vol. 1 fols. 432, 438, 446v, 454, 497v, Of. 14 vol. 24 sec. 9 fol. 23, Of. 18 vol. 7 fols. 184–5v, 188v, 191, 196, 205–6, 210v, 212; linen and wool *alcabala* (1500): APC Of. 18 vol. 7 fols. 136–9.

35 Sub-letting took place, for example, in 1484, 1490 and 1497: APC Of. 14 vol. 17 sec. 9 fol. 31, Of. 18 vol. 3 fol. 705v, Of. 14 vol. 31 sec. 10 fol. 14.

36 Ladero, *La hacienda real*, pp. 69–70.

37 AMC Actas 9.1.1497, 15.1.1500, 11.10.1501, 14.1.1502, 1.4.1502, 26.3.1505. AMC Sec. 18 Ser. 3 No. 9.

38 AMC Actas 27.11.1499.

39 AMC Actas 14.1.1502, 1.4.1502.

40 AGS Patronato Real leg. 3 fol. 145, quoted in Joseph Pérez, *La révolution des 'comunidades' de Castille, 1520–1521* (Bordeaux, 1970), p. 140.

41 AMC Actas 18.1.1497, 9.8.1497, 7.3.1510.

42 AMC Actas 13.1.1503, 8.3.1503.

43 Ladero, *La hacienda real*, pp. 89–92.

44 Ladero, 'Almojarifazgo sevillano y comercio exterior de Andalucía en el siglo XV', *Anuario de Historia Económica y Social*, ii (1969), 72.

45 See Table 2.

46 AMC Sec. 1 Ser. 2 No. 36, copy, 24.2.1494, of John II's privilege of exemption from *portazgo* and *almojarifazgo*; AMC Sec. 1 Ser. 2 No. 40, royal confirmation, 24.3.1491, of Córdoba's *fueros* on this subject. AMC Actas 30.12.1495.

47 The charges for the *servicio*, according to the 1438 *cuaderno*, were as follows:

> Bulls, young bulls (*novillos*), sows and calves separated from their mothers: 3 head per thousand and 18 *mrs* for *guarda* (probably towards the cost of collection).
>
> Pigs: 1 head per thousand and 1 *dinero* (1/10 *maravedí*) per head.
>
> Sheep and goats: 5 head per thousand and 3 *mrs* for *guarda*.
>
> *Ganado merchaniego*: 7 *dineros* per head for cattle, 2 *dineros* for sheep and goats.
>
> (Ladero, *La hacienda real*, pp. 152–66.)

48 AMC Sec. 1 Ser. 2 No. 11 (Sancho IV, 29.11.1288). AMC Actas 28.1.1495, 1.3.1497, 18.1.1499, 30.12.1502.

49 For *servicio* figures see note 19, pp. 210–11. For *moneda forera*, see note 21, p. 211. For *alcabalas*, *tercias*, *almojarifazgo* and *servicio* and *montazgo*, see Table 3. For the proportions of revenue provided by different taxes, see Ladero, *La hacienda real*, p. 41.

50 AMC Actas 1479, fol. 63. See also Table 2.

51 Ladero, 'Almojarifazgo', pp. 71–2.

52 AMC Sec. 1 Ser. 2 No. 34 (privilege of John II, 5.6.1451, in copy of 24.2.1494).

53 Ladero, 'Almojarifazgo', p. 72.

54 AMC Actas 1.10.1479, 12.9.1498, 13.2.1493.

55 See Appendix 2.

56 Carlé, 'Mercaderes', p. 212.

57 AMC Actas 28.9.1479, 10.7.1503, 26.5.1503, 15.9.1503.

58 González Jiménez, 'Ordenanzas', pp. 196–201.

59 AMC Actas 20.3.1503. AMC Sec. 13 Ser. 10 No. 4, fol. 5.

60 APC Of. 14 vol. 10 sec. 3 fol. 35, Of. 18 vol. 1 fol. 729v, Of. 14 vol. 30 sec. 23 fol. 17, Of. 14 vol. 31 sec. 11 fol. 30, Of. 18 vol. 8 fol. 425, Of. 1 vol. 1

fols. 34v–35. AMC Actas 22.6.1513, 11.9.1514. APC Of. 14 vol. 4 sec. 8 fol. 2v, Of. 18 vol. 1 fol. 145v, Of. 18 vol. 5 fol. 1133, Of. 25 vol. 2 fol. 99v.

61 AMC Actas 2.3.1490, 18.7.1496.

62 AMC Sec. 12 Ser. 21 No. 5. AMC Actas 11.1.1493. AMC Sec. 12 Ser. 67 No. 27. AMC Actas 13.1.1500, 1.2.1499.

63 AMC Actas 2.1.1495, 8.7.1495.

64 AMC Actas 7.5.1498.

65 AMC Sec. 12 Ser. 4 No. 14, fols. 342–6v and 352–7. AMC Sec. 14 Ser. 1 No. 3. AMC Actas 1479 fol. 63, 30.8.1501, 3.2.1505 and 8.11.1507.

66 AMC Sec. 14 Ser. 1 No. 3.

67 Montalvo 7-2-19. AMC Actas 15.5.1495, 13.7.1495.

68 AMC Actas 6.4.1479, 25.9.1510, 8.9.1512.

69 AMC Actas 4.9.1506, 4.5.1515.

70 Alfonso X, on 18 March 1254, granted Córdoba council a tax of 500 *mrs* on Moorish inhabitants, and Sancho IV, on 29 November 1288, gave the council the *montazgo* for this purpose (AMC Sec. 1 Ser. 2 Nos. 2 and 8).

71 AMC Actas 1479 fol. 63, 9.7.1497, 3.2.1505, 18.5.1506, 14.1.1499, 4.5.1498.

72 Cabrera is at present working on the lordships of the *alcaides de los donceles* in Chillón, Lucena and Espejo.

73 Emma Solano Ruiz, 'La hacienda de las casas de Medina Sidonia y Arcos en la Andalucía del siglo XV', *Archivo Hispalense*, clxviii (1972), 85–176.

74 AMC Sec. 19 Ser. 20 No. 23. Quintanilla, *Nobleza*, pp. 247, 267.

75 APC Of. 14 vol. 31 sec. 10 fols. 11–14.

76 Cabrera, 'La fortuna de una familia noble castellana, a través de un inventario de mediados del siglo XV', *HID*, ii (1975), 9–42.

77 Cabrera, 'La fortuna', pp. 19–23.

4 CÓRDOBA IN THE REGIONAL ECONOMY

1 See, for example, Jacques Heers, *Gênes au XVe siècle* (Paris, 1971), pp. 311, 321, 326, 331–3; Ruth Pike, *Enterprise and adventure: the Genoese in Seville and the opening of the New World* (Ithaca, 1966), passim; and R. S. Lopez, 'The trade of medieval Europe: the south', *Cambridge Economic History of Europe*, ii (1952), 314.

2 Ladero, 'Los cereales en la Andalucía del siglo XV', *Revista de la Universidad de Madrid*, xviii (1969), 223–4.

3 Ladero, 'Los cereales', and 'Producción y renta cerealeras en el reino de Córdoba a finales del siglo XV', *Andalucía Medieval*, i, 375–96. González Jiménez, 'Las crisis cerealistas en Carmona a fines de la Edad Media', *HID*, iii (1976), 283–307. Ladero and González Jiménez, *Diezmo eclesiástico y producción de cereales en el reino de Sevilla (1408–1503)* (Seville, 1979, 1978 on cover).

4 Volume of grain production in hectolitres

1486	332 150	1492	642 676
1487	422 452	1495	541 218
1488	593 833	1496	512 481
1489	221 674	1502	519 561
1490	430 130	1510	455 321
1491	476 119		

(Ladero, 'Producción y renta cerealeras', p. 376.)

5 *Ibid.*, pp. 376–8.
6 Quoted in Ladero, *Diezmo eclesiástico*, p. 93 and note. See also note on measurements on p. 193.
7 Ladero, 'Producción y rentas cerealeras', pp. 378–9.
8 *Ibid.*, pp. 379–96.
9 APC Of. 14 vol. 10 sec. 24 fols. 8v–9v, Of. 18 vol. 2 fols. 298, 358v–60, vol. 1 fols. 298, 309v–12, 335, vol. 3 fols. 672–4, 977, Of. 14 vol. 5 sec. 12 fols. 27v–8, vol. 19 sec. 8 fols. 6v–7.
10 APC Of. 24 vol. 1 fols. 492–5.
11 APC Of. 14 vol. 5 sec. 12 fol. 23v, vol. 15 sec. 9 fol. 14.
12 Cabrera Muñoz, 'Renta episcopal y producción agraria en el obispado de Córdoba en 1510', *Andalucía Medieval*, i, 397–412.
13 *Ibid.*, pp. 398, 405.
14 *Ibid.*, pp. 401–3.
15 *Ibid.*, pp. 398, 401–3.
16 *Censo* contracts: APC Of. 14 vol. 21 sec. 12 fol. 17v, vol. 28 sec. 4 fol. 14, vol. 29 sec. 24 fol. 139, vol. 36 sec. 4 fol. 21, Of. 18 vol. 1 fol. 304.
Arrendamiento contracts: APC Of. 18 vol. 2 fol. 3v, vol. 2, fol. 204, vol. 3 fols. 1024v–5.
17 González Jiménez, *El concejo de Carmona*, pp. 96–7, 99–102, 123–5.
18 APC Of. 18 vol. 1 fol. 303v, Of. 14 vol. 1 sec. 4 fols. 85, 87, sec. 5 fols. 1v–2, 9, 9v–10.
19 APC Of. 14 vol. 19 sec. 6 fol. 3, vol. 16 sec. 4 fols. 17v–18.
20 T. F. Glick, *Islamic and Christian Spain in the early Middle Ages. Comparative perspectives on social and cultural formation* (Princeton, 1979), pp. 119–20. Leopoldo Torres Balbás, *Ciudades hispanomusulmanas* (2 vols., no place or date), i, 281–2, 295, 298, 345–7. María Concepción Quintanilla Raso, 'Notas sobre el comercio urbano en Córdoba durante la baja Edad Media', *Andalucía Medieval*, i, 413–22.
21 Quintanilla, 'Notas', pp. 414–15. González Jiménez, 'Ordenanzas del concejo de Córdoba (1435)', *HID*, ii (1975), 299.
22 Quintanilla, 'Notas', pp. 416–20.
23 AMC Actas 7.9.1502, 8.5.1504. AMC Sec. 19 Ser. 5 No. 7 (royal provision of 2.3.1493), No. 5, No. 12, No. 17.
24 Pedro Chalmeta Gendrón, *El 'señor del zoco' en España: Edades Media y Moderna, contribución al estudio de la historia del mercado* (Madrid, 1973), pp. 498–9, 511–12. Glick, *Islamic and Christian Spain*, pp. 121–4. González Jiménez, 'Ordenanzas...de Córdoba', pp. 196–8.
25 AMC Actas 9.7.1479, 10.4.1493.
26 AMC Actas 18.1.1497, 30.1.1497, 11.9.1500, 15.10.1501, 15.11.1499.
27 AMC Actas, 13.8.1498, 11.8.1514.
28 González Jiménez, 'Ordenanzas...de Córdoba', pp. 208–9, 292–6. AMC Sec. 6 Ser. 40 No. 2 (royal provision of 15.12.1500).
29 González Jiménez, 'Ordenanzas...de Córdoba', pp. 209, 296. RGS 7.9.1489, 8.7.1489. APC Of. 14 vol. 11 sec. 6 fols. 111–18, Of. 18 vol. 1 fols. 43, 549v–51v, Of. 14 vol. 10 sec. 16 fol. 22, Of. 18 vol. 4 fols. 340–1, vol. 5 fol. 1187v, Of. 14 vol. 29 sec. 24 fol. 15v, Of. 18 vol. 8 fol. 15.
30 AMC Sec. 7 Ser. 8 Nos. 2, 3. RGS 21.11.1478. AMC Sec. 7 Ser. 8 Nos. 6, 7, Sec. 12 Ser. 4 No. 1. AMC Actas 30.9.1493, 18.2.1495, 6.2.1506, 4.1.1510, 8.3.1512. RGS 15.3.1478. AMC Sec. 7 Ser. 8 No. 5.
31 AMC Actas 30.3.1493, 4.7.1513, 16.10.1495, 21.8.1497, 25.8.1497, 22.4.1496,

10.4.1495, 8.8.1498, 9.8.1501, 27.6.1502, 31.8.1502, 4.9.1502, 5.9.1502, 7.9.1502, 17.10.1502.

32 AMC Actas 23.8.1504, 19.2.1505, 8.3.1505, 15.3.1506, 17.4.1506, 29.4.1506, 4.5.1506, 18.5.1506, 7.4.1507, 28.2.1513, 3.8.1513. AMC Sec. 19 Ser. 4 No. 109. AMC Actas 8.3.1514.

33 Eduardo Ibarra y Rodríguez, *El problema cerealista en España durante el reinado de los Reyes Católicos (1475–1516)* (Madrid, 1944).

34 RGS 11.3.1479, 22.5.1479, 15.6.1479.

35 AMC Actas 16.11.1502, 14.7.1504, 31.10.1505, 21.11.1505.

36 AMC Actas 20.10.1505, 20.4.1506, 18.4.1506, 6.6.1506, 27.2.1506, 9.9.1506, 28.9.1506.

37 AMC Actas 5.10.1506, 14.9.1506, 22.11.1507, 16.1.1510, 22.9.1514, 9.10.1514.

38 See note 4 above. Ladero and González Jiménez, *Diezmo eclesiástico*, pp. 89–91, including quotation. AMC Actas 21.2.1506, 22.7.1506, 1.2.1503, 28.11.1502.

39 Charles Julian Bishko, 'The Andalusian municipal mestas in the fourteenth–sixteenth centuries: administrative and social aspects', *Andalucía Medieval*, i, 347–74, especially pp. 372–3.

40 Julius Klein, *The Mesta. A study in Spanish economic history, 1273–1836* (Cambridge, Mass., 1920).

41 John H. Edwards, 'El comercio lanero en Córdoba bajo los Reyes Católicos', *Andalucía Medieval*, i, 423–8, esp. p. 425.

42 Bishko, 'Andalusian municipal mestas', pp. 347–8, 353–4, 366–9.

43 APC Of. 18 vol. 3 fol. 844v. AMC Sec. 5 Ser. 42 Nos. 3, 4, 5 fols. 1–22, Nos. 6, 7.

44 ACC Caj. V No. 65, Caj. Q No. 651. AMC Sec. 1 No. 48.

45 ACC Caj. Q No. 651.

46 AMC Sec. 12 Ser. 2 No. 4. AMC Actas 29.12.1496, 4.1.1497, 27.11.1512, 14.12.1496.

47 AMC Actas 10.4.1495. AMC Sec. 6 Ser. 1 No. 5. AMC Actas, 27.11.1493, 2.12.1493, 20.12.1493. AMC Sec. 6 Ser. 3 No. 4.

48 Bishko, 'Andalusian municipal mestas', pp. 354, 363, 366–9.

49 AMC Sec. 1 No. 48, Sec. 12 Ser. 4 No. 3, fols. 52–3, 62, 77.

50 AMC Sec. 6 Ser. 1 Nos. 7, 16, 18.

51 AMC Sec. 12 Ser. 3 Santaella No. 3, Hornachuelos No. 1, Bujalance No. 1, Ser. 2 Nos. 12, 1, 16, 30.

52 AMC Sec. 12 Ser. 4 No. 3 fols. 209–17. AMC Actas 27.5.1495, 29.10.1503, 6.11.1503. AMC Sec. 12 Ser. 2 Castro No. 5. AMC Actas 22.2.1515, 24.2.1515. Quintanilla, *Nobleza*, p. 200.

53 AMC Actas 4.9.1493, 14.8.1493, 19.6.1500, 12.2.1504.

54 AMC Sec. 12 Ser. 4 No. 3 fols. 134–6.

55 AMC Sec. 6 Ser. 1 No. 27.

56 For full references to this material see Edwards, 'El comercio lanero' or 'Oligarchy and merchant capitalism in lower Andalusia under the Catholic Kings: the case of Córdoba and Jerez de la Frontera', *HID*, iv (1977), 11–33.

57 AMC Actas 10.5.1499.

58 APC Of. 18 vol. 3 fol. 884v.

59 Pérez, *La révolution des 'comunidades' de Castille, 1520–1521*, pp. 97–107.

60 Paulino Iradiel Murugarren, *Evolución de la industria textil castellana en los siglos XIII–XVI* (Salamanca, 1974), pp. 35, 28.

61 AMC Actas 11.3.1498. ACC Actas, iv, fol. 89. APC Of. 14 vol. 4 sec. 16 fol. 29 and vol. 5 sec. 7 fols. 23v–4.
62 Iradiel, *Evolución*, pp. 117, 122. AMC Actas 8.10.1501, 18.11.1500.
63 AMC Actas 5.7.1499, 8.4.1499.
64 AMC Actas 30.8.1493.
65 Iradiel, *Evolución*, pp. 75, 147–53. AMC Actas 31.1.1500 (weavers).
66 González, 'Ordenanzas...de Córdoba', pp. 266, 281. AMC Sec. 6 Ser. 7 No. 3.
67 AMC Actas 22.6.1495, 14.7.1497, 14.6.1499.
68 AMC Actas 16.12.1500.
69 AMC Actas 14.7.1497, 7.12.1498. Iradiel, *Evolución*, pp. 179, 182–3.
70 AMC Actas 8.4.1499, 18.8.1497.
71 AMC Actas 1512 (June), petitions to Cortes.
72 AMC Actas 23.4.1515.

5 THE NOBILITY IN REGIONAL POLITICS

1 Diego de Valera, *Espejo de la verdadera nobleza, Biblioteca de Autores Españoles*, cxvi, 89–116.
2 *Ibid.*, p. 116n.
3 Montalvo 4-1-9.
4. Alfonso García Gallo, *Manual de historia del derecho español*, 4th edn (Madrid, 1971), p. 707.
5 Abbot of Rute, *Historia de la casa de Córdoba, Boletín de la Real Academia de Córdoba*, lxxvii (1958), 249, 259.
6 See Chapter 1, pp. 17–23.
7 A. Matilla Tascón, *Declaratorias de los Reyes Católicos sobre reducción de juros y otras mercedes* (Madrid, 1952), pp. 4–9, 17.
8 *Ibid.*, p. 133. AMC Actas 20.3.1493. For *acostamientos*, see below, pp. 147–8.
9 *Testamento y codicilo de la reina Isabel la Católica* (Madrid, 1969), p. 30.
10 RGS 14.3.1494. AMC Sec. 19 Ser. 20 No. 23. RGS 17.1.1493, 20.8.1492, 25.6.1492.
11 *Fuero Juzgo* 4-5-1
12 *Partidas* 2-15-2. Gregorio López's comments are in the *Códigos* edition.
13 For the laws of Toro, see *Códigos*, vol. vi. The legal and historical origins of the *mayorazgo* are effectively surveyed in Bartolomé Clavero, *Mayorazgo, Propiedad feudal en Castilla, 1369–1836* (Madrid, 1974). Its later history is discussed in an important comparative essay by J. P. Cooper, 'Patterns of inheritance and settlement by great landowners from the fifteenth to the eighteenth centuries', in *Family and inheritance. Rural society in western Europe, 1200–1800*, ed. Jack Goody, Joan Thirsk and E. P. Thompson (Cambridge, 1976), pp. 192–327.
14 Angel González Palencia, *Biblioteca histórica y genealógica*, vol. i: *Mayorazgos españoles* (Madrid, 1929).
15 See, in particular, Jacques Heers, *Le clan familial au Moyen Age* (Paris, 1974), and, for Extremadura, Gerbet, *La noblesse dans le royaume de Castille*.
16 The genealogical information in this chapter was obtained from documents in APC and RAH Salazar y Castro, also from Francisco Fernández de Bethencourt, *Historia genealógica y heráldica de la monarquía española, casa real y grandes de España*, 10 vols. (Madrid, 1897–1920), and Alberto and Arturo García Carraffa, *Enciclopedia heráldica y genealógica hispano-americana*,

88 vols. (Madrid, 1957–63). The last of these works has been used as little as possible, because of its lack of bibliographical references.

17 AMC Actas 5.5.1514–12.6.1514, a document bound into the *actas* of that year.

18 AMC Sec. 2 Ser. 10 No. 1.

19 Lists without documentary reference from a paper delivered at Cuenca in May 1979.

20 APC Of. 14 vol. 31 sec. 22 fols. 304v–6. For the 1496 and 1513 lists of *hidalgos* see n. 18.

21 On urban militias, see Nicolás Tenorio, 'Las milicias de Sevilla', *Revista de Archivos, Bibliotecas y Museos*, xvii (1907), 222–63.

22 *Ibid.*, pp. 234, 241.

23 Some global figures for 1483–7 and 1489 from Ladero, *Castilla y la conquista del reino de Granada* (Valladolid, 1967), pp. 234–90. More detailed figures for royal levies are to be found in AMC Actas 20.12.1495, 21.9.1496, 10.9.1499, 20.12.1499, 23.11.1500, 18.12.1500, 1.3.1501, 8.8.1502, 26.8.1503, 4.9.1503, 10.7.1505, 23.2.1512, 3.12.1512, 26.2.1513, 1.3.1513.

24 Ladero, *Castilla y la conquista*, pp. 234–90, 111–14. Gerbet's figure from her unpublished Cuenca paper.

25 Emilio Meneses García, 'Documentos sobre la caballería de alarde madrileña', *Hispania*, xxi (1961), 323–41. AMC Actas 27.3.1500, 12.11.1515.

26 Ladero, *Castilla y la conquista*, pp. 234–90.

27 Ladero, *Andalucía en el siglo XV*, p. 86.

28 *Ibid.*, pp. 8, 25. Montalvo 7-2-17.

29 Ladero, *Andalucía*, pp. 123–8. AMC Sec. 1 Ser. 10 No. 5, Sec. 1 Ser. 1 No. 43, Sec. 1 Ser. 10 No. 4.

30 Ladero, *Andalucía*, pp. 135–8.

31 *Ibid.*, pp. 127, 146, 143.

32 AMC Sec. 1 Ser. 2 No. 43. Ladero, *Andalucía*, p. 135. ACC Caj. S (reversed) No. 39, Caj. H-vii No. 149.

33 Bethencourt, *Historia genealógica*, vii, 233–4n. Abbot of Rute, *Historia, Boletín de la Real Academia de Córdoba*, lxxxii (1961), 300.

34 RAH Salazar M-49 fols. 72v–3v.

35 RAH Salazar K-37 fols. 191 and verso.

36 RAH Salazar M-49 fols. 75v–6v.

37 Abbot of Rute, *Historia, BRAC*, lxxxii (1961), 356.

38 RAH Salazar M-49 fols. 76v–7v. AHN Osuna leg. 873 no. 8. AMC Actas 14.2.1500, 9.10.1500.

39 AMC Actas 27.10.1501.

40 AMC Actas 18.5.1506, 6.6.1506, 21.6.1506. See also Chapter 4, pp. 111–13.

41 AMC Actas 15.7.1504, 18.11.1504, 4.12.1504, 8.12.1504.

42 AMC Actas 19.8.1506, fol. 72v.

43 AMC Actas 25.3.1507.

44 AMC Actas 17.12.1507.

45 Andrés Bernáldez, *Memorias de los Reyes Católicos*, ed. M. Gómez-Moreno and J. de M. Carriazo (Madrid, 1962). Alonso de Santa Cruz, *Crónica de los Reyes Católicos*, ed. Carriazo, 2 vols. (Seville, 1951). Pedro de Alcocer, *Relaciones de algunas cosas que pasaron*, ed. A. Martín Gomero (Seville, 1872). Juan and Gonzalo Román, *Libro de istorias de los libros...en este ilustre çibdad de diez años, comenzando del año de mil e quinientos fasta el de mil e quinientos e nueve años*, Biblioteca Municipal de Jerez, MS 81 est. C no. 1.

46 Bernáldez, *Memorias*, p. 540.
47 RAH 9-1-1-A-12. Bernáldez, *Memorias*, pp. 541–2.
48 Bernáldez, *Memorias*, pp. 542–3. Alcocer, *Relaciones*, pp. 26–7. RAH Salazar K-37 fols. 196–7.
49 Bartolomé Yun Casalilla, *Crisis de subsistencias y conflictividad social en Córdoba a principios del siglo XVI* (Córdoba, 1980), pp. 196–208. Quintanilla, *Nobleza*, pp. 169–72.
50 Alcocer, *Relaciones*, p. 27, AMC Actas 21.8.1510, 26.2.1511. Quintanilla, *Nobleza*, pp. 151–3.
51 AMC Actas 27.10.1511, 16.1.1512, 28.1.1512, 30.4.1512.
52 AMC Actas 15.7.1513, 17.7.1513, 27.7.1513, 6.2.1514, 20.3.1514.
53 AMC Actas 20.7.1515.

6 RELIGION AND SOCIETY

1 Ladero, 'Producción y renta cereales', *Andalucía Medieval*, i, 387–8
2 Ladero and González Jiménez, *Diezmo eclesiástico*, p. 26.
3 Teodomiro Ramírez de Arellano, *Paseos por Córdoba o sean apuntes para su historia*, 3rd edn (Córdoba, 1976), pp. 101, 156, 289, 468–9, 550, 206, 31, 147, 563, 413, 358, 528–9, 523–4. Nieto, 'La reforma del clero regular en Córdoba (1400–1450)', in *Andalucía medieval. Nuevos estudios* (Córdoba, 1979), pp. 219–28.
4 Antonio Collantes de Terán, 'Los señoríos andaluces, análisis de su evolución territorial en la Edad Media', *HID*, vi (1979), 8 (offprint). RGS 1497, fol. 307.
5 Ladero, 'Producción y renta cereales', pp. 393–6. Emilio Cabrera, 'Renta episcopal y producción agraria en el obispado de Córdoba en 1510', *Andalucía Medieval*, i, 406–10.
6 Cabrera, 'Renta', pp. 409–10.
7 Ramírez de Arellano, *Paseos*, pp. 25, 413, 206, 563, 147. Nieto, 'La reforma', pp. 220–6.
8 Ramírez de Arellano, *Paseos*, pp. 41, 137, 207.
9 *Ibid.*, pp. 144, 25.
10 APC Of. 14 vol. 30 sec. 10 fols. 7–25.
11 RAH Morales C-14 fols. 847–9v.
12 Marie-Claude Gerbet, 'Les confréries religieuses à Cáceres de 1467 à 1523', *MCV*, vii (1971), 75–113. Evidence for noble *cofradías* in the Córdoba area is confined to the lordship of Priego. See M. C. Quintanilla Raso, *Nobleza y señoríos en el reino de Córdoba. La casa de Aguilar (siglos XIV y XV)* (Córdoba, 1979), pp. 86–7.
13 RAH Morales C-14, fols. 845, 845v–6. AMC Actas 21.4.1503.
14 APC Of. 14 vol. 8 sec. 3 fols. 14–19, vol. 11 sec. 6 fols. 111–15, vol. 13 sec. 11 fols. 123–8, vol. 16 sec. 3 fols. 10–19, sec. 5 fols. 4v–6v, sec. 7 fols. 61–5, sec. 11 fols. 31v–4, vol. 37 sec. 15 fols. 28–9, vol. 43 sec. 1 fols. 1–4.
15 APC Of. 14 vol. 41 sec. 4 fols. 14–20. Some details concerning the religious patronage of Doña Catalina and her son in their lordships are provided by Quintanilla, *Nobleza y señoríos*, p. 156.
16 APC Of. 14 vol. 41 sec. 19 fols. 1–12 (6.11.1507).
17 APC Of. 14 vol. 8 sec. 3 fols. 14–19, vol. 11 sec. 6 fols. 111–15, vol. 12 sec. 4 fols. 63–5, sec. 7 fols. 1–4, vol. 13 sec. 11 fols. 110–12, 123–8, vol. 16 sec. 4 fols. 3–4, 4v–7, vol. 17 sec. 1 fols. 7–13, vol. 43 sec. 1 fols. 1–4. Of. 18 vol. 3 fols. 877–81v, vol. 4 fols. 245v–53.

18 José Sánchez Herrero, *Las diócesis del reino de León. Siglos XIV y XV* (León, 1978).

19 The best general surveys of Catholic reform in late medieval Castile are by Tarsicio de Azcona, *Isabel la Católica* (Madrid, 1964), pp. 425–98, 557–622, on the 1474–1516 period and, more generally, J. N. Hillgarth, *The Spanish kingdoms, 1250–1516* (2 vols., Oxford, 1968), ii, 88–125, 394–410.

20 Azcona, *Isabel*, pp. 568–70, Hillgarth, *The Spanish kingdoms*, ii, 402. Nieto, 'La reforma', pp. 221, 224–5.

21 Ramírez de Arellano, *Paseos*, pp. 585–6. Azcona, *Isabel*, pp. 53, 168–9, 681, 579. For examples of synodal and conciliar legislation, see Sánchez Herrero, *Concilios provinciales y sínodos toledanos de los siglos XIV y XV* (La Laguna, 1976), and F. Javier Fernández Conde, *Gutierre de Toledo, obispo de Oviedo (1377–1389). Reforma eclesiástica en la Asturias bajomedieval* (Oviedo, 1978).

22 Ladero, 'Producción y renta cerealeras', *Andalucía Medieval*, i, 387–8.

23 Antonio García y García, Francisco Cantelar Rodríguez, Manuel Nieto Cumplido, *Catálogo de los manuscritos e incunables de la catedral de Córdoba* (Salamanca, 1976), pp. xxxviii–xli, lvii–lx, lxxi–lxxiv. Nieto, *La miniatura en la catedral de Córdoba* (Cordoba, 1973), pp. 32–4.

24 García y García et al., *Catálogo*, pp. lxv–lxx (*Statuto fecho en favor de los estudiantes* in ACC Actas, iii, fols. 103–5v). ACC Actas iii, fol. 81v (3–4 Jan. 1464) and fol. 132 (28.8.1471). See also Richard L. Kagan, *Students and society in early modern Spain* (Baltimore and London, 1974).

25 Ladero, 'Los mudéjares de Castilla en la baja Edad Media', *HID*, v (1978), 15–16 (offprint). Nieto, 'La crisis demográfica y social del siglo XIV en Córdoba', *Anales del Instituto Luis de Góngora*, iii (1972), 31–2.

26 Ladero, 'Los mudéjares', pp. 22–36. RGS 1–1480 fol. 46, v–1480 fol. 87.

27 RGS 20.1.1488, 2.4.1490. AMC Actas 20.5.1495, 15.7.1495.

28 Ladero, 'Los mudéjares', p. 39.

29 Angus MacKay, 'The ballad and the frontier in late mediaeval Spain', *Bulletin of Hispanic Studies*, liii (1976), 15–33. 'Jerónimo', *Córdoba en el siglo XV*, ed. and trans. Manuel Nieto Cumplido (Córdoba, 1973). For a comparison with contemporary Italian and Spanish descriptions of cities see Robert B. Tate, 'The civic humanism of Alfonso de Palencia', *Renaissance and Modern Studies*, xxiii (1979), 36–40.

30 Jerónimo, *Córdoba*, pp. 50–1. Nieto, *La miniatura*, pl. 56.

31 Nieto, *Corrientes artísticas en la Córdoba medieval cristiana* (Córdoba, 1975) (no page numbers), and *La miniatura*, pp. 19–36.

32 Francisco Cantera Burgos, *Sinagogas de Toledo, Segovia y Córdoba* (Madrid, 1973), pp. 153–4.

33 Nieto, 'Luchas nobiliarias y movimientos populares en Córdoba a fines del siglo XIV', in Manuel Riu Riu, Cristóbal Torres, Manuel Nieto Cumplido, *Tres estudios de historia medieval andaluza* (Córdoba, 1977), pp. 43–6.

34 Fritz Baer, *Die Juden im christlichen Spanien*, i, pt 2, pp. 232–3 (Henry III, Segovia, 16.6.1391), 245 (Aliseda, 13.6.1396). Nieto, 'Luchas nobiliarias', p. 43.

35 AMC Actas 23.3.1479. Baer, *Die Juden*, i, pt 2, pp. 348–9. Luis Suárez Fernández, *Documentos acerca de la expulsión de los judíos* (Valladolid, 1964), pp. 35–6.

36 Hillgarth, *The Spanish kingdoms*, ii, 144.

37 Eloy Benito Ruano, *Los orígenes del problema converso* (Barcelona, 1976), pp. 85–92, 44–5.

38 Nieto, 'La revuelta contra los conversos de Córdoba en 1473', *Homenaje a*

Antón de Montoro en el V centenario de su muerte (Montoro, 1977), p. 35.

39 Diego de Valera, *Memorial de diversas hazañas*, ed. Juan de Mata Carriazo (Madrid, 1941), pp. 240–3. Alfonso de Palencia, *Décadas*, trans. A. Paz y Melia (Madrid, 1904–9), iii, 107–16. See also Nieto, 'La revuelta', pp. 31–49.

40 Palencia, *Décadas*, iii, pp. 107–10. Montalvo 7-2-9. Diego Pérez, *Pragmáticas*, law 65, fol. 55. Nieto, 'La revuelta', pp. 36–40, 44–5.

41 ACC Actas, iv, fol. 142v.

42 RGS 8.2.1484, 21.2.1484, 20.12.1484, 20.2.1485, 15.2.1485, 15.6.1486, 4.4.1487, 4.1487, 7.4.1487, 8.4.1487, 29.8.1487, 26.2.1490, 30.4.1485, 24.9,1491, 27.1.1492. ACC Caj. L No. 513 (28.3.1487), Caj. G No. 247 (17.2.1492).

43 *El tumbo de los Reyes Católicos del concejo de Sevilla*, ed. Juan de Mata Carriazo, iii, 159–62. ACC Caj. L No. 513. APC Of. 14 vol. 41 sec. 4 fols. 6–7.

44 RGS 28.3.1487, 4.4.1487, 3.11.1488, 26.1.1489. ACC Caj. F No. 420.

45 RGS 8.7.1487. Henry C. Lea, 'Lucero the inquisitor', *American Historical Review*, ii (1896–7), 611–26. Yun, *Crisis*, pp. 209–15.

46 ACC Actas, vi, fol. 30v (10.5.1498). Lea, 'Lucero', pp. 612–13, 625.

47 Rodrigo Blázquez to the marquis of Priego, in A. Paz y Melia, *Series de los más importantes documentos del archivo del excmo Sr Duque de Medinaceli* (Madrid, 1915), *Primera serie*, doc. 96. For a fuller account of these episodes see Edwards, 'La révolte du marquis de Priego à Cordoue en 1508: un symptôme des tensions d'une société urbaine', *MCV*, xii (1976), 165–72.

48 AMC Actas, 1.2.1514.

49 Benito, *Los orígenes*, pp. 51–2. Other works supporting this view include Alonso de Cartagena, *Defensorium unitatis christianae*, ed. P. Manuel Alonso (Madrid, 1943); Fernán Díaz de Toledo, *Instrucción del relator para el obispo de Cuenca, a favor de la nación hebrea*, in Cartagena, *Defensorium*, pp. 343–56; Lope de Barrientos' reply in *Defensorium*, pp. 324–38; Juan de Torquemada, *Tractatus contra madianitas et ismaelitas*, ed. Nicolás López Martínez and Vicente Proaño Gil (Burgos, 1957).

50 Philippe Wolff, 'The 1391 pogrom in Spain. Social crisis or not?', *Past and Present*, no. 50 (1971), 4–18. Angus MacKay, 'Popular movements and pogroms in fifteenth-century Castile', *Past and Present*, no. 55 (1972), 35–67. Nieto, 'Luchas nobiliarias' and 'La revuelta', passim.

51 Manuel González Jiménez, 'Beguinos en Castilla. Nota sobre un documento sevillano', *HID*, iv (1977), 109–14. Francesco Guicciardini, 'Relación de España escrita', in *Viaje a España de Francesco Guicciardini*, ed. José María Alonso Gamo (Valencia, 1952), p. 70.

Select bibliography

A. MANUSCRIPT SOURCES

(i) Real Academia de la Historia, Madrid

Colección Salazar y Castro. Transcriptions from seignorial archives, indexed by A. Vargas-Zúñiga and B. Cuartero y Huerta in *Indice de la colección de Don Luis de Salazar y Castro.*
Madrid, 1949–

Colección Morales. References to original manuscripts and copies collected by Manuel Nieto in his *Corpus mediaevale cordubense* (see below)

Morales, Andrés de. *Historia general de la muy leal ciudad de Córdoba y de sus nobilísimas familias.* 2 vols., 1620–62. MS ref. 9-4-1-H 11/12

(ii) Archivo Municipal de Córdoba

Sección 1a   Historia
  Serie 1   Fuero (1241)
  Serie 2   Reales privilegios
  Serie 10   Castillos y fortalezas

Sección 2   Antiguo régimen político-administrativo
  Serie 1   Capítulos de Cortes
  Serie 2   Corregidores
  Serie 3   Alcaldes mayores
  Serie 8   Veinticuatros
  Serie 10   Nobles e hijosdalgo
  Serie 13   Santa Hermandad
  Serie 17   Caballeros cuantiosos
  Serie 20   Jurados
  Serie 21   Escribanos públicos
  Serie 27   Alguaciles ordinarios
  Serie 29   Señoríos territoriales
  Serie 30   Señorío de la ciudad de Córdoba sobre las villas de Fuenteovejuna, Gahete, Hinojosa y Belmez

Sección 5   Patrimonio municipal
  Serie 21   Dehesa de Navas del Moro
  Serie 29   Dehesa de Trassierra
  Serie 31   Villalobillos
  Serie 32   Dehesas de Samonosas y La Parrilla

Serie 42   Derechos sobre el Puerto del Guijo
Serie 43   Almojarifazgo

Sección 6   Agricultura, industria, comercio
Serie 1   As above. Processes concerning usurpation of council lands
Serie 3   Concejo de la Mesta
Serie 7   Fábricas de tejidos
Serie 18   Fábricas de jabón
Serie 44   Abasto de granos

Sección 7   Policía urbana y rural
Serie 7   Terrenos realengos
Serie 8   Caza y pesca

Sección 12   Estadística
Serie 1   As above. Boundary disputes.
Serie 2   Predíos rústicos en el término de Córdoba
Serie 3   As above. Various individual areas
Serie 4   Sentencias de términos

Sección 13   Legislación
Serie 1   Reales resoluciones
Serie 2   Recopilación de reales disposiciones
Serie 10   Ordenanzas municipales

Sección 16   Asuntos judiciales
Serie 4   Pleitos civiles

Sección 18   Servicios prestados al Estado
Serie 1   Rentas reales
Serie 3   Alcabalas

Sección 19   Archivos particulares
Serie 1   Actas capitulares, 1479, 1493, 1495–1516
Serie 4   Archivo del cabildo de los señores jurados

(iii) Archivo de Protocolos de Córdoba
Office 1   from 1512
Office 14   from 1442
Office 18   from 1482
Office 24   from 1507
Office 25   from 1508
Office 33   from 1510
Office 37   from 1516

The above dates refer to the earliest surviving register in each office.

(iv) Archivo Catedralicio de Córdoba
Actas capitulares 1474–1516
Other individual documents have been used and the archive's card catalogue, compiled by Manuel Nieto under the title, *Corpus mediaevale cordubense*,

has been of value. The *Corpus* also includes references to material in the *Registro general del sello*, the *Colección Morales*, the Archivo de Medinaceli (Seville) and other manuscript and printed sources.

B. PRINTED SOURCES

(i) Primary sources

Alcocer, Pedro de. *Relaciones de algunas cosas que pasaron en estos reinos desde que murió la reina católica doña Isabel hasta que se acabaron las comunidades en la ciudad de Toledo.* Ed. Antonio Martín Gomero. Seville, 1872

Archivo General de Simancas. Catalogue 5. *Patronato real.* Ed. Amalia Prieto Cantero. 2 vols. Valladolid, 1946–9

Archivo General de Simancas. Catalogue 13. *Registro general del sello, 1454–95.* 12 vols. Valladolid, 1950–74

Archivo Municipal de Sevilla. *El tumbo de los Reyes Católicos del concejo de Sevilla.* Ed. Juan de Mata Carriazo. 5 vols. (1474–92). Seville, 1968–71

Bernáldez, Andrés. *Memorias de los Reyes Católicos.* Ed. Manuel Gómez-Moreno and Juan de Mata Carriazo. Madrid, 1962

Capítulos de corregidores. Capítulos hechos por el Rey e la Reyna nuestros señores. En los quales contienen las cosas que an de guardar e conplir los governadores, assistentes, juezes de residencia e alcaldes de las ciudades, villas e lugares de sus reynos e señoríos, hechos en la muy noble e leal ciudad de Sevilla a ix de junio de mil e quinientos. Seville, 1500

Cartagena, Alonso de. *Defensorium unitatis christianae.* Ed. P. Manuel Alonso. Madrid, 1943

Códigos españoles concordados y anotados, Los. 12 vols. Madrid, 1847–51

Colón, Hernando. *Descripción y cosmografía de España,* or *Itinerario.* Ed. Antonio Blázquez. 3 vols. Madrid, 1915. Also in *Boletín de la Real Sociedad Geográfica* (1904–8)

Cortes de los antiguos reinos de León y Castilla. 5 vols. Madrid, 1861–1903

Díaz de Toledo, Fernán. *Instrucción del relator para el obispo de Cuenca a favor de la nación hebrea,* in Cartagena, *Defensorium* (see above), pp. 343–56

Edrisi. *Description de l'Afrique et de l'Espagne.* Arabic text with French trans., ed. R. Dozy and M. J. de Goeje. 1st edn 1866, repr. Leiden, 1968

Fuero de Usagre. Ed. Rafael de Ureña and Adolfo Bonilla. Madrid, 1907

García y García, A., Cantelar Rodríguez, F., Nieto Cumplido, M. *Catálogo de los manuscritos e incunables de la catedral de Córdoba.* Salamanca. 1976

González, T. *Colección de cédulas, cartas patentes, provisiones, reales órdenes... concedidas a varios pueblos y corporaciones de la Corona de Castilla.* 6 vols. Madrid, 1829–33

Guicciardini, Francesco. 'Relación de España escrita', in *Viaje a España de Francesco Guicciardini.* Ed. José María Alonso Gamo. Valencia, 1952

Herrera, Gabriel Alonso de. *Agricultura general que trata de la labranza del campo y sus particularidades.* Madrid, 1513 and other edns

Jerónimo (sic). *Descriptio Cordubae.* Ed. and trans. Manuel Nieto Cumplido. Córdoba, 1973

Montalvo, A. Díaz de. *Leyes de España.* Edn used printed at Zamora, 1485

Ordenanzas del concejo de Carmona. Ed. Manuel González Jiménez. Seville, 1972

Ordenanzas del concejo de Córdoba (1435). Ed. M. González Jiménez. *HID,* ii (1975), 67–97

Palencia, Alfonso de. *Crónica de Enrique IV* or *Decádas*. Trans. A. Paz y Melia. 5 vols. Madrid, 1904–9

Paz y Melia, A. *Series de los más importantes documentos del archivo y biblioteca del Excmo Sr Duque de Medinaceli.* 1st series (*Historia*). Madrid, 1915

Pérez, Lic. Diego. *Pragmáticas de los Reyes Católicos.* Medina del Campo, 1549

Pulgar, Hernando del. *Crónica de los Reyes Católicos.* Ed. Juan de Mata Carriazo. 2 vols. Madrid, 1943

Ramírez, Juan. *Pragmáticas de los Reyes Católicos.* Alcalá de Henares, 1503

Santa Cruz, Alonso de. *Crónica de los Reyes Católicos.* Ed. Juan de Mata Carriazo. 2 vols. Seville, 1951

Siete Partidas de Alfonso X. Ed. Real Academia de la Historia. 3 vols. Madrid, 1807

Testamento y codicilo de la reina Isabel la Católica. Madrid, 1969

Torquemada, Juan de. *Tractatus contra madianitas et ismaelitas.* Ed. Nicolás López Martínez and Vicente Proaño Gil. Burgos, 1957

Valera, Mosén Diego de. *Crónica de los Reyes Católicos.* Ed. Juan de Mata Carriazo. Madrid, 1927

Espejo de la verdadera nobleza, Biblioteca de Autores Españoles, cxvi, 89–116

Memorial de diversas hazañas. Ed. Juan de Mata Carriazo. Madrid, 1941

(ii) Secondary sources

Actas del Primer Congreso de Historia de Andalucía (*1976*), *Andalucía Medieval.* 2 vols. Córdoba, 1978 (Referred to as *Andalucía Medieval*)

Azcona, Tarsicio de. *Isabel la Católica. Estudio crítico de su vida y reinado.* Madrid, 1964

Baer, Fritz. *Die Juden im christlichen Spanien,* 1 pt 2: *Kastilien/Inquisitionakten.* Berlin, 1929–36, repr. 1970

Basas Fernández, Manuel. 'Burgos en el comercio lanero del siglo XVI', *Moneda y Crédito,* lxxvii (1961), 37–68

'La estabilización monetaria bajo los Reyes Católicos', *Boletín de Estudios Económicos,* xlvii (1959), 121–39

Benito Ruano, Eloy. *Los orígenes del problema converso.* Barcelona, 1976

Bishko, Charles Julian. 'The Andalusian municipal mestas in the fourteenth–sixteenth centuries: administrative and social aspects', *Andalucía Medieval,* i, 347–74

Braudel, Fernand. *Capitalism and material life, 1400–1800.* London, 1973

Cabrera Muñoz, Emilio. *El condado de Belalcázar (1444–1516). Aportación al estudio del régimen señorial en la baja Edad Media.* Córdoba, 1977

'La fortuna de una familia noble castellana, a través de un inventario de mediados del siglo XV', *HID,* ii (1975), 9–42

'Renta episcopal y producción agraria en el obispado de Córdoba en 1510', *Andalucía Medieval,* i, 397–412

'Tierras realengas y tierras de señorío a fines de la Edad Media. Distribución geográfica y niveles de población', *Andalucía Medieval,* i, 295–308

Cabrera, E., Ibarra, F., Martínez R., Moros, A., Villegas, M., 'La sublevación de Fuenteovejuna, contemplada en su V centenario', *Andalucía Medieval,* ii, 113–22

Cabrillana N. 'Villages desértés en Espagne', in *Villages desértés et histoire économique, XIe–XVIIIe siècle,* Paris, 1965, pp. 461–512

Cantera Burgos, Francisco. *Sinagogas de Toledo, Segovia y Córdoba.* Madrid, 1973

Carande, Ramón. *Sevilla, fortaleza y mercado. Las tierras, las gentes y la administración de la ciudad en el siglo XIV.* Seville, 1975

Carlé, María del Carmen. 'Mercaderes en Castilla, 1252–1512', *Cuadernos de Historia de España*, xxi–xxii (1954), 146–328

Cedillo, Conde de. *Contribuciones y impuestos en León y Castilla durante la Edad Media.* Madrid, 1896

Chalmeta Gendrón, Pedro. *El 'señor del zoco' en España: Edades Media y Moderna, contribuciún al estudio de la historia del mercado.* Madrid, 1973

Clavero, Bartolomé. *Mayorazgo: propiedad feudal en Castilla, 1369–1836.* Madrid, 1974

Clemencín, Diego. *Elogio de la Reina Católica, Doña Isabel.* Memorias de la Academia de la Historia, vi. Madrid, 1821

Collantes de Terán, Antonio. 'Le latifundium sévillan aux XIVe et XVe siècles. Ebauche d'une problématique', *MCV*, xii (1976), 101–25

'Nuevas poblaciones del siglo XV en el reino de Sevilla', *Cuadernos de Historia anexos a Hispania*, vii (1977), 283–336

'Los señoríos andaluces, análisis de su evolución territorial en la Edad Media', *HID*, vi (1979)

Sevilla en la baja Edad Media. La ciudad y los hombres. Seville, 1977

Contreras y López de Ayala, A. *Los gremios españoles.* Madrid, 1944

Cooper, J. P. 'Patterns of inheritance and settlement by great landowners from the fifteenth to the eighteenth centuries', in Jack Goody, Joan Thirsk and E. P. Thompson (eds.), *Family and inheritance. Rural society in western Europe, 1200–1800.* Cambridge, 1976.

Drain, Michel, and Ponsot, Pierre. 'Les paysages agraires de l'Andalousie occidentale au début du XVIe siècle, d'après l'*Itinerario* de Hernando Colón', *MCV*, ii (1966), 73–85

Edwards, John H. 'El comercio lanero en Córdoba bajo los Reyes Católicos', *Andalucía Medieval*, i, 423–8

'Oligarchy and merchant capitalism in lower Andalusia under the Catholic Kings: the case of Córdoba and Jerez de la Frontera', *HID*, iv (1977), 11–33

'La révolte du marquis de Priego à Cordoue en 1508: un symptôme des tensions d'une société urbaine', *MCV*, xii (1976), 165–72

España, atlas y índices de sus términos municipales, 2 vols. Madrid, 1969

Fernández Conde, F. Javier. *Gutierre de Toledo, obispo de Oviedo (1377–1389). Reforma eclesiástica en la Asturias bajomedieval.* Oviedo, 1978

Fernández de Bethencourt, Francisco. *Historia genealógica y heráldica de la monarquía española, casa real y grandes de España.* 10 vols. Madrid, 1897–1920

Fernández de Córdoba, Francisco, Abbot of Rute. *Historia de la casa de Córdoba.* Córdoba n.d. Published in instalments in *Boletín de la Real Academia de Córdoba* from vol. lxx (1954)

Fernández Duro, Cesáreo. 'Noticias de la vida y obra de Gonzalo de Ayora y fragmentos de su crónica inédita', *Boletín de la Real Academia de la Historia*, xvii (1890), 433–75

García Carraffa, Alberto and Arturo. *Enciclopedia heráldica y genealógica hispano-americana.* 88 vols. Madrid, 1957–63

García de Cortázar, J. A. *Historia de España Alfaguara,* vol. ii: *La época medieval.* Madrid, 1973

García de Valdeavellano, Luis. *Curso de historia de las instituciones españolas, de los orígenes al final de la Edad Media.* Madrid, 1968

García Gallo, Alfonso. *Manual de historia del derecho español.* 4th edn. Madrid, 1971

Gerbet, Marie-Claude. 'Les confréries religieuses à Cáceres de 1467 à 1523', *MCV*, vii (1971), 75–113

La noblesse dans le royaume de Castille. Etude sur ses structures sociales en Estrémadure de 1454 á 1516. Paris, 1979

Glick, T. F. *Islamic and Christian Spain in the Early Middle Ages. Comparative perspectives on social and cultural formation.* Princeton, 1979

Gómez Bravo, Juan. *Catálogo de los obispos de Córdoba y breve noticia histórica de su iglesia catedral y obispado.* 2 vols. Córdoba, 1778

González, Julio. *Repartimiento de Sevilla.* 2 vols. Madrid, 1951

González Alonso, Benjamín. *El corregidor castellano, 1348–1808.* Madrid, 1970

González Jiménez, Manuel. 'Aspectos de la economía rural andaluza del siglo XV', in *Huelva en la Andalucía del siglo XV*, Huelva, 1976, pp. 13–36

'Beguinos en Castilla. Notas sobre un documento sevillano', *HID*, iv (1977), 104–14

El concejo de Carmona a fines de la Edad Media, 1464–1523. Seville, 1973

'Las crisis cerealistas en Carmona a fines de la Edad Media', *HID*, iii (1976), 283–307

La repoblacíon de la zona de Sevilla en el siglo XIV. Estudio y documentos. Seville, 1975

González Palencia, Angel. *Mayorazgos españoles. Biblioteca histórica y genealógica*, i, Madrid, 1929

Gual Camarena, Miguel. 'Para una mapa de la industria textil hispana en la Edad Media', *Anuario de Estudios Medievales*, iv (1967), 109–68

'Para una mapa de la sal hispana', in *Homenaje a Jaime Vicens Vives*, i (1965), 483–97

Guilarte, Alfonso María. *El régimen señorial en el siglo XVI.* Madrid, 1962

Heers, Jacques. *Le clan familial au Moyen Age.* Paris, 1974

Gênes au XVe siècle. Paris, 1971

Hernández Jiménez, Félix. 'El camino de Córdoba a Toledo en la época musulmana', *Al Andalus*, xxiv (1959), 1–62

'Gafiq, Gahet, Gahet=Belalcázar', *Al Andalus*, ix (1944), 71–109

Hillgarth, J. N. *The Spanish kingdoms, 1250–1516.* 2 vols. Oxford, 1976–8

Ibarra y Rodríguez, E. *El problema cerealista en España durante el reinado de los Reyes Católicos (1475–1516).* Madrid, 1944

Iradiel Murugarren, Paulino. *Evolución de la industria textil castellana en los siglos XIII–XVI.* Salamanca, 1974

Kagan, Richard L. *Students and society in early modern Spain.* Baltimore and London, 1974

Klein, Julius. *The Mesta. A study in Spanish economic history, 1273–1836.* Cambridge, Mass., 1920

Ladero Quesada, Miguel Angel. 'Algunos datos para la historia económica de las órdenes militares de Santiago y Calatrava en el siglo XV', *Hispania*, xxx (1970), 637–62

'Almojarifazgo sevillano y comercio exterior de Andalucía en el siglo XV', *Anuario de Historia Económica y Social*, ii (1969), 69–115

Andalucía en el siglo XV. Estudios de historia política. Madrid, 1973

Castilla y la conquista del reino de Granada. Valladolid, 1967.

'Los cereales en la Andalucía del siglo XV', *Revista de la Universidad de Madrid*, xviii (1969), 223–40

'La hacienda castellana de los Reyes Católicos, 1493–1504', *Moneda y Crédito*, ciii (1967), 81–112

La hacienda real castellana entre 1480 y 1492. Valladolid, 1967

La hacienda real de Castilla en el siglo XV. La Laguna, 1973

'Los mudéjares de Castilla en la baja Edad Media', *HID*, v (1978)

'La población de Andalucía en el siglo XV. Notas provisionales', *Anuario de Historia Económica y Social*, ii (1969), 479–85

'Producción y rentas cerealeras en el reino de Córdoba a finales del siglo XV', *Andalucía Medieval*, i, 375–96

Ladero Quesada, M. A., and González Jiménez, M. *Diezmo eclesiástico y producción de cereales en el reino de Sevilla (1408–1503)*. Seville, 1979 (1978 on cover)

Lea, Henry C. 'Lucero the inquisitor', *American Historical Review*, ii (1896–7), 611–26

López Martínez, Celestino. *La Santa Hermandad de los Reyes Católicos*. Seville, 1921

Lunenfeld, M. *The council of the Santa Hermandad, a study of the pacification forces of Ferdinand and Isabella*. Coral Gables, Fla., 1970

MacKay, Angus. 'The ballad and the frontier in late mediaeval Spain', *Bulletin of Hispanic Studies*, liii (1976), 15–33

'Popular movements and pogroms in fifteenth-century Castile', *Past and Present*, no. 55 (1972), 35–67

Spain in the Middle Ages, from frontier to empire. London, 1977

Madoz, Pascual. *Diccionario geográfico–estadístico–histórico de España y sus posesiones de ultramar*. 16 vols. Madrid, 1848–50

Matilla Tascón, A. *Declaratorias de los Reyes Católicos sobre reducción de juros y otras mercedes*. Madrid, 1952

Mazo Romero, Fernando. 'Los Suárez de Figueroa y el señorío de Feria', *HID*, i (1974), 140–50

'Tensiones sociales en el municipio cordobés en la primera mitad del siglo XV', *Andalucía Medieval*, ii, 85–112

Mendizábal, Francisco. 'En torno a la real chancillería de Valladolid', *Hidalguía*, vi (1958), 357–64

'La real chancillería de Valladolid', *Revista de Archivos, Bibliotecas y Museos*, 3rd series, xxx (1914), 61–72, 243–64, 437–52; xxxi (1914), 95–112, 459–67

Meneses García, Emilio. 'Documentos sobre la caballería de alarde madrileña', *Hispania*, xxi (1961), 323–41

Mitre Fernández, Emilio. 'Córdoba y su campiña. Una comarca fronteriza al comienzo del siglo XV', *Cuadernos de Estudios Medievales*, i (Granada, 1973)

La extensión del régimen de corregidores en el reinado de Enrique III. Valladolid, 1969

Moxó, Salvador de. 'De la nobleza vieja a la nobleza nueva. La transformación nobiliaria castellana en la baja Edad Media', *Cuadernos de Historia anexos a Hispania*, iii (1969), 1–209

'El señorío, legado medieval', *Cuadernos de Historia anexos a Hispania*, i (1967), 105–18

'Exenciones tributarias en Castilla a fines de la Edad Media', *Hispania*, xxi (1961), 163–88

La alcabala: sobre sus orígenes, concepto y naturaleza. Madrid, 1963

'Los señoríos', *Hispania*, xxiv (1964), 185–236, 399–430

Muñoz Vázquez, M. 'Notas sobre el repartimiento de tierras que hizo el rey don Fernando III en Córdoba y su término', *Boletín de la Real Academia de Córdoba*, no. 71 (1954), 251–70

Nieto Cumplido, Manuel. *Corrientes artísticas en la Córdoba medieval cristiana.* Córdoba, 1975

'La crisis demográfica y social del siglo XIV en Córdoba', *Anales del Instituto Luis de Góngora*, iii (1972), 25–34

La miniatura en la catedral de Córdoba. Córdoba, 1973

'La reforma del clero regular en Córdoba (1400–1450)', *Andalucía medieval. Nuevos estudios*, Córdoba, 1979, pp. 219–28.

'La revuelta contra los conversos de Córdoba en 1473', *Homenaje a Antón de de Montoro en el V centenario de su muerte*, Montoro, 1977, pp. 29–49

'Luchas nobiliarias y movimientos populares en Córdoba a fines del siglo XIV', in Manuel Riu Riu, Cristóbal Torres, and Manuel Nieto Cumplido, *Tres estudios de historia medieval andaluza*, Córdoba, 1977, 11–65

Ocaña Torrejón, Juan. *Historia de la villa de Pedroche y su comarca.* Córdoba, 1962

Oliveros de Castro, María Teresa, and Jordana de Pozas, Julio. *La agricultura en tiempo de los Reyes Católicos.* Madrid, 1968

Ortí Belmonte, Miguel Angel. 'El fuero de Córdoba y las clases sociales en la ciudad. Mudéjares y judíos en la Edad Media', *Boletín de la Real Academia de Córdoba* yr 25 (1954), 7–94

Pérez, Joseph. *La révolution des 'comunidades' de Castille, 1520–1521.* Bordeaux, 1970

Pérez-Embid, Florentino. 'Navigation et commerce dans le port de Seville au bas Moyen Age', *Le Moyen Age* (1969), 263–90, 479–502

Pike, Ruth. *Enterprise and adventure: the Genoese in Seville and the opening of the New World.* Ithaca, 1966

Procter, Evelyn S. *Curia and Cortes in León and Castile, 1072–1295.* Cambridge, 1980

Quintanilla Raso, M. C. *Nobleza y señoríos en el reino de Córdoba. La casa de Aguilar (siglos XIV y XV).* Córdoba, 1979

'Notas sobre el comercio urbano en Córdoba durante la baja Edad Media', *Andalucía Medieval*, i, 413–22

Ramírez de Arellano, Rafael. 'Estudios biográficos, ii, Gonzalo de Ayora', *Boletín de la Real Academia de la Historia*, xli (1902), 293–324

Historia de Córdoba desde su fundación hasta la muerte de Isabel la Católica. 4 vols. Ciudad Real, 1915–17

'Rebelión de Fuente Obejuna contra el comendador mayor de Calatrava', *Boletín de la Real Academia de la Historia*, xix (1901), 446–512

Ramírez de Arellano, Teodomiro. *Paseos por Córdoba o sean apuntes para su historia.* 3rd edn. Córdoba, 1976

Sánchez Herrero, José. *Concilios provinciales y sínodos toledanos de los siglos XIV y XV.* La Laguna, 1976

Las diócesis del reino de León. Siglos XIV y XV. León, 1978

Solano Ruiz, Emma. 'La hacienda de las casas de Medina Sidonia y Arcos en la Andalucía del siglo XV', *Archivo Hispalense*, clxviii (1972), 85–176

Sopranis, Hipólito Sancho de. *Historia de Jerez de la Frontera desde su incorporación a los dominios cristianos.* 2 vols. Jerez, 1964–5

Suárez Fernández, Luis. *Documentos acerca de la expulsión de los judíos.* Valladolid, 1964

'Evolución histórica de las hermandades castellanas', *Cuadernos de Historia de España*, xvi (1951), 5–78

Nobleza y monarquia en la estructura política castellana del siglo XV. Valladolid, 1959

Tate, Robert B. 'The civic humanism of Alfonso de Palencia', *Renaissance and Modern Studies*, xxiii (1979), 25–44

Tenorio, Nicolás. 'Las milicias de Sevilla', *Revista de Archivos, Bibliotecas y Museos*, xvii (1907), 222–63

Torres Balbás, Leopoldo. *Ciudades hispanomusulmanas*. 2 vols. No place or date *Resumen histórico del urbanismo en España*. 2nd edn. Madrid, 1968

Ubieto Arteta, Antonio. 'Cronología del desarrollo de la Peste Negra en la península ibérica', *Cuadernos de Historia anexos a Hispania*, v (1975), 47–66

Ulloa, Modesto. *La hacienda real de Castilla en el reinado de Felipe II*. Rome, 1963

Valverde y Perales, Francisco. *Historia de la villa de Baena*. 2nd edn. Córdoba, 1969

Vicens Vives, Jaime. *Historia social y economía de España y America*. 5 vols. Barcelona, 1957–9

Wolff, Philippe. 'The 1391 pogrom in Spain. Social crisis or not?', *Past and Present*, no. 50 (1971), 4–18

Yun Casalilla, Bartolomé. *Crisis de subsistencias y conflictividad social en Córdoba a principios del siglo XVI*. Córdoba, 1980

Index

accountants (*contadores*), municipal, 27, 43

acostamientos, 14, 135, 147–8

actas capitulares, 46, 145

Adamuz, 4, 20, 95, 97, 99, 114, 166, 167; castle, 148

adelantado mayor, 28

aduana, see customs

agriculture: methods of cultivation, 2–6; municipal ordinances, 3–4

aguadores, rent, 84

Aguayo, Alfonso de, *veinticuatro*, 106; Alonso Ruiz de, *jurado*, 160; Diego de, *veinticuatro*, 108; family, 96, 139, 152; Fernán Ruiz de, *chantre*, 165, 182; Francisco de, *veinticuatro*, 186; Pedro de, *veinticuatro*, 170–1, 183; Rodrigo de, *veinticuatro*, 171

Aguila, Lic. de, 106

Aguilar, 10, 19, 21, 105, 121; house of, x, 21, 54, 133–4, 140, 141, 189

Aguilar, D. Alonso de, lord of Aguilar, *alcalde mayor*, 29, 30, 89, 90–1, 103, 121–3, 133–4, 135, 140, 146, 147, 148–54, 156, 160, 171, 183–4

Aguilarejo, 98

Ajarquía, *see* Córdoba, Ajarquía

alarifes, 27

alcabalas, 57, 59, 60, 69–77, 80, 86, 90, 91, 108, 135, 138, 190

alcaicería, 74, 85, 101–3

alcaides (governors) of castles, 49, 135, 161–2, 189

alcaides de los donceles, 55, 87, 98, 122; *and see* Diego Fernández de Córdoba

Alcalá de Henares, ordinances of, 15, 144

Alcalá la Real, 150

alcaldes de la real casa y corte, 39

alcaldes de las dehesas, 42, 117

alcaldes de los hijosdalgo, 54–5, 65

alcaldes, of trades, 42–3

alcaldes mayores, see magistrates

Alcántara, military order of, 19, 20

Alcaracejos, 3, 20

Alcaudete, 21; convent, 172; lords of, 122

Alcolea, Puente de, 20, 51, 99, 125, 148

Alcudia, valley, 114

Aldea del Río, 20, 89; castle, 149

alférez, 26, 41 160

Alfonso, prince, 148–9

Alfonso X, king of Castile, 1, 8, 13, 14, 18, 23, 25, 102, 127, 136

Alfonso XI, king of Castile, 19, 22, 25, 27, 35, 70

Algallarín, *cortijo* of, 97

Algeciras, 70

alguacil, mayor or *menor, see* constables

alhóndiga (granary), 73, 102, 110

Aljarafe, of Seville, 9, 11–12, 60

Almedilla, *cortijo* of, 98

Almena (Granada), 135

Almodóvar del Río, 4, 20, 99, 107, 125; castle, 18, 49, 107, 162

almogávares, 6

almojarifazgo castellano, 76, 78, 80, 81, 86, 103, 135; in *tierra*, 81–2, 89, 135

almojarifazgo sevillano, 59, 60, 69, 80, 86, 90, 135, 190

almojarifes, see almojarifazgo

almotacenazgo, 82–3, 103–4; *fieles* of, 42

almotacenes, 103

almotaclacía, 103

Alonso, Martín, *jurado*, 106

Alonso Rodrigo, labourer, 98

Andújar, 18

Angulo, Alfonso Martínez de, *veinticuatro, procurador mayor*, 114; family, 96, 139, 152; D. Martín Fernández de, bishop of Córdoba, 175, 176

Añora, 3, 20, 55

Antequera (Málaga), 115, 125; governorship, 159

231